WHAT PEOPLE ARE SAYIN
THE WORSHIPING AR

Wow! Rory has done it again! *The Worshiping Artist* is the most theological yet applicable resource on worship I've seen. Rory does a masterful job of teaching the core competencies of worship yet relating them to everyday life and the circumstances we face in arts ministries. Thanks, Rory! Our teams already enjoy a deeper understanding of our calling and abilities because of your previous books. I anticipate an even greater impact with *The Worshiping Artist.*

Larry Harrison, Worship and Teaching Pastor,
Henderson Hills Baptist Church

Rory helps you consider what matters most: it is not about serving in worship as part of my life—but integrating a lifestyle of worship into my service—this book will be a great tool to go through and *grow* through as a team.

Connie Leachman, Executive Producer,
Living Word Community Church

The Worshiping Artist—it's fresh, biblical, eye-opening, practical, substantial, helpful, provocative, instructive, debunking (tired stereotypes); wisdom for the "in-the-trenches-worship-leader" drawn from worship-leader-creatives of the Bible and the Church's history. One of the best guides for Worship Leaders I've seen in my forty years of worship ministry!

Rev. Byron Spradlin, President, Artists in
Christian Testimony International

A must read for anyone wanting to grow as a private worshiper or as a public ministry leader. Practical, biblical, and refreshing. I highly recommend it to those looking to enrich their personal worship experience.

Rick Muchow

In today's complex and often controversial landscape of worship within the local church, Rory has written the definitive textbook/handbook to help us create God-honoring and culturally relevant worship environments—an incredible resource!

Dennis Worley, Music and Worship Minister,
Brentwood Baptist Church

Rory Noland has produced his most mature work yet with *The Worshiping Artist* In the past, he has taught us servanthood, he has taught us how to thrive as artists, now, most importantly, he has taught us to worship. Amidst all the self-absorption and self-congratulation of the "contemporary church," Rory Noland points us back to God and his magnificent attributes. And he does it in a way that integrates the senses into his maturing theology. This book will be useful to Christian artists everywhere because it points them back to the ultimate Artist. What lessons there are to be learned!

TONY PAYNE, Director, Conservatory of Music, Wheaton College

Rory Nolan has again written a must-read for all worship leaders—a primer on worship, a peek into the mind and heart of the artist, and a thorough biblical challenge to Godly leadership. Above all, this is a pastoral book—written with a deep love for the church and for those who lead in worship. This book both affirms and challenges: gently pulling us up and encouraging us at the same time. For the seasoned worship leader, Noland affirms core beliefs. For the less experienced, Noland offers pages of "aha" moments.

RANDALL BRADLEY, Professor of Church Music, Director of the Church Music Program and the Center for Christian Music Studies, Baylor School of Music

I definitely want to recommend Rory's new book to any worship leader or worship team. This book contains the nuts and bolts of what it takes to worship the Lord. Developing his material around the three questions—Who is God? Who am I (in God's view)? What is God asking me to do?—has challenged me in simplifying my approach to leading others in worship. As you read *The Worshiping Artist* you will realize that Rory has developed a systematic theology for the worshiping artist that will be a reference book that you can return to again and again as you experience worship privately and lead others in worship publicly. What a great reminder to me of the basic building blocks and essentials that must continue to stay in my life and heart as I seek to lead others into the presence of the Lord. The questions and practical guide at the end of each chapter challenged me personally and would stretch any worship team that plans to lead an authentic worship experiences.

DAN FERGUSON, Worship Arts Director, Park Avenue Baptist Church

7-07

Matt,
What a blessing it is to do ministry with such a godly guy!
We love you, [illegible]

the Worshiping Artist

equipping you and your ministry team
to ***lead others in worship***

Oh how we believe in you!
love,
Perry

rory **noland** author of
The Heart of the Artist

ZONDERVAN.com/
AUTHORTRACKER
follow your favorite authors

We want to hear from you. Please send your comments about this book to us in care of zreview@zondervan.com. Thank you.

The Worshiping Artist

Requests for information should be addressed to:

Zondervan, *Grand Rapids, Michigan 49530*

Library of Congress Cataloging-in-Publication Data

Noland, Rory.
The worshiping artist: equipping you and your ministry team to lead others in worship / Rory Noland.
p. cm.
Includes bibliographical references.
ISBN-13: 978-0-310-27334-9
ISBN-10: 0-310-27334-x
1. Public worship. 2. Christian Leadership. 3. Christianity and art. I. Title.
BV15.N65 2006
264.0088'7 - dc22 2006037569

Interior design by Mark Sheeres

Printed in the United States of America

07 08 09 10 11 12 • 10 9 8 7 6 5 4 3 2 1

Contents

List of Illustrations

Foreword by Chuck Fromm

From the mid-seventies to the mid-eighties I visited Willow Creek Community Church on several occasions. My own journey as music publisher and producer, caught up in the gale force winds of the Jesus movement, took me across the nation and the world. At the time a well-disciplined group of talented men and women was emerging, and they were bringing about a radical, imaginative change in worship style, often sparked by a simple guitar and drum accompaniments. These leaders rapidly forged a new community at Willow Creek, noted for communicating the good news of Jesus Christ in a manner that was truly both good *and* news.

Since then, those men and women have become mentors for subsequent generations around the nation and the world. The true test of their giftedness and calling is not just their relevance during those early days of an extraordinary revival but also how their ideas have continued to grow and mature.

That is the story of Rory Noland, the author of the work I am privileged to commend to you here. Please read the instruction in this book carefully; reflect on it and pay heed to it. Rarely can you find such a unique combination of biblical truth and practical experience from a single source.

Rory speaks as not just a survivor of change but as one who has learned to surrender to God alone in the process. His words carry the authoritative echo of an elder-teacher from the ancient house of Asaph, but he speaks in our present context as a brother and "fellow artist." Being a "worshiping artist" is not a new idea for Rory, it has been his life.

A constant theme in the life of any artist is the discovery of an identity, the ongoing pain and struggle of imaging out something from deep within the soul. The final product is an artifact that invites the involvement of others, that asks them to experience a new insight, to share in the artist's wonder, joy, and even suffering.

Rory shares his own discovery with us. He gives us a primer in a biblical theology of worship. For example, he points to the first time the term *worship* is used in the Scriptures—when Abraham is called upon to experience the heart of God in the suffering of sacrificing his only son. Rory reminds us that the worship artist's work must always be balanced with the devotional life of a humble, face-down, worshiping servant. Be ready for hard work and sacrificial demands.

As you read this book, you'll need to dust off your Bible. Rory takes us to the Scriptures that unscramble the identity of those called to serve in God's house of prayer. Just as many Old Testament prophecies gave Jesus an early clue to his own identity and ministry, Rory challenges his fellow artists to discover their own calling in these ancient prophetic writings. It is in this personal enactment of Scripture—and its ultimate revoicing in the heart of the worship artist—that the word becomes alive and the art transcends mere performance.

Rory is most instructive when he reminds us that worship is not ultimately about the rituals we enact but rather the transformation that takes place in God's house, a place of partnership between those called to serve as "Levites and priests"—that is, "pastors and worship artists"—and God himself.

To lead, Rory reminds us, you must know the way. He doesn't simply give the reader abstract principles and platitudes. Instead, he offers illustrative models that relate to his own experience. He invites us to become apprentices to a master teacher, to learn the spiritual disciplines required to be a servant of prayer, a minstrel in the house of God. He instructs us to take off our shoes in the presence of a Holy God as we move from our *American Idol* culture to the ancient tradition of the "icon." An idol points to itself, while an icon, ultimately, points to God.

This book itself is a sacrificial offering of praise, as Rory graciously invites us to learn through his own transparency the faithfulness of God and his sufficiency in our weakness.

Charles E. Fromm, Founder and Publisher,
Worship Leader Magazine, February 16, 2007

Introduction

Help! I'm a Back-Row Choir Guy Leading Worship!

Of all the creatures both in sea and land
Only to Man thou hast made known thy ways,
And put the pen alone into his hand,
And made him Secretary of thy praise.

From "Providence" by George Herbert

An astute guitar player recently asked me, "How should I prepare myself spiritually to lead worship?" He practiced his guitar regularly and never missed rehearsal, yet he sensed intuitively that leading worship demanded spiritual preparation as well. His question, echoed by dozens of other church artists I've met, served as the motivation for writing this book.

In the Bible, artists are often at the forefront of worship. In Psalm 68:25, David describes a team of artists leading a procession of worshipers into the sanctuary: "In front are the singers, after them the musicians; with them are the maidens playing tambourines." Jehoshaphat once assembled a choir to lead an army of worshipers into battle (2 Chronicles 20).

Much like David's praise team or Jehoshaphat's worship choir, artists today are on the front lines of worship ministry. In fact, unlike any other time in church history, worship today is led predominantly by teams of artists. While some are on staff at the church, the majority are volunteers with day jobs during the week. Yet, on weekends they serve at their church. For example, they play in the praise band, sing in the worship choir, or help in the audiovisual area. The majority of these church artists are neither seminary graduates nor even Bible college alumni, yet they are called upon every week to lead hundreds, sometimes thousands, of people in worship.

Given the responsibility of such a vital priestly function, one would assume that every artist would make spiritual preparation top priority. Unfortunately, so much time goes into other tasks such as rehearsing, practicing, and/or setting up, that there is little or no time left for spiritual preparation, especially for the average volunteer with family and job obligations.

To complicate matters, some church artists don't readily view themselves as worship leaders. For so long, that title has traditionally been given to the "up-front" paid professional at the church—the person who puts the worship order together and speaks during transitions. However, today there is a growing realization that if you're using your artistic gifts to facilitate worship in any way, you are indeed leading worship. Whether you sing, play, write, paint, act, dance, mix sound, run lyric slides, or direct lighting, whether you solo or sing in the choir, whether you lead visibly "up front" or labor behind the scenes, the congregation follows your lead. Hence, you are a worship leader. Or to use the phrase most people are using these days, you are a "lead worshiper."

While this may be a new concept for some, I continually hear worship pastors address all their artists (not just the musicians) as "fellow worship leaders." One young leader told his team, "I'm not the only worship leader here; we're *all* leading worship." Last year I heard a pastor in Florida address his artists and thank them for their commitment and faithfulness to ministry. Then he reminded them that, no matter their role, they were all worship leaders. Afterward, I overheard a vocalist soberly exclaim, "Wow! I'm just a back-row choir guy; I never thought of myself as a worship leader before." This realization amounted to a new calling for this man and changed the way he approached his role in the choir.

The goal of this book is to help you prepare your heart and soul for leading others in worship. The first part defines worship and delves into the heart of worship, which is to encounter God and be transformed by his character. The second part provides the basic theology one needs to know in order to lead others in worship by examining the truth about who God is and who we are. The third part analyzes the spiritual practices of some ancient worship leaders and suggests ways for us to apply those principles in worship today.

This book is written for all artists who are involved in any way with the worship services at their church—the musicians, media team, technical help, dancers, actors, visual artists, writers, and producers. When David wrote, "Praise him, you servants of the Lord, you who minister in the house of the Lord" (Psalm 135:1–2), he was referring to all of us who facilitate worship. As we "minister in the house of the Lord," may we all grow in our understanding of what it means to be a worshiping artist.

part one

Worshiping in Spirit

God is spirit, and his worshipers must worship in spirit.

John 4:24

Because God is spirit, he is not confined to time, place, or other physical limitations. Therefore, we must worship him in spirit; we must connect with him on a soul level. Contrary to common belief, the soul is not separate from the mind or body, but is the life center of every human being. The soul integrates every facet of our being—our thoughts, feelings, convictions, relationships, as well as our physical bodies. The soul represents the deepest part of who we are. That's the level on which God wants to relate to us, the point at which we meet him in worship.

Worship may at times seem ethereal, or "other worldly," but it is never divorced from the "real world." We tend to regard Sunday as relegated for spiritual things, like going to church, singing, and praying. The rest of the week, then, is devoted to the "real stuff" of life—work, soccer games, carpooling, and PTO meetings. However, worship and all other spiritual activities are every bit a part of the real world because they bring God into all of who we are and all we do. Also, worship deals with the soul, the only part of us that's going to live forever. For that reason, it could be safely argued that worship *is* the real world.

chapter one

Growing as a Private Worshiper

> This evening as my sunset becomes a sunrise for someone else, I repeat once again my day's mantra, "You, O Lord, are my lamp, my God who lights my darkness. . . ." In the praying of these few lines I have found sufficient nourishment on this desert day.
>
> From *A Tree Full of Angels*
> by Macrina Wiederkehr

Troy slept through his alarm this morning. He finally woke up after his wife jabbed him in the side and asked, "Aren't you supposed to sing at church this morning?" At that, Troy flew out of bed, threw on some clothes, and was out the door. That's how his day started and it only got worse from there.

It's normally a half-hour drive from Troy's house to the church, but with no traffic and all green lights, the trip is cut to twenty minutes. That would put him arriving in the middle of sound check—not bad, considering the circumstances. However, Troy hit every red light. And maybe it was because he was in a hurry, but every red light seemed longer than usual. He was growing impatient. About halfway to church, he came upon a stop sign with no other cars in sight. He slowed down but then sped through the intersection without stopping. Just then a squad car pulled out from a side street with lights flashing. Troy promptly pulled over.

"Are you in a hurry?" the officer asked.

"Yes, I'm late for church," Troy confessed, hoping that speeding for a noble cause would get him off the hook.

"License and registration," the officer curtly demanded. "I'm going to cite you for running a stop sign. There are a lot of little kids in this neighborhood."

While the policeman wrote up the ticket, Troy tried to call the church on his cell phone, but he couldn't get through. He tried to call the music director, but all he got was voice mail. Troy had never been late for a sound check before. He managed a construction company and prided himself on being dependable and responsible, so he was very upset with himself for being tardy.

By the time he arrived, Troy had missed the entire sound check. He apologized profusely to his team leader, who promptly caught him up to speed on all the final instructions he had missed. Then before he had time to catch his breath, Troy was on the platform singing the first worship chorus.

However, he immediately discovered that he was not in good voice. He sounded like a cat with a hair ball. He tried to quietly clear his throat, but to no avail. Then he started coughing, so loud in fact that the guitar player came over and offered him a bottle of water. Troy soon recovered, but started the second song in the wrong place and forgot the tag at the end. The third song was even worse. The music director had assigned a solo to Troy, but Troy couldn't remember whether he was supposed to sing the first or second verse. He opted for the second verse; he guessed wrong. After the band intro, there was an awkward silence. The music director looked back anxiously, so Troy jumped in, mid sentence, stumbling over words and fumbling for the right pitch. He was embarrassed. The rest of the worship set went without incident, but the whole time Troy kept thinking about the solo he messed up.

After the service, Troy was walking to the parking lot with Susan and Buddy, a married couple on the team. Susan plays piano and Buddy plays drums. Just then, the pastor approached them with exciting news. "I just want you to know," he said, "that a man I've been praying for this past year accepted Christ this morning, and it was during the worship time that he sensed God speaking to him. I want to thank you all for the part you played this morning in my friend's coming to salvation. That was certainly one of the most anointed worship times our church has ever had."

As the pastor hustled happily to his car, Troy and his friends stood there in this strange mix of shock, disbelief, and joy. "Wow!" Troy finally spoke up. "I'm thrilled that someone found Christ, but that worship time felt anything but anointed. I don't know about you guys, but my head was not in the game this morning. It was all pretty much a blur to me."

"Me too," said Susan. "I'm still learning how to read chord charts, so I've got my head in the music stand the whole time. But I think that's the worst we've ever sounded."

"Well, it always feels like a whirlwind of activity to me," added Buddy. "I'm pretty much in my own little world behind those drum shields. I can barely hear the singers. Sometimes I have no idea where we are. All I'm thinking about is not messing up."

They all laughed, but Troy looked concerned. "Aren't we supposed to be thinking about the Lord during worship?"

"Of course we are," answered Buddy, "but how can we focus on the Lord when there's so much other stuff to think about? You know what I mean—tempos, transitions, solos, and, by the way, where are we in the chart?" They all laughed.

"You're right," Susan chimed in. "If we don't concentrate on what we're doing, we could have a train wreck up on the platform, and then no one would be able to worship."

Troy pushed further. "Is it okay then to be thinking about other things besides the Lord while we're leading worship?"

"I don't see any other way around it," Susan replied.

"Me neither," agreed Buddy.

Questions for Group Discussion

1. Why were the three artists in our story shocked that someone found Christ during worship that morning?

2. Why did worship feel like a "blur" to Troy and some of the others?

3. Is there anything Troy could have done differently to prepare his heart and mind for worship?

4. Have you ever left a worship experience feeling like you weren't able to connect with God, only to hear everyone else describe it as "deeply meaningful" or even "anointed"? If so, how do you account for that?

5. Has worship ever felt like a whirlwind of activity to you, devoid of God's presence? If so, what contributed to that?

6. What can be done to always make sure one's "head is in the game" while leading worship?

7. Is it possible to focus totally on the Lord while leading worship? Why or why not?

8. How does one stay focused on the Lord amidst all the necessary details demanded by the task of leading worship?

9. Is there anything you could do personally to simplify your role in leading worship?

10. Is there anything you could do personally to minimize distractions as you lead worship?

WHAT IS WORSHIP?

A pastor stopped me recently and asked, "What's the next big innovation on the horizon for worship?" He believes the "worship movement" is in a rut and needs "a shot in the arm." Not long after that, a couple colleagues called to ask, "Who's the next big, up-and-coming worship leader?" They both felt that the "worship scene" needed a new spark. Then a friend who is disillusioned with the worship at his church posed this question, "Do you know any churches in my area that are doing worship right?"

I can't help but notice that these well-meaning questions illustrate the fact that our concept of worship has become far too narrow. I'm a musician, I write worship music, but I would be the first one to admit that worship is much more than singing catchy little tunes in church. Simply put, worship is our response to the presence of God. Therefore, worship is more than merely an emotional "feel good" experience; it is more than a program at church or a concert by my favorite worship leader. Worship is participatory; it is not something done to me by a worship band. In fact, worship is not about me at all; worship is all about God. And, if we allow it, worship can transform us.

Created to Worship

According to 1 Peter 2:9, we were created to worship God: "You are a chosen people, a royal priesthood, a holy nation, a people belonging to God, that you may declare the praises of him who called you out of darkness into his wonderful light." In Isaiah, God refers to his people as those "I formed for myself that they may proclaim my praise" (Isaiah 43:21).

Worship is part of our identity as Christians. In Acts 18:7, a man named Titius Justus is identified as a "worshiper of God," as is Lydia in Acts 16:14. In the same way, every Christian is a worshiper of God through Jesus Christ.

Philippians 3:3 points out that true believers are ones who "worship by the Spirit of God, who glory in Christ Jesus, and who put no confidence in the flesh."

Destined to Worship

Worship is also our destiny because it is one of the primary activities of heaven. Now many of us, if we're totally honest, dread the prospect of worshiping for eternity, as if it's going to be one very long church service. But I assure you that heavenly worship is going to be far more captivating than anything you've ever experienced. The book of Revelation offers an exhilarating glimpse of worship in heaven. As much as words can do it justice, here's a brief snapshot:

> Then I looked and heard the voice of many angels, numbering thousands upon thousands, and ten thousand times ten thousand. They encircled the throne and the living creatures and the elders. In a loud voice they sang:
>
> "Worthy is the Lamb, who was slain,
> to receive power and wealth and wisdom and strength
> and honor and glory and praise!" ...
>
> And he carried me away in the Spirit to a mountain great and high, and showed me the Holy City, Jerusalem, coming down out of heaven from God. It shone with the glory of God, and its brilliance was like that of a very precious jewel, like a jasper, clear as crystal.... I did not see a temple in the city, because the Lord God Almighty and the Lamb are its temple. The city does not need the sun or the moon to shine on it, for the glory of God gives it light, and the Lamb is its lamp. (Revelation 5:11–12; 21:10–11, 22–23)

Notice that there is no need for the sun or moon to light heaven's way—for God's glory shines brilliantly enough to light the entire heavenly realm. No wonder the heavens constantly erupt with spontaneous worship.

Compelled to Worship

Recently I heard a worship leader tell an auditorium full of young people that they needed to worship loud enough to make God smile. This leader meant well, but unfortunately he made God sound childish and egotistical, as if he sits up in heaven pouting unless we flatter him with praise. Does God need us to worship him? Is he so insecure that he needs us to tell him how great and wonderful he is all the time? The answer is no to both questions. God doesn't need anything; he's God. He delights in our worship, but the truth is, we're the ones who need to worship.

C. S. Lewis contends that we delight to worship and we can't help doing it.[1] Indeed, praise comes quite naturally to human beings. Parents sing the praises of their children. Lovers heap praise upon each other. Pet owners adore their pets. We praise what we enjoy, and oftentimes it's spontaneous; we can't hold back, but instead erupt with adulation. We applaud a good meal, movie, or TV show. We cheer our favorite sports teams, celebrities, and entertainers. We celebrate those who display talent, honor heroes who exhibit valor, and immortalize those who embody greatness.

In much the same way, when we truly encounter God we are enamored with his glory and can't help but overflow with joy. As C. S. Lewis says:

> The Scotch catechism says that man's chief end is "to glorify God and enjoy Him forever." But . . . these are the same thing. Fully to enjoy is to glorify. In commanding us to glorify Him, God is inviting us to enjoy Him.[2]

Worship Is a Way of Life

In the Bible, the word *worship* refers to a specific activity as well as an ongoing lifestyle. When the psalmist wrote, "Come, let us bow down in worship, let us kneel before the Lord our Maker" (Psalm 95:6), he was speaking of the activity most of us know as corporate worship, where the church gathers together to praise God. The first-century church worshiped together regularly: "Every day they continued to meet together in the temple courts. They broke bread in their homes and ate together with glad and sincere hearts, praising God and enjoying the favor of all the people" (Acts 2:46–47).

One of the most exciting developments in Christendom over the past few decades has been the resurgence of corporate worship. In fact, when it comes to choosing churches, people these days are just as apt to consider the quality of the "worship times" as they are the effectiveness of the teaching. In recent years, praise music has become increasingly popular, prompting even some secular recording labels to get into the "worship market." In spite of all this happy progress, and the impressive showing in sales, it's important to remember that worship is not merely a new genre within the music business. In fact, worship is more than just music; it's a lifestyle.

When the prophet Jonah said, "I am a Hebrew and I worship the Lord" (Jonah 1:9), he was describing an ongoing lifestyle. The apostle Paul said, "I worship the God of our fathers as a follower of the Way" (Acts 24:14). Clearly then, worship is not something we do only on Sundays, it is a way of life. David said, "I will extol the Lord at *all* times; his praise will *always* be on my lips" (Psalm 34:1, emphasis mine). The writer of Hebrews instructs us to "continually offer to God a sacrifice of praise" (Hebrews 13:15).

Sadly, too many Christians are unfamiliar with this broader concept of worship. When we think of worship, we too often picture a large group of people standing with their eyes closed, passionately singing with their hands raised heavenward—like the cover of many worship CDs. No doubt the corporate worship experience can be extremely powerful, but when the singing ends, we're not done worshiping! We can worship God on our own—one-on-one—as private worshipers, and experience the power and privilege of worship every day. The first step in becoming a worshiping artist, and an effective lead worshiper, is to become a vibrant private worshiper. You can't lead others in an experience that you yourself aren't having regularly.

KEYS TO GROWING AS A PRIVATE WORSHIPER

Private worshipers understand that our God is a personal God. His presence is manifest whenever two or three are gathered in his name (Matthew 18:20), but he also desires one-on-one fellowship with each of us. Jesus said, "Here I am! I stand at the door and knock. If anyone hears my voice and opens the door, I will come in and eat with them, and they with me" (Revelation 3:20 TNIV). King David composed seventy-three beautiful psalms of praise and became known as Israel's beloved singer of songs (2 Samuel 23:1). David's enduring contribution can be traced to those early years he spent alone in the fields tending his father's sheep. That's where he learned to worship God privately.

Because personal worshipers enjoy the fruits of worship on a regular basis, they tend to engage more fully and contribute more wholeheartedly to corporate worship. As author Jerry Bridges notes:

> The vitality and genuineness of corporate worship is to a large degree dependent upon the vitality of our individual private worship. If we aren't spending time daily worshiping God, we're not apt to contribute to the corporate experience of worship. If we aren't worshiping God during the week, how can we expect to genuinely participate in it on Sunday morning? We may indeed go through the motions and think we have worshiped, but how can we honor and adore One on Sunday whom we have not taken time to praise and give thanks to during the week?[3]

Personal worshipers, therefore, tend to take the corporate worship experience home with them and bring their private worship experience to church with them, thus enhancing the worship service. If a church wanted to take the next step in improving its worship, I wouldn't rush to change the program or find a new worship leader. I would encourage every member to become a personal worshiper. Can you imagine a church comprised largely of people who worshiped privately during the week and then came together on Sunday to worship? Their hearts would be so primed for worship, it wouldn't matter whether the music was traditional, contemporary, or blended. Any worship leader would have an easy time getting a congregation like that to engage. In fact, they might not even need a worship leader!

God is the one who initiates worship. He reveals himself to us and we respond accordingly. Since we don't initiate worship, is there anything we can do to increase our receptivity to God? I believe there are three things we can do to respond to God as private worshipers:

1. Make ourselves increasingly present to God.
2. Set aside time regularly for private worship.
3. Offer ourselves completely to God.

Make Yourself Increasingly Present to God

At the risk of sounding irreverent, I'd have to admit that I've learned a great deal about worship from our family dog. Pepper, a black miniature poodle, was part of our family for seventeen years. Our main reason for buying the dog was so that our two sons would have a boyhood companion. However, from the beginning Pepper would have nothing to do with the boys or me. Instead, he idolized my wife, Sue. He followed her wherever she went and went on hunger strikes whenever she was away. Pepper always positioned himself as close to Master Sue as possible, guarding her like a hawk. Whenever I got within six feet of my wife, the dog would sit up, roll his eyes (I'm not kidding, he rolled his eyes), as if to say, "Oh, you again. State your business and leave." Whenever we all gathered to watch television, Pepper always sat with his back to the picture, facing my wife, attentively watching the "Sue Channel." Pepper constantly lived in the presence of his master.

Similarly, you and I are always in the presence of God; there is never a moment when he is absent. "Am I not a God near at hand ... and not a God far off? declares the Lord. Can anyone hide out in a corner where I can't see him?... Am I not present everywhere, whether seen or unseen?" (Jeremiah 23:23–24 MSG). Theologians describe God as "omnipresent," meaning that he is everywhere, always present. "Who is able to build a temple for him, since the heavens, even the highest heavens, cannot contain him?" (2 Chronicles 2:6). God has no limits or boundaries.

If you ever wonder, *God where are you?* his answer is always, "I'm right here." According to Acts 17:27, "He is not far from each one of us." The psalmist adds that there is nowhere you could go and not find God:

> Where can I go from your Spirit?
> Where can I flee from your presence?
> If I go up to the heavens, you are there;
> if I make my bed in the depths, you are there.
> If I rise on the wings of the dawn,
> if I settle on the far side of the sea,
> even there your hand will guide me,
> your right hand will hold me fast.
> If I say, "Surely the darkness will hide me
> and the light become night around me,"
> even the darkness will not be dark to you;
> the night will shine like the day,
> for darkness is as light to you.
>
> Psalm 139:7–12

We can pray to God anywhere, anytime because he is everywhere all the time. God is with you as you drive to work, as you sit through meetings, as you carpool, as you clean the house, and as you walk the halls at school. The problem is, more often than not, we are oblivious to God's presence. We're too busy, too preoccupied. We're like Jacob. When he woke up to the fact that he had been visited by God, he exclaimed, "Surely the Lord is in this place, and I was not aware of it" (Genesis 28:16).

Since God is always with us, serious worshipers are on the alert for God's presence in all they do. Jerry Bridges suggests that we "live all of life in a conscious awareness of God's constant presence."[4] Attentiveness to God prompted the psalmist to say, "My mouth is filled with your praise, declaring your splendor all day long" (Psalm 71:8). I like the way Bob Rognlien puts it in his book *Experiential Worship*, "The question is not whether *God* is present to *us*; the question is how present *we* are to God."[5]

In the Song of Solomon, the female protagonist has one of my favorite lines in all of Scripture. She says, "I slept but my heart was awake. Listen! My lover is knocking" (Song of Songs 5:2). Personal worshipers cultivate an "awakened heart," one that is tuned to God's presence in their lives. I know a businessman who shuts his office door for five minutes of silence every morning. Others post Bible verses around their homes or offices to remind them of the Lord. An artist friend of mine listens to worship music while she paints. Another friend takes the scenic route home from work every day so he can catch the sunset. Private worshipers remind themselves of God's presence amidst their regular routines.

Set Aside Time Regularly for Private Worship

Early in my spiritual journey, I learned an acronym that made worship a vital part of my daily devotions. ACTS stands for adoration, confession, thanksgiving, and supplication—all vital components of an effective prayer life. The first part of that sequence taught me, more than anything else, how to worship God privately. I used to praise God for whatever attribute of his came to mind, sometimes writing a worshipful paragraph in my journal or composing a brief psalm or poem.

Since those early days, I've adopted the habit of reading a psalm a day. Every morning I select a psalm and read it all the way through to get the general idea. If the psalm is a long one, I often divide it into sections. Then, because the Psalter contains hundreds of references to the nature of God, I read the passage a second time and stop at any word or phrase that seems to resonate with me. Usually it's a name or attribute of God, which I'll then use as a springboard for private worship. I'll also try to recall that theme later during the day, especially when praying before meals. Doing so enables worship to permeate my day in much the same way David describes in Psalm 44:8: "In God we make our boast all day long."

Should you wish to adopt this approach, I also suggest praying over the name or attribute of God you select. For example, ascribing to God strength and glory might prompt you to pray, "God, I praise you for being mighty and strong. Please show your strength and power in this area of my life" (then name a specific area in which you're struggling).

If you ever feel like you're in a rut with devotions, try injecting more worship into your routine. However, private worship doesn't have to be confined only to one's quiet times. Nor does it need to be long and involved. I know people who sing along with a worship CD as they drive to work. A good friend of mine, who would never claim to be a singer, likes to sing worship choruses when she's alone and will even make up her own praise songs. A worship leader I know steals off to the church sanctuary during the week when it's empty, guitar in hand, and worships God one-on-one.

Some people use regular occurrences throughout their day as reminders to worship. For example, they set their watch to go off at a certain time each day, at which point they stop whatever they're doing and worship. Whenever some people drive by a church, they're prompted to praise God.

When you make worship a regular routine, you'll find yourself in a worshipful mindset throughout the day. So whether it's daily, every other day, or weekly, I invite you to set aside time specifically for private worship.

Offer Yourself Completely to God

In Romans 12:1, the apostle Paul urges us to offer our bodies as "living sacrifices, holy and pleasing to God—this is your spiritual act of worship." According to William Barclay, this verse captures what real worship is:

> "So," Paul says "take your body; take all the tasks that you have to do every day; take the ordinary work of the shop, the office, the factory, the shipyard, the mine; and offer all that as an act of worship to God. . . ."
>
> True worship is the offering to God of one's body and all that one does every day with it. Real worship is not the offering to God of a liturgy, however noble, and a ritual, however magnificent. *Real worship is the offering of everyday life to him.*[6]

Every glimpse of God's glory is an invitation to submit to his lordship in every area of our lives. So offering ourselves completely to God is an act of worship. Paul instructs us to present our bodies as living and holy sacrifices because our bodies represent all of us—our thoughts, feelings, and actions. Jesus said, "Love the Lord your God with all your heart and with all your soul and with all your mind and with all your strength" (Mark 12:30).

Worship is holistic, involving every facet of our being. The words that come out of our mouths can either be life-giving or they can be cutting, slanderous, and hateful. Our minds can either think pure thoughts or impure ones. Our faces can either radiate light or reflect darkness. Our hands can either serve others or ourselves. Our feet can either run to sin or away from it. Our sexuality can be enjoyed as God intended or it can be misused.

If worship is giving all of ourselves to God, then everything we do is potentially an act of worship. We are instructed to acknowledge the Lord in all we do (Proverbs 3:6). So how we live our lives is how we praise God. As Louie Giglio writes in *The Air I Breathe*:

> The point is this: Everything on earth (except sin) can be done as an act of worship to God. Everything we do *is* worship when we do it for Him, displaying His face as we go.
>
> The question is not *what* you do, but *who* you do it for.
>
> Your calling is to turn your place in life into a place of true worship.
>
> To do whatever you do in a way that will reflect God's heart to those around you.
>
> It's to worship ... as you live your life.[7]

Colossians 3:17 says, "And whatever you do, whether in word or deed, do it all in the name of the Lord Jesus." What do you spend the majority of your time doing? As you work, raise a family, go to school, serve at church, or do your art, what would it look like for you to do each of those things as an act of worship? Or consider the activities or tasks you will be doing in the next twenty-four hours. How would doing those activities to the glory of God change the way you do them? Is there any area of your life that isn't given over completely to God? Why not offer that to him as an act of worship? Let's examine two areas in which we are continually challenged to give ourselves to the Lord as an act of worship.

Say No to Sin as an Act of Worship

It's impossible to discuss giving yourself completely to God without addressing the issue of sin. Indeed, sin is not to be taken lightly. In the book of Amos, God rebukes the nation of Israel for their hypocritical worship: "I hate, I despise your religious feasts; I cannot stand your assemblies.... Away with the noise of your songs! I will not listen to the music of your harps" (Amos 5:21, 23).

Regarding sin and temptation, many Christians are unclear about what God does and what we must do for ourselves. "Letting go and letting God" is not a wise approach for dealing with temptation if it abdicates personal responsibility for the choices we make. Leviticus 22:31–32 reveals both God's role and our responsibility: "Keep my commands and follow them.... I am the Lord, who makes you holy." God has delivered us from sin; he is making us holy. But he expects us, when given the chance, to choose godliness over disobedience. "Therefore do not let sin reign in your mortal body so that you obey its evil desires" (Romans 6:12). With the help of the Holy Spirit, we have the ability to resist sin, but the responsibility for using that power lands squarely on our shoulders. In *The Pursuit of Holiness*, Jerry Bridges writes:

> It is time for us Christians to face up to our responsibility for holiness. Too often we say we are "defeated" by this or that sin. No, we are not defeated; we are simply disobedient....
>
> We need to brace ourselves up, and to realize that we are responsible for our thoughts, attitudes, and actions. We need to reckon on the fact that we died to sin's reign, that it no longer has any dominion over us, that God has united us with the risen Christ in all His power, and has given us the Holy Spirit to work in us. Only as we accept our responsibility and appropriate God's provisions will we make any progress in our pursuit of holiness.[8]

Since the garden of Eden, it's been typical of human nature to shift the blame for our wrongdoing to someone or something else. Adam blamed both Eve and God when he said, "The woman you put here with me—she gave me some fruit from the tree, and I ate it" (Genesis 3:12). Too often we blame our bad choices on an addiction, our family upbringing, or the fact that we have "issues" or unmet needs. The fact is, we choose to sin. That's why Ephesians 4:26, for example, says, "In your anger do not sin." The Bible recognizes that people get angry, but it advises against acting out of anger. So take responsibility for your actions. Be angry, be sad, be mistreated, be without ... but do not sin.

Of course, this is not to say that it's easy to resist temptation. However, worship can be a powerful weapon against temptation. Psalm 8:2 says that God has "ordained praise ... to silence the foe and the avenger." I know a young man who struggles with impure thoughts, so every time he's tempted to look lustfully at a woman, he shifts gears and quietly praises God for the beauty with which he created her.

Obedience itself is an act of worship. In the Old Testament, a bull or lamb was actually sacrificed as a "burnt offering" during worship. However, as 1 Samuel 15:22 illustrates, it's not the sacrifice that God is after—it's our obedience: "Does the Lord delight in burnt offerings and sacrifices as much as in obeying the voice of the Lord? To obey is better than sacrifice."

In 1660, the Dutch artist Jan Steen completed his painting entitled *Bathsheba Receiving David's Letter* (plate 1). The painting effectively captures Bathsheba at a crossroad. In the foreground she stands holding the invitation from King David. Her ornately draped bed in the background, be it highly suggestive, implies that she knew full well David's intentions. The king's palace can be seen off in the distance through her window. There he awaits her reply, as does the ominous messenger to the right. Bathsheba looks back at us as if to say, "What should I do?"

Interestingly, Steen's Bathsheba looks more Dutch than Jewish. She's even dressed, not in Old Testament costume, but like a seventeenth-century Dutch girl. By contemporizing the scene for his day, Steen essentially dramatizes the fact that temptation is a universal dilemma. Like Bathsheba, we too stand at many a crossroads where we must choose right from wrong, to obey or disobey, God's way or our own way. My fellow artists, may obedience be for you an extension of worship. Say yes to God and no to sin as a definitive act of worship.

Give of Your Resources as an Act of Worship

In my years of pastoring artists, I've observed glaring inconsistencies when it comes to personal stewardship. Putting it bluntly, too many artists contribute little or nothing financially to their church.

Some are going through hard times economically, and I wouldn't expect them to be giving. In those cases, the church community should help out in any way possible. At my church, a single mom serving in the music ministry who was struggling to make ends meet was graciously given a new car. Bags of groceries were donated to the family of a man who lost his job. And at an orchestra rehearsal, a collection was taken to help provide a new French horn for a young man whose family couldn't afford one. These acts of charity are characteristic of a healthy ministry.

However, the majority of the artists I work with are far from destitute. Yet they don't put anything in the offering plate. When you consider how much the average church pays for sound equipment, microphones, lighting, and video equipment, it's a shame that the team that utilizes those things the most barely contributes to funding them. One volunteer told me that instead of giving money to his church, he gave his time. Somehow it was an either/or proposition in his mind. While it's important to give time, it doesn't constitute the same level of sacrifice that giving financially entails. Besides, it still doesn't help pay for that expensive new soundboard the church just bought. Another person once told me she was too strapped financially to give, yet she always dressed in the latest fashion, bought new CDs regularly, and went out for lunch every day. Giving forces us to prioritize according to our convictions. Jesus said, "For where your treasure is, there your heart will be also" (Matthew 6:21).

You don't have to be rich to give money to your home church. During the first century, a horrible famine arose in the Middle East and Christians from other parts of the known world were asked to give relief to their suffering brothers and sisters. The churches in Macedonia drew honorable mention because they gave abundantly even though they were extremely poor. Paul reports that they gave "beyond their ability. Entirely on their own, they urgently pleaded with us for the privilege of sharing in this service to the saints" (2 Corinthians 8:3–4). Paul further explains that their generosity was a reflection of their commitment to Christ, saying "they gave themselves first to the Lord and then to us in keeping with God's will" (2 Corinthians 8:5). Indeed, sometimes it's the poorest people who have the biggest hearts.

Bear in mind that giving always costs something. Yet God rewards givers. In Malachi 3:10, he lays down the gauntlet and says, "Bring the whole tithe into the storehouse.... Test me in this ... and see if I will not throw open the floodgates of heaven and pour out so much blessing that you will not have room enough for it." God blesses those who give. Jesus reiterated the same promise: "Give, and it will be given to you" (Luke 6:38). Paul taught that "whoever sows sparingly will also reap sparingly, and whoever sows generously will also reap generously" (2 Corinthians 9:6). Evidently, one can never out-give God.

In many church services, the offering occurs in conjunction with a hymn or praise chorus. In such cases, it's not uncommon for the pastor or worship leader to say, "Let's worship the Lord now with our tithes and offerings." As Psalm 96:8 points out, giving is an extension of worship: "Ascribe to the Lord the glory due his name; bring an offering and come into his courts." With that in mind, I urge all artists to give whatever you can monetarily as an act of worship. It's one of the most fitting ways to say thank you to the Lord for all he's given to you. The offering is also an opportunity to express another important facet of worship—joy—for we are instructed to always give cheerfully (2 Corinthians 9:7).

In a lot of churches, it's standard to give 10 percent of your earnings. The scriptural basis for the tithe is found in Leviticus 27:30: "A tithe of everything from the land, whether grain from the soil or fruit from the trees, belongs to the Lord; it is holy to the Lord" (see also Deuteronomy 12:6; 14:22). However, most church leaders would agree that the tithe is a starting point, not a hard-and-fast rule. We need to ask God how much we should give, because everything we have is from him and belongs to him anyway. Scripture says that "each of you should give what you have decided in your heart to give, not reluctantly or under compulsion, for God loves a cheerful giver" (2 Corinthians 9:7 TNIV). As always, be open to God challenging you in this area. If you absolutely have no money to give, then let the plate pass by. You can start giving again as soon as you're able. If you currently give 1 percent, I challenge you to increase it to 2 percent. If you're at 5 percent, can you make it 6 percent? If you're already tithing, but can give more, by all means do so.

The amount we give is not as important to the Lord as the heart of the giver. That's why Jesus commended a poor widow for putting what amounted to a fraction of a cent in the offering plate; that was all she had and she gave it to the Lord (Mark 12:41–44). So, my fellow artists, give as an act of worship.

GOD IS SEEKING WORSHIPERS

In the scenario that opened this chapter, Troy slept through his alarm, was late for church, and fumbled his way through leading worship. Every church artist has had experiences when things went woefully wrong during a service. No matter how well rehearsed you are, equipment malfunction, unforeseen problems, and honest mistakes can greatly hinder one's ability to lead worship. I've observed that those artists who are also private worshipers are most often able to lead effectively through such adversity. The service doesn't become a blur to them like it was for Troy. Worship is so ingrained in them that they're able to rise above such challenges.

According to 2 Chronicles 16:9, God is constantly on the lookout for people who are open to an encounter with him: "For the eyes of the Lord range throughout the earth to strengthen those whose hearts are fully committed to him." Of course, God doesn't confine his search to Sundays only. He regularly scans the planet for serious worshipers. David exclaimed, "Every day I will praise you and extol your name for ever and ever" (Psalm 145:2). My fellow artist, may you be counted among those who worship the Lord privately as well as corporately.

Follow-up Questions for Group Discussion

1. Why do you worship?

2. How do you think growing as a private worshiper could affect one's ability to lead worship?

3. Which one of the following suggestions can best help you grow as a private worshiper?

   _____Make yourself increasingly present to God

   _____Set aside time regularly for private worship

   _____Offer yourself completely to God

4. What are you already doing to make yourself present to God throughout your day?

5. How can you make yourself more present to God at work, home, or school?

6. Whether it's daily, every other day, or weekly, what time can you set aside for private worship?

7. If you already practice private worship, what can you do to deepen the experience or bring variety to it?

8. What would it look like for you to work, raise a family, go to school, serve at church, or do your art to the glory of God?

9. Name the part of your job or domestic responsibilities that you enjoy the least. How would doing that task to the glory of God change how you go about it?

10. Do you agree that worship can be a powerful tool in battling temptation? Why or why not?

Personal Action Steps

1. Read Colossians 3:23. Consider all the activities you'll be doing in the next twenty-four hours and ponder how doing them "for the Lord" might change the way you do those activities.

2. Read a different psalm every day this week, pick out a name or attribute of God, and write down any thoughts or feelings you have in relation to it.

3. Ask the Lord to reveal to you if there is any area of your life that isn't given completely over to him. Offer that as an act of worship.

4. Are you honoring God sufficiently with your finances? If not, make the necessary changes in order to offer your resources as a suitable act of worship.

5. Express artistically what it means for you to worship God privately.

chapter two

Encountering the Character of God

I made a cloister of my body and a garden of my soul.... Year after year, I built the walls. But in the center I made a garden that I left open to heaven, and I invited God to walk there. And God came to me.... God filled me, and the rapture of those moments was so pure and so powerful that the cloister walls were leveled. I had no more need for walls.... God was my protection.

From *Children of God* by Mary Doria Russell

Last week during rehearsal, the worship team at Springfield Community Church got into an animated discussion about worship and ministry. It all started when Sharon, a vocalist, expressed concern that the congregation at their early Sunday morning service doesn't worship as enthusiastically as at the later service. "I feel like we're working so hard to get them to participate," she sighed.

Several reasons were offered: because it's early, the congregation might not be awake yet, the crowd is smaller, and there aren't as many young people in attendance. However, Shaline, another vocalist, expressed a deeper concern. "It feels like there is a chasm, some kind of barrier, between us and the congregation. I wish there was something we could do to pull them in."

"It's so hard to get people to sing sometimes," added Haley, their keyboard player. Everybody nodded in agreement.

Then Kyle, their lead guitarist, spoke up. "Hey, I've got an idea. Let's stand at the back after the service and greet people as they leave. Maybe if we reach out to them, they'll get to know us and feel more comfortable singing."

"That's a great idea!" roared Chuck their leader. "Let's do it this week!"

So that Sunday after the first service, all the artists gathered with the pastor at the door, greeted everyone, shook hands, and wished them all a good week. Afterward, the artists discussed their experience backstage as they were getting ready to start the second service.

"I heard a lot of encouraging words," Shaline said excitedly, "a lot of good comments about the band and the singers."

"Me too," Kyle added. "People were surprised when I told them we're all volunteers. They said we sound so professional. One guy even asked me if we have any CDs for sale."

They all laughed. Then Sharon said, "Yeah, I had several people tell me how much they love the music here at Springfield Community. Some even admitted they come just for the music."

Haley added, "Yeah, and people really like those nature videos too."

Throughout this exchange, Kyle noticed that Chuck was quiet and pensive. "What's wrong, Chuck?"

"Did you hear any comments about the worship? Don't get me wrong; I'm glad people appreciate our music. But did any of them mention that they experienced God's presence during worship this morning? Or that they connected with God in a meaningful way?"

One by one, they all shook their heads no.

"Okay, let's go further back," Chuck said. "In the last six months, has anyone in our congregation mentioned that they met God at any of our services? How about the past year? Anyone? How about ever?

Again, no response.

Chuck sighed. "I'm afraid we have a bigger problem on our hands than we thought."

Questions for Group Discussion

1. Why do you suppose the artists heard such superficial feedback about the worship at their church?
2. How would you articulate the problem Chuck refers to at the end of this scenario?
3. Do you agree with Chuck's conclusion?
4. What can be done to help the people of Springfield Community Church connect with God more deeply during worship?
5. Describe how these artists could have tactfully turned the adulation they received into an opportunity to share on a deeper level with congregation members.
6. Generally speaking, is there anything churches do that actually inhibits people from experiencing God? If so, what?
7. What type of feedback have you heard recently about the worship at your own church?

8. What type of comments would you most like to hear from your congregation concerning the corporate worship times?

9. When was the last time you left church feeling like you met God? Describe your experience.

10. Aside from the results in this story, what do you think of Kyle's idea of having the artists greet people at the door?

ENCOUNTERING GOD MEANS EXPERIENCING HIS CHARACTER

A good friend of mine is going through a divorce. Her husband left her and their two teenagers for another woman. In spite of all the hardship, she recently shared with me that her faith is what's keeping her going, and that God's presence has been very real to her throughout this ordeal. However, there is a specific aspect of God's presence that is especially meaningful to her these days. "It's not a disinterested kind of presence," she explained, "but an extremely attentive one. I'm convinced that God is watching out for me." Her words reminded me of Psalm 116:1–2: "I love the Lord, for he heard my voice; he heard my cry for mercy.... He turned his ear to me." The New American Standard translation reads: "He has inclined His ear to me." The psalmist paints a poignant picture of God leaning over the railing of heaven, bending his ear our way, and hearing every cry for help. Needless to say, my friend worships God with added vigor these days.

As stated in the previous chapter, worship is our response to the presence of God. However, as my friend would attest, it is not some vague notion of God that captivates us, but most often a specific quality, or attribute. Romans 1:20 asserts that "since the creation of the world God's invisible qualities—his eternal power and divine nature—have been clearly seen, being understood from what has been made, so that men are without excuse." Thus to encounter God is to experience his character. God reveals to us his grace, for example, or his love, or his power and, unless we're oblivious to his presence, we are moved to worship him. "In view of God's mercy," Paul calls us to worship in Romans 12:1. It is no accident that our most endearing hymns and worship choruses focus on God's character: "Great Is Thy Faithfulness," "A Mighty Fortress Is Our God," "Amazing Grace," "Immortal Invisible," "What a Friend We Have in Jesus."

The Attributes of God Reveal His Character

The attributes of God then are foundational to worship. We worship God for who he is. When David dedicated the temple, he erupted into glorious praise. Notice all the attributes of God he listed:

> Yours, O Lord, is the greatness and the power and the glory and the majesty and the splendor, for everything in heaven and earth is yours. Yours, O Lord, is the kingdom; you are exalted as head over all. Wealth and honor come from you; you are the ruler of all things. In your hands are strength and power to exalt and give strength to all. Now, our God, we give you thanks, and praise your glorious name. (1 Chronicles 29:11–13)

Every attribute of God reveals something significant about who he is. Chapter 5 examines in detail some of the attributes of God. For now, though, the following list provides a brief overview of those attributes.

God is . . .

compassionate
faithful
forgiving
gentle
glorious
good
gracious
holy
immense
immutable
infinite
jealous
just
kind
loving
majestic
merciful
omnipotent
omnipresent
omniscient
patient
perfect
powerful
sovereign
strong
transcendent
true
wise

The Names of God Reveal His Character

The ancient Hebrews had several names for God because no one name could adequately describe God. Each name highlights a specific facet of God's personality. For example:

Our Adequacy
All-Sufficient God
Almighty God
Awesome God
The Beginning and the End
Our Burden Bearer
Our Comforter
Our Confidence
Our Conqueror
Consuming Fire
Counselor
The Creator
Our Deliverer
Our Encouragement
Father
Forgiver
Fortress
Friend
Giver of Every Good Gift
God With Us
Good Shepherd
Our Guide
The Head of the Church
Our Healer
Our Help
Our Hope
Our Joy
Judge
King of Kings
Our Lamp
Lord of All
Marvelous
Master
Most High God
Name Above All Names
Our Peace
Our Protector
Our Provider
Our Redeemer
Our Refuge
Restorer
Rewarder
Our Righteousness
Our Rock
Our Salvation
Our Sanctification
Our Satisfaction
Our Shelter
Our Song
Our Sure Foundation
Our Sustainer
Our Teacher

It's important to note that the names of God reveal character traits that operate, for the most part, on our behalf. God is our righteousness and peace, our shepherd and healer, and so on. I've recently experienced God as Faithful

Provider. Some time ago, I sensed God nudging me to leave my job as a church music director and start a ministry that specializes in ministering to artists in the church—a risky career move to say the least. For twenty years, I had been the music director at a fairly visible and influential church, and the thought of leaving such a prestigious position, with its fixed income and regular pay-checks, was scary. What worried me most was whether or not I could make a living in this new harebrained venture.

Then one morning I read in Psalm 34 that those who seek the Lord "lack nothing" (vv. 4–9). At a time when I felt insecure about providing for my family, God reminded me that he is my provider. A few days later, I read Psalm 42:11 and I was reminded that God is my hope: "Why are you downcast, O my soul? Why so disturbed within me? Put your hope in God, for I will yet praise him, my Savior and my God." Every day that week, I worshiped God with a lump in my throat.

I've learned time and again that, amidst adversity, my help truly is in the name of the Lord (Psalm 124:8). I wholeheartedly agree with the psalmist who wrote, "Praise the Lord. Praise, O servants of the Lord, praise the name of the Lord. Let the name of the Lord be praised, both now and forevermore. From the rising of the sun to the place where it sets, the name of the Lord is to be praised" (Psalm 113:1–3).

The Works of God Reveal His Character

We not only worship God for who he is but also for what he's done. Psalm 66:5 reads, "Come and see what God has done, his awesome deeds for humankind!" (TNIV). God's actions are not only etched throughout history, they are a vital part of our own personal stories.

Psalm 52:9 exclaims, "I will praise you forever for what you have done." Like the psalmist, we can all look back on our lives and see evidence of God's activity. I see God's hand in bringing me to faith, gracing me with a wonderful wife and two sons, and in preparing me for ministry. I recount his provision when finances were tight. I revel in him bringing our younger son safely home from two combat deployments in Iraq. And that's just the tip of the iceberg! My life is a virtual portfolio of God's goodness. And so is yours because our God is not one to sit idly by and watch the world go around; he is actively involved in our lives. As Deuteronomy 3:24 reveals, God's actions reflect his character: "O Sovereign Lord, you have begun to show to your servant your greatness and your strong hand. For what god is there in heaven or on earth who can do the deeds and mighty works you do?"

WHATEVER CHARACTERISTIC GOD REVEALS IS EXACTLY WHAT WE NEED

It's no accident that my friend going through the divorce encountered God as a loving, caring, and attentive presence. It appears that God went out of his way to assure her that he was there for her at a time when she felt abandoned and alone. That's very common; whatever characteristic God chooses to reveal to us is exactly what we need at the time. According to the Puritan writer Thomas Brooks, it's as if God is saying:

> You shall have as true an interest in all my attributes for your good, as they are mine for my own glory.... My grace, saith God, shall be yours to pardon you, and my power shall be yours to protect you, and my wisdom shall be yours to direct you, and my goodness shall be yours to relieve you, and my mercy shall be yours to supply you, and my glory shall be yours to crown you.[1]

Isaiah Experiences God's Holiness

In Isaiah 6, the prophet receives a vision of God's holiness. The scene is a virtual feast for the senses. Isaiah sees the Lord "seated on a throne, high and exalted," and the train of his robe fills the temple. Angels everywhere are calling out to each other with deafeningly loud voices, "Holy, holy, holy is the Lord Almighty; the whole earth is full of his glory." The doorposts and thresholds shake and the temple fills with smoke. There stands Isaiah, eyes as wide as saucers, knees shaking, and a huge lump in his throat. With a quivering voice he cries out, "Woe to me! I am ruined! For I am a man of unclean lips." Isaiah is beside himself. All he catches is but a glimpse of God's holiness, and he realizes that even his best efforts fall far short of God's righteousness. Then an angel flies to Isaiah with a burning coal in his hand, touches his mouth with it and says, "Your guilt is taken away and your sin atoned for." One can only imagine the depth of emotion that consumes Isaiah at this point: overwhelming gratitude, boundless joy, and unspeakable peace.

Have you ever wondered why God chose to reveal his holiness to Isaiah? He could have impressed Isaiah with his might, his mercy, or his love. Why his holiness? And why did the angel touch Isaiah's lips while proclaiming forgiveness? Why not touch his head or his hands or feet? Evidently, this rapturous scene turned out to be Isaiah's commissioning ceremony as a prophet. Now if he was to be God's spokesman, there were a few things Isaiah needed to get straight in order to serve the Lord. It's as if God is saying, "Always remember, Isaiah, you are the mouthpiece of a holy God. Every time you speak on my behalf, you represent me. And because your lips will be the tools of your trade, I am anointing your mouth and the words that emanate from it."

Moses Experiences God's Goodness

In Exodus 33, Moses asks to see God's glory. In complying with this request, God reveals a specific character trait—his goodness. And the Lord says, "I will cause all my goodness to pass in front of you, and I will proclaim my name, the Lord, in your presence. I will have mercy on whom I will have mercy, and I will have compassion on whom I will have compassion" (v. 19).

It's no coincidence that, of all the character traits God could have disclosed, he elected to reveal his goodness to Moses. For this was right after Moses got so angry over the disobedience of his people that he threw down the tablets containing the Ten Commandments and smashed them to bits. However, that wasn't the first time Moses lost his cool. He exploded at his people (Numbers 20:10–11), at Pharaoh (Exodus 11:8), and he even killed a man out of anger (Exodus 2:11–12). Perhaps God revealed his goodness to Moses because he wanted the patriarch to be more merciful and patient—two traits inherent in God's goodness. In fact, before God dictates the Ten Commandments for the second time, he reminds Moses that he is a "compassionate and gracious God, slow to anger, abounding in love and faithfulness, maintaining love to thousands, and forgiving wickedness, rebellion and sin" (Exodus 34:6–7). It's as if God is saying, "Hey, Moe, if you're going to represent me, we need to do something about that temper of yours!" Apparently it worked, for Moses took a more humble and compassionate approach in his second attempt at presenting God's commandments (see Exodus 34:29–32).

Thomas Experiences God's Patience

After his resurrection, Jesus appeared to his disciples.

> Now Thomas (called Didymus), one of the Twelve, was not with the disciples when Jesus came. So the other disciples told him, "We have seen the Lord!"

> But he said to them, "Unless I see the nail marks in his hands and put my finger where the nails were, and put my hand into his side, I will not believe it."
>
> A week later his disciples were in the house again, and Thomas was with them. Though the doors were locked, Jesus came and stood among them and said, "Peace be with you!" Then he said to Thomas, "Put your finger here; see my hands. Reach out your hand and put it into my side. Stop doubting and believe."
>
> Thomas said to him, "My Lord and my God!" (John 20:24–28)

Poor Thomas. He will be forever known as a doubter, a skeptic. Yet there is a bit of Thomas in all of us. We all have periods, or at least moments, of uncertainty, confusion, or mistrust. And like many of us with artistic temperaments, Thomas was apparently negative, pessimistic, and cynical by nature. For example, in spite of all the reliable reports to the contrary, Thomas was convinced Jesus was still dead. Instead of simply saying, "I'll believe it when I see it," he laid out some rather gruesome stipulations. "Until I stick my finger through his puncture wounds," he said, "I will not believe." On another occasion, Jesus insisted on going to Bethany to heal Lazarus even though the religious leaders there had threatened to kill him. Assuming the worst, Thomas's gloomy response sounds fatalistic. Far from triumphant, he dejectedly said something like, "Well, okay, let's all go to Bethany and die" (John 11:16).

Thomas not only seems prone to depression, he appears to be a loner as well. The first time the risen Christ appeared to his disciples, Thomas was nowhere to be found. At a time when he desperately needed the strength and support of his band of brothers, Thomas withdrew. No doubt he was in despair. Witnessing those bloodthirsty nails driven through his Lord's hands and feet and that deadly spear thrust through his side undoubtedly left a horrific impression on Thomas. Yet he chose to suffer alone in his anguish.

Jesus could have harshly rebuked Thomas for being weak, faithless, and full of self-pity. He could have sharply reprimanded him for deserting the others, but instead Christ displayed patience. A week later, Jesus appeared again. This time Thomas was among them, so Jesus specifically invited him to touch his wounds. The Italian painter Caravaggio captured the scene brilliantly in his masterpiece *The Incredulity of Saint Thomas* (plate 2). In the painting, Thomas's cloak is torn at the shoulder, perhaps symbolic of the disciple's frailty and brokenness. As Thomas leans forward peering intently, Jesus gently guides his finger into the wound on his right side. Two other disciples sheepishly look over Thomas's shoulder. While Jesus' face registers loving patience, Thomas's eyes radiate overwhelming astonishment. He is no longer a doubter. Despondent disbelief has been transformed into blessed assurance, and Thomas passionately proclaims, "My Lord and my God!"

Interestingly, this was not the only time Jesus exhibited patience with Thomas. In John 14, Jesus told his disciples that he was going to prepare a place for them. He said, "And if I go and prepare a place for you, I will come back and take you to be with me that you also may be where I am. You know the way to the place where I am going" (vv. 3–4). This cryptic remark undoubtedly left several disciples scratching their heads. Yet Thomas was the only one honest enough to admit he didn't understand and courageous enough to speak up. "Lord," he said, "we don't know where you are going, so how can we know the way?" (v. 5). Without a hint of frustration or anger, Jesus answered, "I am the way and the truth and the life. No one comes to the Father except through me" (v. 6).

Thomas was wired up like many of us. He had moments of doubt, he was easily discouraged, and he didn't always "get it" when it came to spiritual things. Yet Christ never gave up on Thomas, but lovingly reached out to him. In the same way, God is patient with our weaknesses and shortcomings.

Encountering the Character of God in Scripture

God reveals himself extensively throughout Scripture. "In the beginning was the Word, and the Word was with God, and the Word was God" (John 1:1). Second Timothy 3:16 reveals that "all Scripture is God-breathed." In other words, God's spirit, character, and nature permeate the Bible. If you want to know how God thinks and acts, read his Word.

God also reveals himself through his son, Jesus Christ. "The Word became flesh and made his dwelling among us. We have seen his glory, the glory of the One and Only, who came from the Father, full of grace and truth" (John 1:14). Every person in the Bible who encountered Christ experienced God's character in some deeply meaningful way. For example, the woman caught in adultery experienced mercy, the blind man experienced healing, and Lazarus experienced God's power. Jesus said, "Anyone who has seen me has seen the Father"

(John 14:9). So if you want details on how God relates personally to people, look intently at Jesus Christ, especially as he's presented in the Gospels.

The Bible is our most comprehensive authority on the character of God. So whether studying the Bible rigorously or reading devotionally, always be on the lookout for names or attributes of God. As you read, ask yourself, "Does this passage reveal anything specific about who God is?"

Encountering the Character of God during Corporate Worship

I have an embarrassing confession to make: I suffer from Worship ADD, Worship Attention Deficit Disorder. The malady strikes only when I'm in church. The symptoms include lack of focus, a faraway look in the eyes, and the impression that I'm not all "there"; it's like my brain is having an out-of-body experience. Most services at my church begin when the band (a contemporary rhythm section) kicks into something upbeat and energetic. The lyrics to the first worship chorus come up on the screen, the singers start to sing, and the congregation joins in. At this point, I'm alert and fully engaged. But within five minutes my mind begins to wander and I become completely distracted. My mouth might be moving, but I'm not thinking at all about what I'm singing. Instead, I'll be thinking about what I'm going to do after church, what new movies I'd like to see, the phone calls I need to make, etc. I am reminded of the words of King Claudius in Hamlet: "My words fly up, my thoughts remain below; words without thoughts never to heaven go."[2]

Apparently I'm not the only one suffering with Worship ADD. Gary Thomas writes:

> It amazes me how casually I can sing songs of deep, almost heroic commitment. It's as if I think, *As long as I'm singing, the words I say don't really matter. God knows it's just a song.* While my mind wanders I promise to bow before the Lord, to proclaim his name to the ends of the earth, and to go so far as to die to express my faith. Yet these words may be sung with scarcely more emotion than I feel when I'm ordering a hamburger. How often do we Christians "take the Lord's name in vain" during our worship?[3]

It must break God's heart when we mindlessly go through the motions during worship. Worshiping without conviction is what prompted Jesus to lament, "These people honor me with their lips, but their hearts are far from me" (Matthew 15:8).

The Cure for Worship ADD

Worship leader/songwriter Andy Park notes that

> As we worship, the Spirit of God enlightens us about different aspects of God's nature. At times, he illumines my understanding about God's unconditional love. I catch a glimpse of the Father's heart of tender mercy. Over and over again I am amazed that his love is not like human love—it is never conditional on our performance. At other times I am awestruck by his holiness, his majesty and his transcendent power.[4]

To remedy my Worship ADD, I've been trying to be more attentive to the names and attributes of God during corporate worship. While singing along with the congregation, I search the lyrics for any characteristics, descriptions, or names of God, and I emphasize those portions and sing them with greater energy. A few weeks ago, we sang a chorus at church that praised Christ as our redeemer. My spirit camped on that title and it reminded me that I am redeemed; I have been freed from my old nature to live as a new man in Christ. It strengthened my resolve to say no to sin and yes to God. Those thoughts lasted only a few seconds, but they helped me focus on the Lord, and isn't that what we're supposed to do during worship?

Don't allow corporate worship to digress into merely a sing-along time before the sermon. In 1 Corinthians 14:15, Paul says, "I will sing with my spirit, but I will also sing with my mind." So the next time you're in church singing hymns or worship choruses, I encourage you to interact intellectually and emotionally with lyrics that point directly to God.

It's Not About Us

File this under "Worship Leaders Say the Darnedest Things." A couple songs into the worship set, I heard a worship leader say, "I love you, Lord. You make me feel so good. I've had a bad week and I came to church this morning feeling pretty down. But as soon as I started singing and lifting up the name of Jesus, my spirit started to soar." Throughout the service, the worship leader's comments were laced with "I," "my," and "me." He referred to himself more often than to the Lord. While it's important to personalize worship, we must remember that worship is not about us; it's about God. "Not to us, O Lord, not to us but to your name be the glory, because of your love and faithfulness" (Psalm 115:1). By focusing on the attributes of God, we insure that our worship will be God-centered instead of me-centered. David wrote, "I have seen you in the sanctuary and beheld your power and your glory (Psalm 63:2).

Get Me to the Church on Time

In many North American churches, I've observed a significant number of people missing when the service begins, as it often does, with worship. In some cases, half the congregation doesn't show up until ten minutes into the first worship set. Not only is it disheartening for those leading, it's more difficult to engage with God if you plop down in your seat midway through worship. In my opinion, the only ones excused for arriving late to church are any disabled worshipers and parents of small children, who often have to make a mad dash to be on time. The rest of us should do everything we can not only to get to church on time but to prepare our hearts beforehand.

The way we approach corporate worship impacts our ability to engage. For that reason, the Puritan author Stephen Charnock suggests we set our sights on the attributes of God as we enter into worship:

> God ... is a Spirit of infinite majesty, therefore we must come before him with reverence; he is a Spirit infinitely high, therefore we must offer up our sacrifices with the deepest humility; he is a Spirit infinitely holy, therefore we must address him with purity; he is a Spirit infinitely glorious, we must therefore acknowledge his excellency in all that we do.[5]

I know many who play a worship CD while driving to church. Others turn the radio off and pray. Some people arrive early so they can enjoy a few moments of quiet before the service starts. Still others read a psalm or the featured Scripture of the day. These are just a few examples of ways to prepare one's heart for worship.

Avoid Worship Wars

The most controversial religious issue of Jesus' day centered upon worship styles. Big shock, huh? The woman at the well, for example, tried to pull Jesus into the ongoing debate over which venue was more suitable for worship:

"'Sir,' the woman said, 'I can see that you are a prophet. Our fathers worshiped on this mountain, but you Jews claim that the place where we must worship is in Jerusalem.' Jesus declared, 'Believe me, woman, a time is coming when you will worship the Father neither on this mountain nor in Jerusalem.... A time is coming and has now come when the true worshipers will worship the Father in spirit and truth" (John 4:19–21, 23).

This poor woman was so hung up on which mountain was more spiritual that she missed the essence of worship, which is God. In fact, he was standing right in front of her in the flesh!

Likewise, modern churchgoers have a bad habit of fixating on non-essentials—the style of music, the pastor's wardrobe, the worship leader's hairstyle—and we miss the essence of worship, which is the character of God. Furthermore, when we allow worship, the most beautiful expression of Christian unity, to become a source of contention, we grieve the heart of God. I recently met a woman whose father is no longer speaking to her because she's spearheading the contemporary service at her church. As an elder at the church, her father is vehemently opposed to current worship styles. I can't help but ask: Is this really worth fighting about?

Practice Tolerance

I believe the most urgent issue facing the church today is our need for tolerance. I'm not referring to a mere "grin and bear it" type of acquiescence, but to something much deeper and more proactive. The local church should be a community of grace where all people feel loved and accepted regardless of race, social standing, or spiritual maturity. Romans 15:7 simply says, "Accept one another, then, just as Christ accepted you, in order to bring praise to God." Accepting others means that we refrain from being petty or hypercritical. Instead of trying to change people into what we want them to be, we celebrate their uniqueness. Ephesians 4:2 encourages us to "be completely humble and gentle; be patient, bearing with one another in love." James 4:11 (NASB) reads, "Do not speak against one another," and James 5:9 (NASB) says, "Do not complain, brethren, against one another, so that you yourselves may not be judged."

Ironically, the church's need for tolerance is most acute in issues pertaining to worship. In many churches, there is total agreement about whom we worship, but sharp division over how to worship, and musical style is at the crux of the controversy. The battle lines are drawn between traditional and contemporary, young and old, your music and my music. If we can't tolerate each other's musical preferences, how are we going to tolerate each other's differing personalities, backgrounds, ethnicities, and political views?

We've all seen examples of intolerance. There's the disgruntled parishioner who sits through the service with his or her arms folded across the chest, stubbornly refusing to sing. Or the church veteran who's offended by the new "ungodly" music and threatens to leave or quit tithing. Or the young person who mocks the older generation's music for being "unspiritual" or "inauthentic." In spite of these strong opinions, the Bible does not endorse one style of music over another, so no type of music is more holy than another. In fact, there is no such thing as a Christian style of music; the only thing "Christian" about Christian music is the lyrics. If you think worship in heaven is going to be confined to old English hymns, you're in for a huge surprise. For worship in heaven will be an exhilarating mix of musical styles—from Gregorian chant to hip-hop. So learn to deal with it now! If during corporate worship you concentrate on the names and attributes of God presented in the lyrics of every praise song or hymn, you will be able to effectively worship regardless of the style of music.

I recently celebrated my fiftieth birthday (and I use the word "celebrated" facetiously). After receiving an invitation by mail to join the AARP (American Association of Retired Persons) and suffering the brunt of numerous senior citizen jokes, I began to contemplate what kind of person I'd eventually like to be in my old age. I've come to the conclusion that I want to be the most loving, caring, open-minded, hippest, on-fire-for-Christ senior citizen I can be. In *A Turbulent Peace*, Ray Waddle writes:

> My heroes include any elderly persons who keep the flame lit, who still feel inspiration and outrage at ideas, current events, history, movies, books, national tragedies, spring flowers, the passing parade. Somehow they take it all in. Life enlarges their spirit, becomes fuel for the remaining journey, seasoned with humor, not bitterness. They age with dignity. Part of the dignity is keeping the inevitable heartbreak framed by larger perspectives and by going deeper into the grief, not denying it. The alternative is that other strategy of the heart, the hardening of it.[6]

Here's my challenge to any other aging boomers out there like me: let tolerance begin with us. Let's encourage the next generation of worship leaders to sing a "new song"—their own song—unto the Lord (Psalm 96:1). Let's get behind them in their efforts to be creative and relevant to today's culture. And let's support fully their desire for deep authentic worship. In other words, let's graciously pass the baton on to the next generation with our fullest blessing.

Encountering the Character of God in Others

God often chooses to reveal himself through other people. In fact, some of God's attributes, like his love, compassion, or approval, are best experienced through others. When King Saul threatened his life, David fled and wandered like a fugitive in the wilderness. However, Jonathan, who was not only David's friend but Saul's son, found David and "helped him find strength in God" (1 Samuel 23:16). At a time when David felt utterly hopeless, God encouraged him through his friend Jonathan.

In Colossians 4:7–11, Paul lists by name a group of men who proved to be a source of encouragement to him. One senses that God ministered deeply to Paul through these men, especially during times of great discouragement.

I too have struggled with discouragement at various points in my life. Like most artists, my musical career, specifically in regard to writing and playing, has been a mixed bag of victories and defeats. What has kept me going all these years, though, is the encouragement I've received along the way, much of which I suspect has been orchestrated by God. After all, Romans 15:5 describes God as a giver of encouragement. On those occasions when I've been particularly disheartened, I've sought comfort from the Lord. Sometimes the only prayer I could muster was simply, *Lord, I'm so down. Please encourage me.* Then, often within days, I'd receive a letter, a phone call, or an email from someone—sometimes someone I didn't even know—with warm words about my music. I know it sounds uncanny, and some might consider it mere coincidence, but because I had prayed, and because the encouragement came seemingly out of the blue, from sources I least expected, I'm convinced God was somehow behind those revitalizing words of support.

Ironically, the biggest obstacle to experiencing God through others is our inability to receive from others. I've wrestled with this. In the past, when someone complimented me, I was always quick to change the subject or deflect the encouragement to someone else. As a result, I was much better at giving encouragement than receiving it, not because I was intrinsically magnanimous, but because I was prideful and arrogant. You see, I hated feeling like a "charity case" or "needy." According to my dysfunctional way of thinking, that was vulnerable and weak. So my superiority and self-sufficiency prevented me from hearing and receiving encouragement. However, as I've grown older, I'm happy to report that I'm making progress in this area. While I still occasionally change the subject or deflect compliments, afterward I'll often look back on the conversation and acknowledge the encouragement intended. After all, those encouraging words might actually be coming from God himself.

Encountering the Character of God in Art

Artists learn from art. While nonartists might see little or no meaning behind a work of art, we glean valuable insights. For believers, these insights often have spiritual connotations. At a retreat not long ago, a woman spoke of her encounter with God through a secular "pop" song. Earlier that week, she was in her car and a love song came on the radio that she had heard hundreds of times. But this time, the song took on a whole new meaning because she heard the lyrics as if God was speaking them directly to her, boldly reminding her that he loves her. The song was not a "Christian song," yet this dear sister experienced God's love through it.

I've had many similar experiences with paintings, novels, plays, and movies. One that comes instantly to mind is the 1983 film *A Christmas Story*. In the movie, nine-year-old Ralphie Parker wants nothing more for Christmas than a Red Ryder BB gun. However, all the adults in his life pour cold water on Ralphie's dream. His parents, teacher, and even Santa Claus warn him of the inevitable danger of owning a BB gun: "You'll shoot your eye out." As Ralphie schemes to overcome his parents' BB gun phobia, we get a humorous glimpse of what it was like to grow up in a small Indiana town in the 1940s, part of which meant dealing with bullies. One such bully, Scut Farcus, constantly harasses Ralphie and his friends on their way to and from school every day. Just when Ralphie has taken all the discouragement he can take, and his beloved BB gun seems furthest out of reach, Scut Farcus corners him. This time, though, instead of cowering, Ralphie's anger and frustration boil over. He charges the bully, takes him down, and starts punching him while screaming a torrent of obscenities. Ralphie's mom is quickly summoned to rescue the school bully from the fury of her son.

Back home, Ralphie is cleaned up and sent to his room. There he waits, pained with remorse and fearing the worst punishment imaginable from his father when he returns home from work. But Ralphie never gets what he deserves because his mother intervenes on his behalf. She mentions the fight to her husband during dinner, but then immediately changes the subject as if the matter had already been taken care of. Ralphie is shocked. With renewed respect for his mother, the narrator reminiscing as the adult Ralphie says, "From then on things were different between me and my mother."

"The Scut Farcus Affair," as it's referred to in the movie, deepened my understanding of God's mercy. Like Ralphie, I too have lashed out in anger and frustration. I too have received mercy undeserved, and I too am continually shocked by God's mercy and grace.

Movies and other art forms are frequently a means for us to experience God. So whether it's a movie, a painting, a symphony, or another form of artistic expression, look for the character of God in art.

Encountering the Character of God in Nature

My wife, Sue, is a devoted nature lover and has taught me much about finding God within the designs of creation. Because of her, I appreciate the nuances, the diversity, and the rhythms of nature. For example, every spring and fall we run outside when we hear the sandhill cranes flying over our house and we cheer them on. To us, their migration signals the change of the seasons.

Sue tends to observe things in nature that very few people even notice. One time while watching some birds splashing around in a birdbath, Sue pointed out that all the birds jump into the bowl, immerse fully in the water, and get completely drenched—except for cardinals. You'll never see a cardinal (at least not in our neck of the woods) frolicking in the birdbath because they prefer showers. They're more apt to stand under a lawn sprinkler or out in a soft rain. I had never picked up on this before.

On another occasion, Sue asked, "Have you ever noticed that when most birds drink, they lift their heads straight up and let the water slide down their throats? But doves never lift up their heads when they drink; they slurp." As I watched the birds I immediately saw what she was describing.

Every time Sue mentions these fascinating tidbits about nature, I can't help but think that God must be pleased that one of his children notices the details of his handiwork. I also can't help but be moved to worship God for the beauty and wonder of his creation. The poet Elizabeth Barrett Browning wrote:

> Earth's crammed with heaven,
> And every common bush afire with God;
> But only he who sees, takes off his shoes,
> The rest sit round it and pluck blackberries,
> And daub their natural faces unaware.[7]

Psalm 19:1–2 proclaims that God's glory is on display throughout the universe day and night: "The heavens declare the glory of God; the skies proclaim the work of his hands. Day after day they pour forth speech; night after night they display knowledge." So the next time you're outside—sitting, walking, or driving—take a moment to observe the various ways God reveals himself to us through creation. The sun reminds us that Jesus is the light of the world (John 8:12). The stars call to mind the fact that God has numbered and named them all (Psalm 147:4). Every sunrise recalls that God's compassions are new every morning (Lamentations 3:22–23). Snow, for those of us "lucky" enough to have to shovel it, provides a vivid picture of the atoning work of grace: "Though your sins are like scarlet, they shall be as white as snow" (Isaiah 1:18).

In summary, whether reading Scripture, interacting with others, singing in corporate worship, or out in nature, be attentive not only to God's presence but also to his character. Jesus said, "Whoever has my commands and keeps them is the one who loves me. Anyone who loves me will be loved by my Father, and I too will love them and show myself to them" (John 14:21 TNIV). God promises to disclose himself personally to those who truly love him, so let's not miss it!

Follow-Up Questions for Group Discussion

1. What names or attributes of God would you add to those listed in this chapter?

2. What name or attribute of God has been most meaningful to you lately? Why?

3. What name or attribute of God do you sense you need more of these days?

4. What name or attribute of God stands out as especially prevalent throughout your life?

5. When do you most sense God's presence?

6. Have you witnessed any controversies around the issue of worship? How were they dealt with?

7. Do you agree that tolerance is desperately needed in light of today's "worship wars"? Why or why not?

8. Have you recently experienced God's character through others? Please describe.

9. Have you seen any movies lately (or any other artistic presentation) that spoke to you on a spiritual level? Please describe it.

10. How can those planning worship services be more effective in helping a congregation experience the attributes of God?

Personal Action Steps

1. Read Psalm 111 and pick out all the attributes of God listed.

2. God anointed Isaiah's mouth because words were the tools of his trade—he served God via the spoken word. As an artist, identify the tools of your trade, then write or say a prayer committing those tools to the Lord (i.e., your hands, voice, feet, mind, etc.).

3. As you read Scripture this week, pick out a name or attribute of God as a springboard for worship and prayer.

4. Make a list of your closest friends and the attributes of God you experience most prevalently in each of them.

5. Schedule a nature activity. It could be something as simple as a walk in a park or as involved as a trip to the Grand Canyon.

chapter three

Responding to the Character of God

It was not the Five Mississippi Blind Boys
who lifted me off the ground
that Sunday morning
as I drove down for the paper, some oranges, and
bread.
Nor was it the Dixie Hummingbirds
or the Soul Stirrers, despite their quickening name,
or even the Swan Silvertones
who inspired me to look off over the commotion of
trees
into the open vault of the sky.

No, it was the Sensational Nightingales
who happened to be singing on the gospel
station early that Sunday morning
and must be credited with the bumping up of my
spirit,
the arousal of the mice within.

I have always loved this harmony,
like four, sometimes five trains running
side by side over a contoured landscape—
make that a shimmering, red-dirt landscape,
wildflowers growing along the silver tracks,
lace tablecloths covering the hills,
the men and women in white shirts and dresses
walking in the direction of a tall steeple.

Sunday morning in a perfect Georgia.

But I am not here to describe the sound
of the falsetto whine, sepulchral bass,
alto and tenor fitted snugly in between;
only to witness my own minor ascension
that morning as they sang, so parallel,
about the usual themes,
the garden of suffering,
the beads of blood on the forehead,
the stone before the hillside tomb,
and the ancient rolling waters
we would all have to cross some day.

God bless the Sensational Nightingales,
I thought as I turned up the volume,
God bless their families and their powder blue
suits.
They are a far cry from the quiet kneeling
I was raised with,
a far, hand-clapping cry from the candles
that glowed in the alcoves
and the fixed eyes of saints staring down
from their corners.

Oh, my cap was on straight that Sunday morning
and I was fine keeping the car on the road.
No one would ever have guessed
I was being lifted into the air by nightingales,
hoisted by their beaks like a long banner
that curls across an empty blue sky,
caught up in the annunciation
of these high, most encouraging tidings.

"Sunday Morning with the Sensational
Nightingales" by Billy Collins
(used by permission)

Pastor Mark looked out his office window and noticed the church parking lot was nearly full. As was his habit before every service, he began to pray for people by name as he spotted them streaming from their cars up the walkway to the church. But he was soon startled by a knock at the door. "Come in."

It was Jonah Stevens, head usher. "Pastor, I hate to bother you, but we have a problem. Daniel isn't here yet."

Daniel is the church's worship leader or, more accurately, he's the church's only worship leader. Daniel is extremely talented, plays nine different instruments, sings, and even writes music. And the congregation loves him. However, Daniel isn't much of a team builder; he's pretty much a one-man show, so to speak.

"Isn't he usually late?" Pastor Mark asked.

"Not this late."

Just then Rosie, the church receptionist, came bounding into the pastor's office clutching a handful of messages. "Pastor, Daniel's gig went late last night, he overslept, and then he got a flat tire on his way here."

"Where is he stranded?" Jonah asked. "I'll drive out to get him."

Rosie shook her head. "He's at the Farm and Fleet on 47."

Pastor Mark voiced what they all instantly realized: "By the time you get back, the worship time will be over." He walked back to the window. "If either of you have any hidden talents, now would be the time to speak up." He chuckled.

Jonah and Rosie both stared at their shoes.

"Okay," Pastor Mark said, "do we have anyone else who can lead worship?"

His two compatriots joined Pastor Mark at the window. "I don't know anyone who can sing, especially on such short notice," Rosie said.

"And I certainly don't know anyone who plays an instrument," Jonah added.

Pastor Mark was getting a little frustrated. "You mean to tell me that in a church of three hundred people we have no one else who can sing or play?"

Jonah and Rosie looked at each other. "No one that we know of," Jonah said.

After an awkward silence, Pastor Mark blurted out, "Well I can't carry a tune in a bucket, that's for sure."

"Let's show a video," Rosie suggested, "or we could sing along to a worship CD."

"How about if we just end early?" Jonah offered.

Pastor Mark sighed. "Our people are expecting a worship service."

"But how can we worship without music?" Jonah asked.

"I don't know," Pastor Mark said, "but we're about to find out."

At that, the determined pastor slid his sermon notes into his Bible, walked briskly out of his office, and headed for the sanctuary, urgently praying the entire way. Jonah and Rosie followed, hot on his heels, like two neighbors hurrying to the scene of a serious accident.

On the hour, Pastor Mark walked up to the podium, welcomed his flock, and went through a few announcements. Then without apology, or any reference to Daniel's absence, he invited the congregation to turn to one of his favorite hymns, number 390, "Spirit of God, Descend Upon My Heart." Some in the congregation panicked when they didn't see Daniel at the piano, but everyone else grabbed a hymnal from the pew and started flipping pages.

"Instead of singing, I'd like us to read the words together," Pastor Mark announced. He led and the congregation jumped in:

> Spirit of God, descend upon my heart;
> Wean it from earth, thro' all its pulses move;
> Stoop to my weakness, mighty as Thou art,
> And make me love Thee as I ought to love.[1]

Pastor Mark expounded briefly on the line "Stoop to my weakness, mighty as Thou art," and invited people to share recent examples of God's strength and power in their lives. This sent the church's sound technician running down the aisle with a microphone for everyone to pass around and share. At first it was quiet. After all, the church had never done anything like this before. But after a while, people started to share. One woman praised God for healing her cancer and a man talked about joining AA and overcoming an alcohol addiction. Then the floodgates opened and many examples of answered prayer, blessing, and provision were eagerly shared. Pastor Mark taught the congregation a call and response he improvised on the spot. At the end of each story, he would say, "Thanks be to God!" and the congregation would cheer, applaud, and shout, "Yes, thanks be to God!" After about fifteen minutes, Pastor Mark had to cut off the sharing so they could move on.

He then led the congregation in reading the second verse of the hymn:

> Teach me to feel that Thou art always nigh;
> Teach me the struggles of the soul to bear,
> To check the rising doubt, the rebel sigh;
> Teach me the patience of unanswered prayer.[2]

Pastor Mark hesitated a bit and then asked for prayer concerning his youngest son who was far from God, running with wild friends, and making bad choices. Those closest to the pastor were aware of the situation, but this was the first time he talked publicly about it. It was obviously very painful for him and his wife. A couple times Pastor Mark stopped to clear his throat and catch his breath; his eyes were moist. Sniffles were heard throughout the sanctuary.

Looking out over the congregation, Pastor Mark asked, "What struggles, concerns, and anxieties are you carrying this morning?" He then directed the congregation to form small groups of three or four people right where they were sitting and pray for each other.

The remainder of the service was equally unscripted. They kneeled and prayed the Lord's Prayer together. Then they read Psalm 23 aloud from the hymnal and even observed a brief time of personal confession and silence (without the usual soothing music playing in the background). Pastor Mark asked the congregation to stand and read Psalm 146 together right before his sermon which, by the way, had to be shortened due to time.

After the service, the congregation was ecstatic. Many commented that it had been the most meaningful worship experience they had had in years. Some even said they wouldn't mind worshiping like that all the time. In fact, months later, people were still buzzing about it and asking Pastor Mark, "When are we going to do another one of those nonmusical worship services?"

Questions for Group Discussion

1. What is your opinion of Pastor Mark's solution for being without a worship leader for music that day?

2. Why do you think the congregation responded so favorably to this service?

3. What do you suppose Pastor Mark's church learned from this experience?

4. Had you been in the congregation, what part of this service would have been most meaningful to you?

5. How would you evaluate Pastor Mark's ability as a worship leader?

6. Is there anything you would have done differently had you been in Pastor Mark's shoes?

7. Is the above story a fluke, or is it really possible to have a meaningful worship experience without music? Why or why not?

8. Have you ever experienced a corporate worship time without music? If so, what was it like?

9. Does music ever hinder you from truly worshiping? If so, how would you explain that?

10. Do you have any suggestions of other nonmusical ways to express praise?

ALL-OUT WORSHIP

Our emotions play an important role in worship, but as Rick Warren notes, worship is much more than merely an emotional experience: "Today many equate being emotionally moved by music as being moved by the Spirit, but these are not the same. Real worship happens when your spirit responds to God, not to some musical tone."[3] Thus, worship is an action, a response; it is something we do.

The English word *worship* comes from two words, *worth* and *ship*, and means to "ascribe" or "declare worth." The Hebrew word most often translated as worship actually means to "bow down" or "fall down in reverence." In both cases, it's clear that worship was never intended to be a passive exercise. The title of Dr. Robert Webber's book says it all: *Worship Is a Verb.*

God's glory demands, and deserves, a response. When Peter saw Jesus on the mountain transfigured in all his glory, he offered to erect three tabernacles as a memorial (Matthew 17:1–8). Peter couldn't sit idly by; he had to do something. And given the significance of the event, he had to do something momentous.

In the same way, Jesus invites us to respond to the Father emphatically. He said, "Love the Lord your God with *all* your heart and with *all* your soul and with *all* your mind" (Matthew 22:37, emphasis mine). David held nothing back when he worshiped. He said, "I will praise you, O Lord my God, with all my heart; I will glorify your name forever" (Psalm 86:12). David also "danced before the Lord with all his might" (2 Samuel 6:14). Worship, therefore, is passionate, zealous, uninhibited, all-out engagement with the presence and character of God.

Luke tells the story of a woman who went all out to worship Christ:

> Now one of the Pharisees invited Jesus to have dinner with him, so he went to the Pharisee's house and reclined at the table. When a woman who had lived a sinful life in that town learned that Jesus was eating at the Pharisee's house, she brought an alabaster jar of perfume, and as she stood behind him at his feet weeping, she began to wet his feet with her tears. Then she wiped them with her hair, kissed them and poured perfume on them. (Luke 7:36–38)

This story also underscores the fact that worship can take on a variety of forms. This woman didn't sing or play guitar. She washed the feet of Christ with her tears, wiped them with her hair, and poured out an expensive bottle of perfume. Indeed, we all respond to God's presence and character in different ways. And as we witnessed in the opening scenario, worship doesn't always have to involve music. So as we explore the various biblical ways to worship, identify any that are new to you and consider adding them to your regular worship routine. In doing so, you will add depth and variety to your worship experience.

Give Thanks

Gratitude is the mark of a true worshiper. The psalmist invites us to "come before [God] with thanksgiving" (Psalm 95:2) and to "enter his gates with thanksgiving and his courts with praise; give thanks to him and praise his name" (Psalm 100:4). Colossians 3:16–17 instructs us to "sing psalms, hymns and spiritual songs with gratitude in your hearts to God. And whatever you do, whether in word or deed, do it all in the name of the Lord Jesus, giving thanks to God the Father through him."

In giving thanks, we remember God's blessings, large and small. In his book *Life Together*, Dietrich Bonhoeffer writes:

> In the Christian community thankfulness is just what it is anywhere else in the Christian life. Only he who gives thanks for little things receives the big things. We prevent God from giving us the great spiritual gifts He has in store for us, because we do not give thanks for daily gifts.... We pray for the big things and forget to give thanks for the ordinary, small (and yet really not small) gifts. How can God entrust great things to one who will not thankfully receive from Him the little things?[4]

In chapter 1, I mentioned the acronym ACTS as a helpful tool for devotions. The *A* stands for adoration—worshiping God for who he is. The *T* stands for thanksgiving—thanking God for what he's done. In 1 Chronicles 17:16 David cried out, "Who am I, O Lord God, and what is my family, that you have brought me this far?" Then he goes on to list specifically some of God's blessings in his life and upon Israel. Like David, we too have much for which to be thankful—salvation, our relationship with God, answered prayer, family, friends, church—and that's just for starters. Hebrews 12:28 claims salvation alone as ample reason for thanksgiving: "Therefore, since we are receiving a kingdom that cannot be shaken, let us be thankful, and so worship God acceptably with reverence and awe." So when giving thanks, be specific. A general prayer like *Thank you for our many blessings,* however sincere, doesn't arouse as much gratitude as actually taking the time to enumerate those blessings. Remember, it's not enough to *be* thankful; we must *express* it verbally, in writing, or however appropriate. Remember, worship is a verb!

Sometimes gratitude produces tears. When the foundation was laid for the rebuilding of the temple, Ezra led the people of Israel in a time of worship that turned deeply emotional:

> With praise and thanksgiving they sang to the Lord: "He is good; his love to Israel endures forever." And all the people gave a great shout of praise to the Lord, because the foundation of the house of the Lord was laid. But many of the older priests and Levites and family heads, who had seen the former temple, wept aloud when they saw the foundation of this temple being laid, while many others shouted for joy. No one could distinguish the sound of the shouts of joy from the sound of weeping, because the people made so much noise. And the sound was heard far away. (Ezra 3:11–13)

Similarly, Joseph's reunion with his family was very emotional. "Joseph had his chariot made ready and went to Goshen to meet his father Israel. As soon as Joseph appeared before him, he threw his arms around his father and wept for a long time" (Genesis 46:29). Tears of joy can be profoundly worshipful.

First Thessalonians 5:18 instructs us to "give thanks in all circumstances, for this is God's will for you in Christ Jesus." Even the smallest of blessings is still more than we deserve, so in everything let's give thanks.

Express Praise and Adoration

Praise is simply telling God our thoughts about him. The people of Israel worshiped God during the Passover for sparing their lives (Exodus 12:27). After Ezra read the Word of God, the people worshiped (Nehemiah 8:18, 9:3). The book of Psalms ends with this climactic admonition: "Let everything that has breath praise the Lord. Praise the Lord" (Psalm 150:6).

Adoration is telling God how we feel about him. The Psalmist says, "I love the Lord, for he heard my voice; he heard my cry for mercy" (Psalm 116:1). The introduction to Psalm 18 reveals how David felt about God and why: "David ... sang to the Lord the words of this song when the Lord delivered him from the hand of all his enemies and from the hand of Saul. He said: 'I love you, O Lord, my strength.'"

Jesus inspired praise and adoration wherever he went. At birth, he was worshiped by shepherds as well as Magi (Luke 2:20; Matthew 2:11). Upon seeing Jesus walk on water, the disciples "worshiped him, saying, 'Truly you are the Son of God'" (Matthew 14:33). And when Jesus entered Jerusalem on Palm Sunday the crowd shouted, "Hosanna! Blessed is he who comes in the name of the Lord! Blessed is the King of Israel!" (John 12:13).

In all the examples above, there is an overwhelming sense of awe and reverence toward God. It's the same kind of feeling you and I have when we're utterly captivated by God and we say something deeply heartfelt like, "I love you, Lord, from the bottom of my heart." Or, "God, I praise you from the depths of my being!"

Expressing our deepest thoughts and feelings about God in worship allows us to experience and enjoy him more. C. S. Lewis states that "we delight to praise what we enjoy because the praise not merely expresses but completes the enjoyment."[5]

Get Vocal: Singing, Shouting, and Making a Joyful Noise

Until modern times, singing was common throughout history: soldiers sang as they marched, workers sang in the fields, and families gathered in the parlor to sing around the piano. Today, people don't often sing. Aside from the national anthem at sporting events or the occasional "Happy Birthday" at the office, we're more apt to listen to music rather than make our own. In fact, music has become the background to life; we listen to it while we drive, work, or exercise.

We have become a generation of music consumers, not music makers. Most everyone likes music, but not many sing. Culturally speaking, participatory singing has become a foreign concept.

Those who grew up in the church usually come to accept singing as a normal part of corporate worship. After all, singing has always played a significant role in the church dating back to the New Testament when believers were exhorted to "sing and make music" to the Lord (Ephesians 5:19) and to gratefully "sing psalms, hymns and spiritual songs" (Colossians 3:16). But for those who have little or no church experience, being asked to sing, even in a crowd, is downright weird. To further complicate matters, a significant number of men are uncomfortable singing because they regard it as "womanly." In his book *Why Men Hate Going to Church,* David Murrow writes, "Even among churchgoers, singing is more popular with women than men. We polled our fifteen-hundred-member church: while three-quarters of the women chose praise singing as a top priority, only about half the guys chose it."[6]

In spite of cultural inhibitions, Scripture commands that we sing. Psalm 66:1–4 says:

> Shout with joy to God, all the earth! Sing the glory of his name; make his praise glorious! Say to God, "How awesome are your deeds! So great is your power that your enemies cringe before you. All the earth bows down to you; they sing praise to you, they sing praise to your name."

If that's not clear enough, Psalm 47:6–7 leaves no doubt that we are commanded to sing: "Sing praises to God, sing praises; sing praises to our King, sing praises. For God is the King of all the earth; sing to him a psalm of praise."

The Bible contains well over a hundred references to singing, mostly as worship to God. Moses erupted into a song of praise after the Israelites were delivered from Egypt (Exodus 15), as did David after God delivered him from the hand of Saul (2 Samuel 22). Jesus and the disciples sang a hymn on their way to Gethsemane (Matthew 26:30). The largest book of the Bible is the Psalms, which contains 150 songs of praise and worship nestled at the midpoint of Scripture.

Why Sing?

Given our reluctance to sing and the Bible's insistence on it, let's briefly discuss why human beings sing in the first place. On a primal level, singing engages our emotions; it helps us experience in our hearts what we know to be true in our minds. Take something as simple as the "Doxology," for example:

> Praise God from whom all blessings flow
> Praise Him, all creatures here below.
> Praise Him above, ye heav'nly host.
> Praise Father, Son and Holy Ghost.[7]

Merely reciting those lyrics can be deeply moving, inviting all to worship our triune God. However, singing those words can be even more profound. The spacious rhythm causes the words to come out more slowly than we'd speak them, enabling us to ponder their meaning and to actually visualize heaven and earth worshiping God. The melody, especially as it climbs and soars, elicits a palpable sense of transcendence, majesty, and beauty. Furthermore, singing is very physical. In order to sing, one must breathe deeply, take the words deep into your gut and exhale them boldly and forcefully. Thus, singing combines mind, body, heart, and soul into one dynamic expression.

Calling All Nonsingers

A common misperception about singing is that one must have a good voice to worship. Even some artists who are not vocalists share this misconception. Since they don't sing as well as the "worship team," they don't fully engage in corporate worship. Recently while leading a retreat for artists, I invited everyone to gather around the piano for a time of worship. A few minutes into our first song, I noticed a handful of people hanging out in the back of the room, removed from the rest of the group. When I invited them to join us, one of them replied good-naturedly, "I'm sorry, but singing just ain't my thing, and believe me, my voice is so bad, if I joined in it would ruin worship for everyone else."

I can certainly relate to his reticence. Though I'm a musician, I'm not much of a singer. I'm more of a composer and instrumentalist. So I was relieved when I learned that God doesn't care what I sound like. He looks at my heart, not the quality of my singing voice. Fortunately, worship is not confined to only those who have beautifully trained voices. Scripture invites all of us to sing, shout, or make a joyful noise unto the Lord (Psalms 35:27; 66:1; 81:1 KJV; 95:1–2; 98:4; 100:1). I can't sing that well, but I can certainly shout or make a "joyful noise." While those up front leading worship are expected to have good voices, the rest of us are off the hook. So don't hold back your worship; be vocal, let it rip!

Once during corporate worship at a conference, I was standing among a group of professional singers. I was engulfed in a sea of beautiful voices singing rich harmonies and tasteful ad libs. However, I couldn't help but notice a man's voice a few rows back singing loudly off key. Out of curiosity, I glanced sideways to get a look and I instantly spotted the man. With both hands raised as high as they could go, his face beamed heavenward with tears rolling down his cheeks. He sang every word from the depth of his soul. From that point on, his faulty intonation no longer bothered me, and I could only imagine how beautiful and precious that man's crackly out-of-tune voice sounded to God.

If you love the Lord and you're grateful for all he's done for you, sing his praises at the top of your lungs. That's the spirit behind Psalm 13:5–6: "But I trust in your unfailing love; my heart rejoices in your salvation. I will sing to the Lord, for he has been good to me." Psalm 89:1 adds: "I will sing of the Lord's great love forever; with my mouth I will make your faithfulness known through all generations." Remember, it's not enough to feel affection for God. As Psalm 66:8 points out, worship must be made audible: "Praise our God, O peoples, let the sound of his praise be heard."

Many years ago, I was hiking in the Rocky Mountains with a friend. We arose very early one morning and set out to climb the tallest peak in the valley, some 11,000 feet high. A little before noon we reached the top. The view jolted our flat Midwestern sensibilities; the expanse was majestic, the colors glorious, and the beauty indescribable. We sat silent, completely overwhelmed, for the longest time. Then, without warning, we spontaneously started to sing—worship songs praising God for his majesty, strength, and glory. It didn't matter what we sounded like. We couldn't contain our joy; we had to sing. At that moment, singing was the only medium that came close to capturing our deepest emotions. "Sing to the Lord, for he has done glorious things; let this be known to all the world" (Isaiah 12:5).

Get Physical: Clap, Dance, and Jump for Joy

Do you ever get so excited about the Lord that you physically can't contain yourself? For those times, Scripture gives us the freedom to clap, dance, or jump for joy. Psalm 47:1 reads, "Clap your hands, all you nations; shout to God with cries of joy." Psalm 149:3 encourages us to "praise his name with dancing" (see also Psalm 150:4).

As David Murrow notes, physical expressions of praise appeal especially to men:

> Men are just as emotional as women; they just express themselves differently. So if a church welcomes feminine displays of emotion such as crying, hugging, and hand holding, it's time to welcome masculine displays such as applause, shouts, fist pumping, and high-fives. I'm serious. Men should be allowed to express their love for God in truly masculine ways as long as it is done in good order.[8]

My favorite example of a physical expression of worship comes from Acts 3. Peter and John healed a crippled man, and the man was so overjoyed he "went with them into the temple courts, walking and jumping, and praising God" (v. 8). Now if you can't imagine yourself shouting, clapping, dancing, or leaping for joy in church, or if your church doesn't allow such things, you are still free to try it at home during your private worship time.

Recently I performed my own version of "walking and jumping and praising God." Every day, while our younger son, Joel, was serving two deployments with the Marines in Iraq, my wife and I were on pins and needles, praying for him whenever we heard news about the war or whenever he came to mind. I'll never forget his second homecoming. It was Friday, April 1, 2005. Just before midnight we arrived at the Marine base in Twenty-Nine Palms, California, and parked at the edge of a huge field. In spite of the chill of the desert air, the atmosphere was festive. Children ran playfully up and down the field holding little American flags, wives kept touching up their makeup, and mothers and fathers unfurled "Welcome Home" signs. Three and a half hours later, word came over the loudspeaker that our Marines were approaching. At that moment, hundreds of men, women, and children rushed onto the field and lined up along the fence. When the buses were spotted off in the distance, the crowd erupted into raucous shouting and thunderous applause. As the first group of Marines stepped off the bus, the band started to play. Children jumped up and down while grown men and women cried. Normally shy and reserved, I found myself jumping for joy with tears streaming uncontrollably down my face. I could barely speak, and I didn't have one of those little American flags, so I waved my cell phone in the air. It was quite the little happy dance. I was just so thankful to God that my son was safely home.

Do Your Art as Private Worship

Visual artists often hold "private showings" of their work that are limited to a small intimate gathering of people. In the same way, artists can do their art as private worship. This is not to say that you're only allowed to produce art with blatantly religious themes or that the church should be the only outlet for your work. Your art is always readily available to you as a vehicle for private worship.

If the only time you use your talents to praise God is in public, you're missing the intimate riches of private worship. The exhortation to "make music" to the Lord (Psalm 92:1; 98:5) gives license for all artists to worship God with our art anytime we desire. After all, when God touches your heart, it's quite natural for you, an artist, to respond in the way that's most natural—through your art.

We are made in the image of an extremely creative God. So whenever we create, we bring glory to the Lord. Gary Thomas writes:

> Christians rightly believe that life is a gift given to us by God—something we shouldn't waste. We celebrate God by using the life he has given us to create other things. Whether it's building a business, writing a poem, painting a picture, or planting a garden, creating something can be a profoundly holy experience. Far more than hobbies, these activities can be powerful expressions of worship.[9]

The book of Psalms was written by artists using their gifts to worship God. In fact, the Psalter culminates with an all-out call for every art form to be raised heavenward in worship:

> Praise him with the sounding of the trumpet, praise him with the harp and lyre, praise him with tambourine and dancing, praise him with the strings and flute, praise him with the clash of cymbals, praise him with resounding cymbals. Let everything that has breath praise the Lord. Praise the Lord. (Psalm 150:3–6)

No one will worship God exactly the way you do. No one else will use the exact words, gestures, or methods you do. No one will bring the same personality, perspective, or life experience to worship as you. Furthermore, no one creates or performs exactly like you, so your art makes your praise distinctive. You bring your own unique creativity and style to worship. So whenever the Lord reveals himself to you, grab your guitar, your paintbrush, or your dancing shoes and have at it.

I know of many artists who are discouraged because their church doesn't utilize their talent, and I deeply empathize with them. On one occasion I met a songwriter who was angry at her church for not using her songs. I encouraged her and then asked, "Do you ever use your songs for private worship?" Her answer was no, which saddened me because that's one of the greatest privileges of being an artist—to do your art for the Audience of One. Sometimes during private worship, I have sensed the Lord saying to me, "Sing me one of *your* songs." The idea that our great and awesome God would accept my humble songs as a worship offering never fails to move me to tears.

In a poem entitled "Praise (II)," George Herbert wrote:

> Wherefore with my utmost art
> I will sing thee,
> And the cream of all my heart
> I will bring thee.

Silence

Sometimes the most appropriate response to the presence of God is silence. Daniel bowed in stunned silence after God visited him (Daniel 10:15). Apparently, words were inadequate. Habakkuk 2:20 proclaims, "The Lord is in his holy temple; let all the earth be silent before him." Again, words can be superfluous or insufficient.

You've probably noticed the word *selah* throughout the Psalms (i.e., Psalm 3:2, 4, 8). It often appears at the end of a line or between stanzas. Though the exact meaning of the word is unknown, scholars generally agree that it signifies some kind of pause or instrumental interlude given for silent meditation. These sacred pauses force us to stop and think about what we've just read or heard.

Silence offers us the opportunity to know God on a deeper level, for he has said, "Be still, and know that I am God" (Psalm 46:10). I have a couple worship leader friends who put a great deal of stock in silence and solitude. Jon Klinepeter, from the Church of Wrigleyville in Chicago, says, "The way I most connect with God is through silence. I love to sit quietly before God. No music. No words. Just God's still voice speaking his love into my heart while I think on his greatness." Aaron Niequist, from Mars Hill Bible Church in Grandville, Michigan, enjoys "sitting in silence, contemplating the reality that God is constantly here, and letting Him supernaturally ... powerfully ... intimately ... magically ... actually invade me; it feels like a river in the desert."

During corporate worship, I have found it meaningful at times not to sing, but instead to listen to the words or just be quiet before God. After all, Ecclesiastes 5:2 says, "Do not be quick with your mouth, do not be hasty in your heart to utter anything before God. God is in heaven and you are on earth, so let your words be few."

Postures for Praise

We've already discussed a few ways to involve our bodies in worship, like clapping, dancing, and leaping for joy, but the Bible offers even more options. Unfortunately, physical responses to worship are often maligned for being improper or undignified. Richard Foster asserts that such closed-mindedness inhibits true worship:

> We are to present our bodies to God in a posture consistent with the inner spirit in worship. Standing, clapping, dancing, lifting the hands, lifting the head are postures consistent with the spirit of praise. To sit still looking dour is simply not appropriate for praise. Kneeling, bowing the head, lying prostrate are postures consistent with the spirit of adoration and humility.
>
> We are quick to object to this line of teaching. "People have different temperaments," we argue. "That may appeal to emotional types, but I'm naturally quiet and reserved. It isn't the kind of worship that will meet my need." What we must see is that the real question in worship is not, "What will meet my need?" The real question is, "What kind of worship does God call for?" It is clear that God calls for wholehearted worship. And it is as reasonable to expect wholehearted worship to be physical as to expect it to be cerebral.
>
> Often our "reserved temperament" is little more than fear of what others will think of us, or perhaps unwillingness to humble ourselves before God and others. Of course people have different temperaments, but that must never keep us from worshiping with our whole being.[10]

First Corinthians 6:20 implores us to "honor God with your body." The following, then, are some more ways to involve your physical body in the act of worship.

Standing

The worship leader who commands a congregation to stand as a way to "warm up the crowd" disregards the biblical purpose for standing. When the children of Israel saw the pillar of cloud representing God's presence, "they all stood and worshiped" (Exodus 33:10). After rebuilding the walls of Jerusalem, the people gathered to worship and were instructed to "Stand up and praise the Lord your God, who is from everlasting to everlasting" (Nehemiah 9:5). In both cases the people stood out of respect and veneration. In many cultures, it's customary to stand when a dignitary walks into a room. Thus, standing is an appropriate way to pay tribute and show honor.

Raising Hands

When we raise our hands in worship we are deliberately directing our praise heavenward. David exclaimed, "I will praise you as long as I live, and in your name I will lift up my hands" (Psalm 63:4). Psalm 134:2 exhorts believers to "Lift up your hands in the sanctuary and praise the Lord" (see also 1 Timothy 2:8).

In addition to expressing praise, some people raise hands in conjunction with prayer. It's their way of saying, "Lord, I receive from you whatever you have for me right now." In Psalm 28:2, the psalmist prays, "Hear my cry for mercy as I call to you for help, as I lift up my hands toward your Most Holy Place" (see also Psalm 88:9).

Stretching out an open hand can also be a tangible way to offer yourself to God, in effect saying, "Lord, I give you my heart, my will, and my talent." Such is the gist of David's prayer from Psalm 141:2: "May the lifting up of my hands be like the evening sacrifice."

Unfortunately, the raising of hands during worship has become controversial. I recently spoke about worship at a church, and afterward an elderly woman came up to me and asked gruffly, "Young man, what do you think about people who sing with their hands up in the air all the time?" Assuming by the tone of her voice that she was against it, I mentioned that raising hands is clearly biblical, but that it should never be forced on anyone. "Good answer," she said, and her whole demeanor changed. She smiled, but at the same time started to cry as she told me she used to hate people who raised their hands during worship. As a child, she was taught that such people were only seeking attention because they were weak, emotional, and immature. However, much later in life some close friends expressed a desire to go deeper in worship. They scoured the Bible and were surprised at the number of verses that endorsed, even commanded, the raising of hands in worship. "Now I do it all the time," she told me with glee. "I'm eighty-five years old and I can't stop raising my hands for Jesus." I found her enthusiasm and open-mindedness most refreshing.

Kneeling

Philippians 2:10 announces that "at the name of Jesus every knee should bow, in heaven and on earth and under the earth" (see also Isaiah 45:23; Romans 14:11). Psalm 95:6 says, "Come, let us bow down in worship, let us kneel before the Lord our Maker." Kneeling and bowing down are postures of submission associated with worship.

A popular worship leader brought his band to my church and led us in a rich worship experience. Though this leader is divinely gifted and anointed, my lasting impression of the service came from one of the band members. At one point, the bass player stopped playing, dropped to his knees, and bowed his head. He obviously wasn't performing for his own glory, but for God's.

In the same way, because lead worshipers spend so much time up on the platform, in the spotlight, I highly recommend that we spend a significant amount of time on our knees during private worship.

Facedown

Prostrating flat on the ground, facedown, is a highly demonstrative act of reverence and submission. Many of the Bible's godliest characters did "face plants" when encountering God: Abraham (Genesis 17:3), Moses (Numbers 20:6), David (1 Chronicles 21:16), Ezekiel (Ezekiel 1:28), Daniel (Daniel 10:15), Peter, James, and John (Matthew 17:6). At one point, the entire nation of Israel worshiped facedown (Leviticus 9:24). That must have been quite a sight!

My friend Karla Worley from Nashville recently shared with me her experience with facedown worship: "Sometimes during the day, I get on my knees and curl over with my face to the ground and just get really still and feel my smallness and God's greatness. It's very reorienting."

Humble facedown worship is also prevalent throughout heaven:

> Whenever the living creatures give glory, honor and thanks to him who sits on the throne and who lives for ever and ever, the twenty-four elders fall down

> before him who sits on the throne, and worship him who lives for ever and ever. They lay their crowns before the throne and say:
>
> "You are worthy, our Lord and God,
> to receive glory and honor and power,
> for you created all things,
> and by your will they were created
> and have their being."
>
> Revelation 4:9–11 (see also 1:17; 7:11)

Serve Others

I recently read of a church where once a month, instead of singing a half hour of worship songs, members march down to the church kitchen to make sandwiches for the homeless. Another church recorded a worship CD and gave the proceeds from sales to a local charity. Serving others is the ultimate example of worship as a verb. As Hebrews 13:15–16 asserts, "Through Jesus, therefore, let us continually offer to God a sacrifice of praise—the fruit of lips that confess his name. And do not forget to do good and to share with others, for with such sacrifices God is pleased." One of the Greek words used for worship in the New Testament is *latreuo*, which actually means "to serve" (see Acts 7:42; 24:14; Philippians 3:3). The same word appears as a noun in the phrase "spiritual act of worship" from Romans 12:1, which is translated elsewhere as "spiritual service of worship" (NASB) or "reasonable service" (KJV). Thus, our concept of worship is far too narrow if it doesn't include serving others.

It's unfortunate that the term "worship service" has come to mean a time on Sunday when the church attends to all our spiritual needs. We speak of being "ministered to" by the worship or "fed" by the teaching. We rarely think of church as a service of worship where we minister to God and others. As a result, this purely consumerist approach to church isolates us from, and stifles our witness to, the culture at large. The church that doesn't function beyond its own four walls does not possess the true spirit of worship. Therefore, I challenge you to put hands and feet to your worship—feet that take you outside your comfort zone with hands ready to serve others. St. Francis said, "Preach the gospel of Jesus by every means possible; and, if it's really necessary, you could even use words."

WOULD YOU KNOW WHAT TO DO?

David stood before the nation of Israel and said, "Praise the Lord your God." That was all the instruction he gave.

Poor David. Every beginning worship leader knows you don't just stand up in front of the congregation and say, "Everybody worship! On your mark, get set, go!" That just wouldn't fly in churches today. But apparently that's all the direction David's people needed. For as 1 Chronicles 29:20 describes, the congregation knew exactly what to do: "So they all praised the Lord, the God of their fathers; they bowed low and fell prostrate before the Lord and the king." Obviously, these people had ample practice at responding to the presence of God.

If you were in David's assembly would you have known what to do? Would you have been able to engage, or would you have needed more guidance or instruction? I sincerely hope that cataloguing the various biblical responses to God has given you a few more options for worship and that some new colors have been added to your worship palette.

Follow-up Questions for Group Discussion

1. Which of the options for worship presented in this chapter are you most experienced with?

2. Which options are you least familiar with?

3. How has your upbringing or church background affected your openness to the various types of worship?

4. Have you had any recent prayers answered that you'd like to share?

5. Do you agree with the author's statement that in today's society "participatory singing has become a foreign concept"? Why or why not?

6. What can the church do to engage men who regard singing as "womanly" in worship through song?

7. What was the most meaningful worship experience you've ever had?

8. Do you find it easy or difficult to do what Psalm 46:10 says: "Be still, and know that I am God"? Why?

9. With which "posture for praise" (i.e., standing, raising hands, kneeling, facedown) are you most experienced? Least experienced?

10. In what new ways can your team serve others as an act of worship?

Personal Action Steps

1. Meditate on Psalm 40:5 and make a list of all that you're thankful for at this moment. If it helps to stimulate your thinking, list your blessings under the following categories: spiritual, relational, ministry, job, health, and material.

2. Using your list as a springboard, express gratitude to the Lord in a new and creative way.

3. Set aside time this week to do your art as private worship. For example write, sing, play, dance, or paint your praise to God.

4. Make it a point this week to practice privately the form of worship offered in this chapter in which you are least experienced.

5. Incorporate one of the "postures for praise" into your private worship time this week.

chapter four

How God's Character Shapes Our Character

I could sing better here than I ever had before. As part of these people, even though I stayed in the doorway, I did not recognize my voice or know where it was coming from, but sometimes I felt like I could sing forever . . . there was no sense of performance or judgment, only that the music was breath and food.

Something inside me that was stiff and rotting would feel soft and tender. Somehow the singing wore down all the boundaries and distinctions that kept me so isolated. Sitting there, standing with them to sing, sometimes so shaky and sick that I felt like I might tip over, I felt bigger than myself, like I was being taken care of, tricked into coming back to life.

From *Traveling Mercies* by Anne Lamott

Reuben was head of the audiovisual department at a prominent church, but four years ago he was asked to step down after it was discovered that he was addicted to pornography. Actually, he was relieved when his secret life was uncovered. The guilt and shame had been weighing heavily on him for quite some time. And the constant effort it took to keep from getting caught—all the lies and deception—was very draining. The church elders dealt firmly but lovingly with Reuben. They removed him from leadership and outlined a restoration program that included counseling, accountability, and adherence to some basic spiritual disciplines.

One of the elders, Steve, befriended Reuben throughout the restoration process and still checks in with him at least once a week by phone. Last month, on Steve's recommendation, the elders decided to allow Reuben back into the ministry as a volunteer, contingent upon one final interview with the pastor. So Reuben and Pastor Sam met for lunch at a local restaurant.

After exchanging pleasantries and ordering their food, Pastor Sam asked how the counseling was going. "It's been really hard, but really good," Reuben answered. "I wouldn't wish what I've been through on anyone, but I sure have learned a lot—especially about myself."

"Like what?" Pastor Sam asked enthusiastically as he spread a napkin across his lap.

"Well, my counselor keeps leading me deeper and deeper into why I do porn, encouraging me to face reality—my true self—and it's not always a pretty picture," Reuben said.

"What do you mean?" queried Pastor Sam.

"Obviously, I have a problem with lust," Reuben admitted, "but I'm also a perfectionist. On top of that, I'm just now learning how to deal with anger. I used to be angry pretty much all the time, but especially when things didn't go like I wanted. I'd get angry at everyone around me, at the church, and at God. Then I'd be angry with myself for being angry. Whenever things got really bad, which was pretty much all the time, I just wanted to run away. So I escaped ..."

"Into pornography," Pastor Sam added.

"Exactly." Reuben nodded. "It made me forget all about my troubles."

"But it doesn't last, does it?" Pastor Sam said.

"Oh yeah. That's the problem. It's all a fantasy, and when it's over you've got even more problems on your hands."

"Like what?" asked the pastor.

"Porn prevented me from facing my issues and dealing with them. And eventually, I woke up to the fact that it was stunting my growth spiritually, emotionally, and even socially."

"Socially?" Pastor Sam inquired.

"Well, relationally. You see, I was becoming more and more withdrawn, out of touch with reality—with other people and the world around me."

"Sounds like you've faced the difficult truth about yourself, Reuben. I admire your courage. How's the accountability going?"

Reuben took a drink of water and then replied, "Well, my friendship with Steve, more than anything else, has kept me on the straight and narrow. I've even called him in the middle of the night a few times and asked for prayer. The first year I had a number of relapses, but I haven't looked at pornography for three years now."

"Praise God," Pastor Sam said as the waitress put their food on the table. "I'm really proud of you, Reuben."

"Thanks, Pastor, but honestly, I'm not completely out of the woods yet. This might be a lifelong battle for me. I can't relax my guard and assume I can handle even the most innocent situation. That's why I plan to continue with the accountability."

"That's very wise, Reuben." At that, Pastor Sam blessed the food and they began to eat. Throughout the meal, Pastor Sam asked many more questions, especially about Reuben's spiritual life, which were all answered to the pastor's satisfaction.

As the two men walked out of the restaurant toward their cars, Pastor Sam had one last question. "Reuben, I'm very pleased with your progress, but if you don't mind there's something I've wanted to ask you for some time now."

"Sure, go ahead," Reuben said a bit cautiously.

Pastor Sam shifted uncomfortably. "How could you attend our church for so long, be involved in our worship ministry every week, while doing pornography on the side? Did the worship not affect you?"

Reuben slowly gathered his thoughts. "I suppose it did, but not deep enough I guess. I mean the worship at church is nice and all, but it never really challenged me to change."

Gently, Pastor Sam pressed further, "But didn't your conscience ever bother you during worship?"

"Sure my conscience bothered me," Reuben admitted, "but after a while I just tuned it out. I got good at hiding. I hid my true feelings, my struggles, and my sin. And I hid behind the soundboard. I had a job to do and as long as I stayed busy, I didn't have to face my issues or talk about anything important, like the depleted state of my heart and soul."

Pastor Sam grimaced. "I wonder if there are others in our worship ministry who are hiding like you did. Reuben, do you have any suggestions as to how we can prevent this sort of thing?"

"I don't know," Reuben replied. "I'll have to give that some thought and get back to you."

"Please do," Pastor Sam said.

Questions for Group Discussion

1. What advice do you have for Pastor Sam about helping those in his worship ministry who struggle with addiction and other sin issues?

2. What in your opinion did the church do right in confronting Reuben's addiction?

3. What could the church have done differently in dealing with Reuben's problems?

4. How would you evaluate the importance of Steve's role in Reuben's life?

5. Do you feel as though Reuben is ready to be involved in ministry again? Why or why not?

6. What advice do you have for someone like Reuben who struggles with a bad habit or addiction?

7. Why do you suppose Reuben, though involved in worship every week, never felt challenged to change?

8. Is it realistic to expect worship to transform us? Why or why not?

9. Would you say that worship has changed your life or transformed your character? If so, how?

10. Is it as easy for church artists to hide their struggles as it was for Reuben? Why or why not?

NEUTRINO WORSHIP

The book of Matthew ends triumphantly. Jesus has conquered death and risen from the grave. Just before ascending into heaven, though, Jesus calls his disciples together for one last meeting. "Then the eleven disciples went to Galilee, to the mountain where Jesus had told them to go. When they saw him, they worshiped him" (Matthew 28:16–17). As you'd expect, the most natural response to the resurrected Christ was to bow down in worship before him. However, there's an eerie twist to the story. After reporting that the disciples worshiped Christ, Matthew immediately adds three bone-chilling words: "but some doubted."

I can't tell you how much those three words bothered me when I first noticed them. Face-to-face with the glory of Christ—even worshiping him—some still doubted. Perhaps they doubted their ability to go on without him, as I'm sure I would have if I had been in their sandals. But the fact remains: this momentous worship experience was not enough to assuage their doubts and fears. My dismay quickly turned into conviction when I realized how often I too come away from the most meaningful times of worship completely unchanged. I call this dubious exercise in futility "neutrino worship."

In physics, a neutrino is a subatomic particle, smaller than a neutron, which carries no electrical charge or measurable mass. Because it is electrically neutral, a neutrino is able to pass through solid matter without being affected. In the same way, I all too often let worship pass over me without allowing it to shape my behavior.

Hand in hand with neutrino worship is the mindset that spiritual growth is an option. Some time ago I was sharing the gospel with someone and when I asked if he wanted to accept Christ into his life, he replied, "No, I already did that and it didn't work." "What do you mean it didn't work?" I asked. "Well, nothing changed," he answered. After further discussion, it became apparent that this man had "gone forward" at an evangelistic meeting and concluded that he was thereby set for life. It made me wonder whether this man had merely "accepted Christ" or been truly converted to Christ.

Now I'm not trying to mess with anyone's theology with a statement like that. I'm just trying to clarify that accepting Christ and being transformed are meant to be one and the same. Titus 2:11–12 says, "For the grace of God has appeared that offers salvation to all people. It teaches us to say 'No' to ungodliness and worldly passions, and to live self-controlled, upright and godly lives in this present age" (TNIV). God's character, specifically his grace, compels us to follow him and to grow spiritually. So grace not only saves us, it changes us.

Spiritual growth is a prominent theme throughout the Bible, especially the parables of Christ. Jesus likened our faith to a tree bearing fruit (Matthew 7:17–20), or seed falling on good soil and yielding a huge crop (Matthew 13:3–8), or like wheat growing resiliently among weeds (Matthew 13:24–30). The notion that we accept Christ without being transformed is totally foreign to Scripture. We are to grow in the faith (Ephesians 4:13). "Therefore let us leave the elementary teachings about Christ and go on to maturity" (Hebrews 6:1).

THE ROLE OF WORSHIP IN OUR SPIRITUAL FORMATION

In chapter 2, we noted that Isaiah had a personal encounter with the holiness of God, and he was convicted of his sinfulness. Moses saw God's goodness, and it made him a more compassionate man. Thomas experienced God's patience and he became devout. All three men came face-to-face with a specific attribute of God and it transformed their character. Indeed, one does not truly encounter the character of God and stay the same. When the Lord appeared to Abraham, he proclaimed, "I am God Almighty; walk before me and be blameless" (Genesis 17:1). As Richard Foster writes, "To stand before the Holy One of eternity is to change."[1]

In Romans 12:1, Paul defines worship as offering ourselves to God. Then he goes on to say in the next verse: "Do not conform any longer to the pattern of this world, but be transformed by the renewing of your mind." Thus, Paul is describing a worship experience that is much deeper than some "warm fuzzy" that wears off within seconds. Worship is inherently and ultimately transformational. Second Corinthians 3:18 teaches that when we behold or contemplate God's glory, we are "transformed into his likeness." Thus, we are molded and shaped by the character of God. Every encounter with God comes with an invitation to be renewed into his image (Colossians 3:10). For that reason, worship can play a very significant role in our spiritual formation.

We Become What We Worship

Whether we realize it or not, we all worship something or someone. Whatever occupies the majority of our thoughts or controls our behavior is our god. The first commandment reads, "You shall have no other gods before me" (Exodus 20:3). Today we may not bow down to graven images like the ancients, yet our idols are just as pervasive and perhaps even more pernicious. Money, sex, and power are the most obvious forms of modern-day idolatry, but there are many more. Some idolize intellect, popularity, pleasure, image, or appearance. Others worship material possessions, clothes, sports, or hobbies. Many of us artists put talent, beauty, and even our art above God. Whatever receives more of our devotion than God, whatever dominates our thoughts or controls our behavior more than the Holy Spirit does, is an idol. Jesus said, "Worship the Lord your God, and serve him only" (Matthew 4:10).

Nothing provokes God to jealousy like idolatry. Exodus 34:14 warns, "Do not worship any other god, for the Lord, whose name is Jealous, is a jealous God." God has gone to excruciating lengths to save us and simply will not tolerate anyone or anything getting in the way of our relationship with him. Thus, his is a holy jealousy, born out of love, for God knows how destructive idolatry can be. The hidden danger of idolatry lies in the fact that we become what we worship. In describing false gods, the psalmist says:

> They have mouths, but cannot speak,
>   eyes, but they cannot see;
> they have ears, but cannot hear,
>   noses, but they cannot smell;
> they have hands, but cannot feel,
>   feet, but they cannot walk;
>   nor can they utter a sound with their throats.
> (Here's the clincher.)
> Those who make them will be like them,
>   and so will all who trust in them.
>
> Psalm 115:5–8, (parenthesis mine)

If we worship money, we will become greedy. If we worship sex, we will become lustful. If it's power, we will become corrupt. No wonder Scripture instructs us to "flee from idolatry" (1 Corinthians 10:14). When we worship anything other than God, it makes us miserable: "The sorrows of those will increase who run after other gods" (Psalm 16:4). Idolatry inevitably leads to addictions, compulsions, and destructive behavior robbing us of our dignity and self-respect, sabotaging our work and relationships, and leaving us feeling worthless and empty (Jeremiah 2:5). That's why Paul exhorts us to put to death anything that takes the place of God in our lives (Colossians 3:5). "For sin shall not be your master, because you are not under law, but under grace" (Romans 6:14). When we worship God, we turn our backs on worldly possessions, affections, and addictions and affirm complete allegiance to him. "For this God is our God for ever and ever; he will be our guide even to the end" (Psalm 48:14).

It's not always easy to spot idolatry in ourselves. Until the Holy Spirit brings it to light, we may be unaware how tight a grip something has on us. For that reason, we should pay close attention to anything we're convinced we can't live without. Not that such things are always bad, but they should be put alongside God to determine whether they hold too much power over us.

Sometimes, if we're not careful, idolatry can creep into our hearts quite innocently. When the apostle John received his apocalyptic vision, he bowed down and started worshiping the angel who was merely acting as his tour guide through the heavenly realm. The angel quickly corrected John, saying, "Do not do it! I am a fellow servant with you and with your brothers the prophets and of all who keep the words of this book. Worship God!" (Revelation 22:9).

Like John, church people must guard against idolatry even while serving God. We tend to make "sacred cows" out of the most undeserving candidates. During college, a friend who was an organ major argued that worship was never legitimate unless there was a pipe organ involved. Our adherence to a tradition or a certain way of doing church can become an obsession that's more about us than about God. Though convinced we're doing God's work, such rigidity could actually be stifling that work. Similarly, if our insistence on a particular worship style becomes more important than connecting with God or causes us to judge, malign, or mistreat others, we are worshiping "created things rather than the Creator" (Romans 1:25). And be careful about becoming addicted to the euphoric adrenaline rush that worship can sometimes be. We are not to be worshiping worship. We are to worship the living God.

Fortunately, if we worship Christ, we will become more and more Christlike (Romans 8:29). A good friend of mine recently told me that his life has been continually marked by God's faithfulness. Near tears, my friend cited several examples of God's goodness throughout his life and then said, "In spite of everything I've been through, God has been so faithful to me and my family."

Faithfulness is one of my friend's most admirable traits. Whenever I need prayer, wisdom, or advice, I can always count on him; he's always been there for me. He's also particularly handy, and on many occasions I've seen him drop whatever he was doing to help someone with a household emergency. I've also known him to give (not loan) money to anyone in need. After many years of walking with Christ, God's faithfulness has rubbed off on this man and made him the faithful and loyal friend that he is. We really do become what we worship.

Worship Awakens a Desire for Transformation

Worship awakens a desire to change by challenging our spiritual status quo. Certain hymns and praise choruses, when taken seriously, are guaranteed to rock your boat. Who can sing the classic hymns "I Surrender All," "Have Thine Own Way," or "All for Jesus" without fully considering the implication of those words.

Worship challenges us to take an honest look within. As Howard L. Rice describes, facing one's moral shortcomings is never easy: "God requires honesty from us, and such honesty can be painful. Because God knows us better than we know ourselves, pretending will not work. God's knowledge of us demands that we come to terms with who we really are."[2]

During worship recently I ran across a couple lyric lines that stopped me dead in my tracks. The first line read, "The power of your love is changing me." While singing that line, I had to ask myself, "Is that true of me? Is God's love really changing me?" Another line stated, "Your grace is enough for me," which prompted me to ask, "Is God really all I need to be happy or am I seeking happiness and fulfillment in temporal things?" I didn't come to those questions on my own. Worship brought them to the forefront.

Worship also affirms our intentions to obey God. Spiritual formation is something God initiates and does in us (Philippians 1:6; 2:13). However, it is our responsibility to cooperate with his work in our lives. Worship songs emphasizing faith and commitment give voice to our intentions to follow Christ.

Very often the Holy Spirit uses worship to convict us of sin. One time I was embroiled in a sticky relational conflict with a brother in Christ. I was absolutely convinced I was right and he was completely wrong. Then I came to church. During the first song, we were invited to "humble yourself before the Lord." The next song proclaimed that God "graciously forgives sinners such as I." I was immediately convicted of my pride and arrogance, and realized that my stubbornness was preventing reconciliation. The next morning I apologized and made amends.

Worship Incorporates Tools for Transformation

Though worship is in itself a spiritual discipline, it's one that integrates two other disciplines that foster spiritual growth: Bible reading and prayer. Most hymns, liturgies, and worship songs are based on or taken verbatim from

Scripture. Prayer, whether sung or spoken, includes confession, thanksgiving, intercession, and petition. God's Word shows us how we're supposed to live and prayer helps us get there.

Corporate worship adds two more practices that foster spiritual growth: fellowship and the observance of the sacraments. Fellowship encourages spiritual maturity through accountability, and the sacraments remind us of the redemption story and the grace that spurs us on to obedience.

Worship then is a paradigm for spiritual growth. It teaches us the disciplines required for spiritual formation and challenges us to assimilate those practices into our lives. Spiritual disciplines hold no magical power in and of themselves, but when undertaken with a teachable spirit, create space for God to transform our behavior.

Worship Addresses the Three Most Important Questions in Life

Jesus was fond of posing questions that forced his listeners to wrestle with spiritual issues. To the multitude he asked, "What does it profit a man to gain the world, but lose his soul?" To his disciples he asked, "Who do people say that I am?" To Peter he asked, "Do you love me?" Jesus knew that we can't arrive at the right answers to life's biggest problems if we never ask the right questions. With that in mind, I submit to you what I believe are the three most important questions in life:

1. Who is God?
2. Who am I?
3. What is God inviting me to do?

Answers to these three questions inevitably inform our convictions, establish our values, and determine our behavior. Worship addresses, in various ways, all three of these vital questions. That's what makes worship so powerfully transformational; God reveals himself to us, invites us to be more than we already are, and we respond accordingly.

Who Is God?

I have a friend named Annie who grew up with an overly strict father. As a result, she perceived God as perpetually angry and harsh. Growing up, she lived in constant fear that if she made one false move, she'd miss out on "God's perfect plan" for her life. She became paralyzed by a fear of failure, and understandably so. In her mind, God was a quick-tempered taskmaster who threw down lightning bolts to keep her in line and turned his back on her whenever she failed. Through counseling, Annie began to realize that she had projected her father's personality onto God—that her image of God was more like her father than who God really is. For the first time in her life, Annie seriously asked, "Who is God?"

Most of us go through life with some concept of who God is. The question is whether or not that concept is accurate. Jesus taught that we are to worship the Lord "in spirit and truth" (John 4:23). Worshiping in truth means that we worship God for who he really is—not some god we concocted from distorted religious training and/or a dysfunctional family upbringing, both of which played major roles in Annie's view of God. So a biblical concept of God is a prerequisite for true worship. According to N. T. Wright, "If your idea of God, if your idea of the salvation offered to you in Christ, is vague or remote, your idea of worship will be fuzzy and ill-formed."[3]

Our concept of God not only shapes our worship, it affects everything—how we think, act, and even feel. That's why it's crucial that our image of God be accurate. Richard Foster says, "To think rightly about God is, in an important sense, to have everything right. To think wrongly about God is, in an important sense, to have everything wrong."[4]

Our attempts to identify who God is or describe what he's like can be challenging because God is holy, infinite, and eternal. He is unfathomable, inscrutable, and incomparable (Psalm 145:3; Job 9:10–12; Exodus 15:11). Additionally, any effort to fully explain God is going to fall short because our human understanding is finite, our reasoning is corrupted by sin, and the language we have at our disposal is limited.

Even though we may never be able to fully explain God, he still invites us to know him. And knowing God entails more than merely knowing about him; it means knowing his thoughts and his character. Our great and powerful God is a personal God. In the opening chapters of Genesis, we observe God walking through the garden of Eden (3:8) and conversing with ordinary human beings (3:11; 4:9; 16:8). Because God is personal he invites us to know him intimately. With each of us, he desires the kind of closeness that a loving parent-child relationship offers. In 2 Corinthians 6:18 he says, "I will be a Father to you, and you will be my sons and daughters." Most scholars interpret the passionate husband-wife relationship in the Song of Solomon as an analogy depicting the depth of intimacy that God seeks with us. By inviting us to ponder the attributes of God, worship helps us to know him better.

Intimate knowledge of God can completely change one's outlook on life. In the book of Lamentations, chapter 3, we find Jeremiah greatly distressed and afflicted. He wrongly perceives that God is against him and blames all his problems on the Lord. Listen to the despair, resignation, and hopelessness in Jeremiah's voice:

> I'm the man who has seen trouble,
> trouble coming from the lash of God's anger.
> He took me by the hand and walked me
> into pitch-black darkness.
> Yes, he's given me the back of his hand
> over and over and over again.
>
> He turned me into a scarecrow
> of skin and bones, then broke the bones.
> He hemmed me in, ganged up on me,
> poured on the trouble and hard times.
> He locked me up in deep darkness,
> like a corpse nailed inside a coffin.
>
> He shuts me in so I'll never get out,
> manacles my hands, shackles my feet.
> Even when I cry out and plead for help,
> he locks up my prayers and throws away the key.
> He sets up blockades with quarried limestone.
> He's got me cornered.
>
> He's a prowling bear tracking me down,
> a lion in hiding ready to pounce.
> He knocked me from the path and ripped me to pieces.
> When he finished, there was nothing left of me.
> He took out his bow and arrows
> and used me for target practice.
>
> Lamentations 3:1–12 MSG

Have you ever felt like that? Angry? Despairing? Abandoned by God? We all have, especially during adversity. After Jeremiah rants and raves at God, he quickly realizes that his concept of God is off. In verse 21 he says, "Yet this I call to mind and therefore I have hope." What is it that he recalls? He remembers who God truly is—that he is loving, compassionate, and faithful. "Because of the Lord's great love we are not consumed, for his compassions never fail. They are new every morning; great is your faithfulness" (Lamentations 3:22–23). Recalibrating his concept of God gave Jeremiah a fresh new outlook. That's why C. S. Lewis referred to worship as "inner health made audible."[5]

Who Am I?

It probably won't surprise you to learn that my friend Annie—the one whose father was a strict authoritarian—suffered from a negative self-image. She felt worthless and unlovable all the time and viewed herself as a pitiful failure, a real loser. When her inability to relate to others in a healthy way began to wreak havoc in her marriage and undermine her job performance, Annie was at a crossroads. She could either perpetuate the negative self-image foisted on her during childhood or she could adopt a new identity. Since the former was ruining her life, she chose the latter. Annie knew it wasn't going to be easy to rebuild her self-esteem, but totally captivated by the love of God, she was starting to realize that all those negative voices from her past were a pack of lies. Over time, Annie began to see herself in a much more positive light because she realized that's how God views her.

Most of us tend to define ourselves by what we do. When asked, "Who are you?" we reference our vocation: I'm a teacher, a lawyer, a stay-at-home mom, a software developer. If it's not the job, our self-image stems from our appearance, wealth, or talent. The problem is that beauty fades, wealth is fleeting, and talent is finicky. So self-esteem that is based on what you do instead of who you are goes up and down like a roller coaster.

In order to discover our true identities, wisdom suggests we do what Annie did—turn to the one who created us and knows us better than we know ourselves. According to 1 Corinthians 8:3, "The man who loves God is known by God." David wrote, "O Lord, you have searched me and you know me" (Psalm 139:1, see also Jeremiah 1:5). Even Jesus derived his identity exclusively from

God. When he proclaimed that he is the light of the world, the Pharisees objected. "Why should we believe that you're the light of the world?" they asked. "Just because you say so?" "No," Jesus replied, "because God said so" (see John 8:12–18). Through worship, we discover not only who God is but also who we are.

Some may reject the notion of drawing their identity from God because they assume that God has a very low opinion of them. But nothing could be further from the truth. God is for us, not against us (Romans 8:31). His opinion of us is a lot higher and far more glorious than most of us dare to realize. God looks upon those who claim him as Lord and says, "They are the glorious ones in whom is all my delight" (Psalm 16:3). Jesus said that he had given his disciples the glory that God had given him (John 17:22). Paul wrote that those God justified, he also glorified (Romans 8:30). Indeed, Philippians 2:15 proclaims that we are destined for greatness, to "shine like stars in the universe." God knows our full potential for godly glory and calls us to live up to that every day.

St. Irenaeus is quoted as saying, "The glory of God is the fully alive human being." Sadly, many of us have no idea what a fully alive version of ourselves looks like. But I assure you that such a vision features you at your very best—at peace with God, in harmony with others, content with yourself, free from dysfunction, unencumbered by brokenness, overcoming addictions, growing through adversity, and using your gifts and talents in a meaningful way (Galatians 5:22–23). C. S. Lewis writes that God is intent on making each of us into "a dazzling, radiant, immortal creature, pulsating all through with such energy and joy and wisdom and love as we cannot now imagine, a bright stainless mirror which reflects back to God perfectly (though, of course, on a smaller scale) His own boundless power and delight and goodness."[6]

I'm not a proponent of the "self-esteem movement" within humanist psychology, which censors all negative evaluations of one's conduct and, in effect, fosters total, yet blind, acceptance of even the most irresponsible and destructive behavior. Self-actualization through self-discovery has produced nothing but a preoccupation with self. Any resulting self-esteem is forced and lacks dignity. God's prescription for healthy self-esteem goes far beyond merely "feeling good" about yourself. God has bestowed dignity on the human race by crowning each of us with glory and honor (Psalm 8:5).

Brennan Manning writes:

> My dignity as [God's] child is my most coherent sense of self. When I seek to fashion a self-image from the adulation of others and the inner voice whispers, 'You've arrived; you're a player in the Kingdom enterprise,' there is no truth in that self-concept. When I sink into despondency and the inner voice whispers, 'You are no good, a fraud, a hypocrite, and a dilettante,' there is no truth in any image shaped from that message."[7]

Mary, the mother of Jesus, viewed herself in a whole new light after her personal encounter with God's miraculous power and might:

> And Mary said: "My soul glorifies the Lord and my spirit rejoices in God my Savior, for he has been mindful of the humble state of his servant.
>
> From now on all generations will call me blessed, for the Mighty One has done great things for me—holy is his name." (Luke 1:46–49)

Who is God? Mary says God is her Savior, the "Mighty One," he is holy. In light of who God is, who is Mary? Mary concludes that she is God's humble servant, someone for whom God has done great things, someone whom history will regard as outrageously blessed.

Knowing our true identity in God also provides a sense of personal destiny. When Nehemiah's enemies threatened his life, someone suggested that he quit the building project he had launched and hide out in the temple until the danger was over. But the thought of giving up was completely foreign to Nehemiah. Instead he replied, "Should a man like me run away? Or should one like me go into the temple to save his life? I will not go!" (Nehemiah 6:11). Nehemiah's God-given destiny gave him courage.

Knowing our true identity also sets us free to live it out. The first time somebody introduced me as an author, I looked back over my shoulder, assuming they had me confused with someone else. I had just published my first book, and I wasn't convinced that writing one book qualified me to be an author. When I accepted the fact that writing was part of the identity God was forging in me, I started accepting invitations to speak at conferences and setting aside time to write.

While the Bible states clearly that we are destined to reflect God's image and glory, the problem is that we don't always allow ourselves to live up to that destiny. We live beneath our privilege. We not only forget who God is, we forget who we are. Instead of enjoying the freedom of being fully alive as new creations in Christ, we fall back into our old natures, with their addictions, bad habits, and dysfunctional behavior. Yet the Lord extends an invitation to each of us to be so much more than that. I'm not suggesting that we live in denial about our fatal flaws, but that we stop allowing them to be the final word as to who we are.

What Is God Inviting Me to Do?

As the prophet Isaiah witnessed God's holiness, he heard God say, "Whom shall I send? And who will go for us?" God apparently had an assignment for some willing soul. Without even knowing what the job was, Isaiah shot up his hand and said, "Here I am. Send me!" (Isaiah 6:8). When Paul met Christ on the road to Damascus, his first question was, "Who are you, Lord?" His second questions was, "What shall I do, Lord?" (Acts 22:8–10). Apparently, enthusiastic obedience is a common and natural response to the presence of God.

Whenever God reveals himself to you, whether through his Word, through worship, or any other means, be prepared to act upon what you receive. Daniel 11:32 claims that "the people who know their God will display strength and take action" (NASB). So worship that doesn't eventually motivate us to do something is sentimental gibberish. We are to be doers of the Word, not let it go in one ear and out the other (James 1:22).

Human beings are basically self-centered. We don't want anyone telling us what to do. Instead, we want to do whatever we want, when we want. So the question, What is God inviting me to do? is one we should be asking regularly, even daily, because it not only inspires action, it also fosters character growth through humble submission.

Obedience that's motivated by a genuine encounter with God is healthy obedience. It is driven by gratitude and love rather than a misguided desire to merit God's favor. Most Christians know that you can't earn your way to heaven; that we're saved by grace, not by works. Yet, once saved, we all too often fall back into a subtle works mentality, participating in spiritual activities out of guilt, shame, or obligation. At least that's what I conclude whenever I hear something said like: "I know I should read the Bible and pray more, but I'm just not disciplined enough." Or, "I don't really want to go to church, but I guess I have to." Contrast that with the man who practices solitude because a one-on-one encounter with the God of the Universe is just too inviting to pass up, or the woman who attends church because she often encounters God through worship, fellowship, and biblical teaching.

In Jesus' day, the scribes were men who took the principles laid out in the Old Testament and tried to apply them to every possible situation. Their work resulted in thousands of legalistic rules and regulations. The Pharisees were the ones ardently dedicated to keeping all those rules. Jesus constantly condemned both groups for their hypocrisy and empty ritual (Matthew 5:20; 23:23–35). Instead of mindlessly following rigid rules, true worshipers are motivated to obey by an encounter with the character of God. As Ephesians 2:8–10 illustrates, the movement is always from grace to works:

> For it is by grace you have been saved, through faith—and this not from yourselves, it is the gift of God—not by works, so that no one can boast. For we are God's workmanship, created in Christ Jesus to do good works, which God prepared in advance for us to do.

I have a good friend who grew up in a Christian home with very strict rules. She was never allowed to play cards or watch movies, and her skirts always had to fall far below her knees. On Sundays, she was forbidden to do anything fun like go to the beach. Instead, her family spent practically the entire day at church. Her parents were missionaries with more than a passion for evangelism—they were obsessed with it and constantly needled their kids into witnessing. Every day when my friend came home from school, her mother would ask, "Did you share Christ with anyone today?" In spite of her sheltered upbringing, my friend is surprisingly well adjusted. However, once in a while I'll hear her conclude dejectedly that she's "not a good enough Christian," that she's "not spiritual enough," or that she doesn't "do enough for God."

Even if you've never voiced those exact sentiments, most of us at some point have purposed to "be good" or "obey the rules" so God will give us what we want. According to C. S. Lewis, spiritual vitality has nothing to do with keeping or breaking religious rules:

> People often think of Christian morality as a kind of bargain in which God says, "If you keep a lot of rules I'll reward you, and if you don't I'll do the other thing." I do not think that is the best way of looking at it. I would much rather say that every time you make a choice you are turning the central part of you, the part of you that chooses, into something a little different from what it was before.

> And taking your life as a whole, with all your innumerable choices, all your life long you are slowly turning this central thing either into a heavenly creature or into a hellish creature: either into a creature that is in harmony with God, and with other creatures, and with itself, or else into one that is in a state of war and hatred with God, and with its fellow-creatures, and with itself. To be the one kind of creature is heaven: that is, it is joy and peace and knowledge and power. To be the other means madness, horror, idiocy, rage, impotence, and eternal loneliness. Each of us at each moment is progressing to the one state or the other.[8]

The question, What is God asking me to do? may also prompt us to look in the mirror, face the truth about our flaws, and invite the Holy Spirit to grow us up. Thus, inner confrontation always demands courage. This willingness to be open to the truth about ourselves is best illustrated in David's prayer from Psalm 139: "Search me, O God, and know my heart; test me and know my anxious thoughts. See if there is any offensive way in me, and lead me in the way everlasting" (vv. 23–24).

Here are some questions one could ask that foster healthy self-examination:

- What about me needs to change?
- What attitudes need to be adjusted?
- What sins need to be confessed?
- How can I be less self-centered and more mindful of others today?
- How can I be more loving toward the people in my life?

God never twists arms when he wants us to do something. He simply reveals himself and invites us to follow him. Zacchaeus was a despised tax collector, yet Jesus befriended him. He spent time with Zacchaeus and even stayed at his house. This made such a huge impression on Zacchaeus that he decided to completely change his lifestyle, and he started by giving half his possessions to charity and making amends to anyone he had cheated. No one coerced Zacchaeus into restitution and benevolence. He came face-to-face with the love of Christ and it changed his behavior.

Though an encounter with God often comes with an invitation to act, we don't always hear it during worship because we're moving through life much too fast. Whenever we skim the surface of worship, we diminish its impact on our lives. So as you worship, I pray that you will probe deeply into the character of God—that you'll continually ask, "Who is God? Who am I? And, What is God inviting me to do?"

Follow-up Questions for Group Discussion

1. Have you ever experienced a change in attitude or behavior as a result of worship? If so, describe it.

2. Has the Holy Spirit ever convicted you of sinful thoughts, attitudes, or behavior during worship? Can you share the experience?

3. How can becoming a private worshiper enrich one's prayer life?

4. How can becoming a private worshiper increase one's exposure to Scripture?

5. How has your upbringing shaped your concept of God?

6. Why is it important for lead worshipers to have an accurate concept of God?

7. How can one go about formulating an accurate concept of God in spite of dysfunctional upbringing or distorted religious training?

8. Why is it important for lead worshipers to discover their true identity in Christ?

9. Why is it important for worshipers to heed God's call to take action?

10. If a church insists that transformational worship is a high priority, how might that change the way worship services are planned and conducted?

Personal Action Steps

1. Consider whether there is anything in your life that receives more of your devotion or affection than God and how that affects your spiritual growth.

2. During your devotions and worship this week, make note of any lines or lyrics that convict you of sin or challenge you to grow in character. Record your thoughts in a journal.

3. Identify how someone who grew up in a healthy environment might view God, and compare that with how you grew up and view God.

4. During corporate worship this week, be cognizant of these three questions: Who is God? Who am I? And, What is God inviting me to do?

5. Create or perform something artistic that expresses how God has changed your life.

part two

Worshiping in Truth

Yet a time is coming and has now come when the true worshipers will worship the Father in spirit and truth, for they are the kind of worshipers the Father seeks.

John 4:23

Scripture expresses concern for people who are zealous for God, but whose zeal is not based on accurate knowledge of God (Romans 10:2). The worshiping artist faces the same potential pitfall. If we have all the artistic talent in the world combined with fire and passion, but our concept of God is sketchy, worship will be shallow. Worshiping in truth means that we worship God for who he truly is. Our job, therefore, is to break through all the misconceptions and false assumptions—to present a clear and accurate picture of who God is—and invite people to worship him. Andy Park writes, "Becoming a worship leader isn't about the pursuit of a ministry or a career; it's about the pursuit of a person. Out of knowing God, we make him known—we are first worshipers and then worship leaders."[1]

The next three chapters probe deeper into the questions: Who is God? Who am I? And, What is God inviting me to do? These are not only the three most important questions for spiritual transformation, they provide a working knowledge of basic Christian theology. For that reason, this section draws heavily upon Scripture, often letting the truth of God's Word stand on its own.

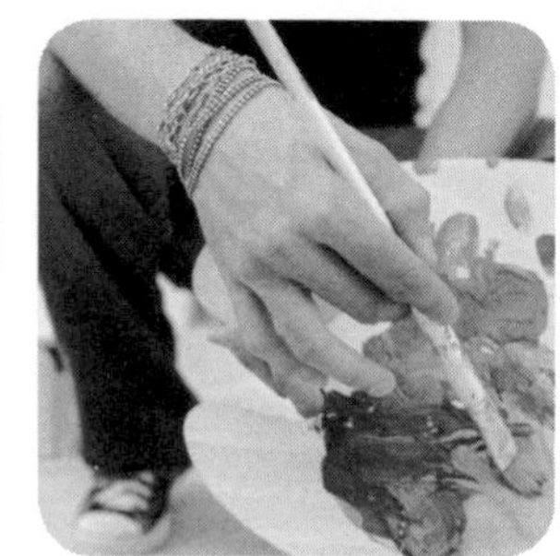

chapter five

Who Is God?

"Nadine and I would sit for hours in her room," she began. "Mostly we would talk about boys or school, but always, by the end of it, we talked about God. The thing I loved about Nadine was that I never felt like she was selling anything. She would talk about God as if she knew Him, as if she had talked to Him on the phone that day."

From *Blue Like Jazz* by Donald Miller

Matty woke up in a cold sweat. It was pitch black. *What time is it? What day is it?* She sat up. Like a neon light on a lonely street, the clock on her nightstand glowed menacingly—2:18. She had been asleep for barely an hour, having tossed and turned the previous three. In an instant, she was reliving the bombshell that was dropped on her after worship team practice. Josh, the church music director, called her into his office and asked her to step down from the team. He explained that the talent level around her had risen several notches over the years and that she wasn't keeping up. She was aware of this trend to some degree and Josh was polite and respectful, but it still hurt. She cried all the way home.

Wide awake now, she flipped on the light, reached for her journal, and started to write:

Dear God,

I am so discouraged. I just want to use my gifts for you. Why does it have to be so hard? I've been singing at that church for nine years and I feel like the rug has just been pulled out from under me. Maybe I'm not as good a singer as I thought I was. I'm embarrassed; I feel stupid and I'm angry. It's hard to be angry at Josh. He works so hard and he's a nice guy and I know he's doing the best he can, but I feel so rejected. I wish he knew me and appreciated me more. I feel so down on myself. And to be honest, God, I'm angry at you. I don't get you sometimes. You tell us to steward our gifts and talents. Well, here I am, Lord, ready and willing to serve. But I'm told I'm not good enough. I'm not pining to be Sally Soloist. I just want to sing on the worship team. So what gives? What am I supposed to do now? Stop singing? Go to another church?

Matty put down her pen and, in her mind, replayed the scene in Josh's office. *It must have been tough on Josh to ask me to step down,* she thought. "Lord, help me forgive Josh," she prayed aloud. Then she turned out the light and tucked herself back into bed, but she was still unable to sleep. *How am I going to explain this to my friends? And what am I going to tell my family when they don't see me up on the platform?* Within minutes, Matty had her journal out and was writing again.

Dear God,

Me again. I'm still struggling, but of course you already know that because you're God. I'm not trying to be a smart aleck. The fact that you're God is just the point. I know you're supposed to make all things work together for good, so I'd say you've got your work cut out for you on this one, because I don't see how any good can come out of this at all. I'm sorry, God, but I'm having trouble trusting right now. My faith is shaken. Sometimes you seem like a complete stranger to me. I can't figure you out. I thought you were a good God. I thought you cared about me. I thought you loved me. Please help me.

Matty closed her journal. She had nothing more to say and no more tears left to cry. Physically exhausted and emotionally drained, she finally nodded off to sleep.

Questions for Group Discussion

1. What emotions is Matty exhibiting in response to being removed from the worship team?

2. Do you think Matty is dealing with her pain and disappointment in a healthy way? Why or why not?

3. Do you think Josh handled the situation well? If not, what should he have done differently?

4. How can Matty communicate truthfully to her friends and family about her removal from the worship team in a way that preserves her dignity and honors Josh and the church?

5. How would you characterize Matty's relationship with God right now?

6. Do you think Matty should leave the church or stop singing? Why or why not?

7. What are some signs that Matty has an accurate view of God?

8. What are some indications that she's struggling in her understanding of God?

9. Is it okay to question God's goodness? Why or why not?

10. What's the best way to cultivate an accurate concept of God?

OUR TRIUNE GOD

I've spent most of my life trying to get my arms around the concept of the Trinity only to realize that I'll probably never fully comprehend it. That's because the Trinity is an attempt to explain the unexplainable: how God can be three entities and one at the same time. In spite of this profound mystery, one thing that is very clear is that the Trinity illustrates how God works in the world. Basically, the Trinity celebrates the fact that our transcendent God is not detached from this world, but is completely engaged with it. He gave himself sacrificially for us, continues to take our pain upon himself, and guides us along life's journey. He abides with us, invites us to abide with him, and grants us the power to do his work in the world. According to N. T. Wright, the Trinity "is the doctrine that assures us that our visiting of the sick, our teaching of the young, our creating of beauty, our praying and working for justice and peace in the world, are not simply us doing something for God; they are God acting in and through us."[1]

The Trinity is also the perfect model of true community. There are three distinct persons, all equal yet submitted to each other, united in purpose, immersed in intimacy, and fully enveloped by love, joy, and peace. And it is not a closed community. The best news of all is that we are invited into this radiant fellowship (John 17:3, 21; 1 Corinthians 1:9; 1 John 1:3). As Larry Crabb says, "The Trinity is a party happening, and we've been invited."[2] Paul echoes the same sentiment as he wraps up his second letter to the Corinthians: "May the grace of the Lord Jesus Christ, and the love of God, and the fellowship of the Holy Spirit be with you all" (2 Corinthians 13:14).

The Holy Trinity icon painted around 1425 by Andrei Rublev effectively captures the deep sense of community among Father, Son, and Holy Spirit (plate 3). The picture draws on the story from Genesis 18 where three nameless visitors appear to Abraham and Sarah, promising the elderly couple that they will conceive a son. The early church regarded this as a revelation of the Trinity. In the painting, three figures are seated in a circle, the symbol of unity, perfection, and eternity. Apart from their clothing, they are identical. Neither male nor female, their eyes are fixed on each other; each head is inclined submissively toward one of the others. Over the years, experts have differed over the identities of the figures, but the one in the middle is generally regarded as God the Father. On the left is Jesus the Son, and the Holy Spirit is seated on the right. The Father's hand gestures toward a gold chalice containing the blood of the Lamb, thereby representing the sacrifice that makes communion with the Trinity available to us. At the top there is a tree representing not only the oaks of Mamre, where Abraham and Sarah lived, but also the Tree of Life from the garden of Eden. Over Christ is a building symbolizing the church and above the Holy Spirit is a mountain, a common symbol of God's glory and power throughout Scripture. Henri Nouwen referred to the fellowship of the Trinity as a "house of love" and taught that our ability to live in this love holds the key for "being in the world without being of it." Commenting on Rublev's painting, Nouwen writes:

> Through the contemplation of this icon we come to see with our inner eyes that all engagements in this world can bear fruit only when they take place within this divine circle.... We can study, teach, write and hold a regular job. We can do all of this without ever having to leave the house of love.[3]

THE ATTRIBUTES OF GOD

In addition to an appreciation of the Trinity, lead worshipers must understand who God is from a biblical perspective. After all, you can't inspire others to know God in deeper ways if you don't know him yourself. As you work through the characteristics of God presented in this chapter, keep in mind that no one attribute offers us a complete picture of God. He is all these things and so much more. Add to every attribute, for example, the fact that God is also infinite, perfect, and eternal (Psalm 147:5; 1 Timothy 1:17; Deuteronomy 32:4; Daniel 4:3). To say that God is good is only a fraction of the story. He is infinitely, perfectly, and eternally good. And because God is infinite and eternal, we will never run out of reasons to worship him. Every time we encounter God, now and forever, some new facet of his glory is waiting to be discovered.

Furthermore, God's attributes are not separate from each other; each one relates to and informs the others. For example, you can't celebrate his love and ignore his holiness. As J. I. Packer writes, God is loving *and* holy:

> Sentimental ideas of His love as an indulgent, benevolent softness, divorced from moral standards and concerns, must therefore be ruled out from the start. God's love is holy love. The God whom Jesus made known is not a God who is indifferent to moral distinctions, but a God who loves righteousness and hates iniquity.[4]

The following therefore is a devotional study of ten selected attributes of God as revealed in Scripture. This is by no means an exhaustive study, but merely a starting point for those who hunger to know God more deeply. Feel free to return to any of these brief meditations during your private worship or even use them in the context of corporate worship.

God Is Sovereign

Our God is infinitely, perfectly, and eternally sovereign; he reigns supreme. He alone is Lord over all creation. "The Lord is God in heaven above and on the earth below. There is no other.... For the Lord your God is God of gods and Lord of lords, the great God." (Deuteronomy 4:39; 10:17). Our Sovereign God is ultimately and exclusively in control. He cannot be commanded, controlled, or manipulated. Daniel 4:35 informs us that God has full authority to do as he desires: "He does as he pleases with the powers of heaven and the peoples of the earth. No one can hold back his hand or say to him: 'What have you done?'" No wonder all of heaven constantly shouts, "Hallelujah! For our Lord God Almighty reigns" (Revelation 19:6).

Just as God the Father is sovereign, God the Son has been exalted to the highest place and been given the name above all names, "that at the name of

Jesus every knee should bow, in heaven and on earth and under the earth, and every tongue confess that Jesus Christ is Lord, to the glory of God the Father" (Philippians 2:9–11). Indeed, Jesus is seated at the right hand of the Father "far above all rule and authority, power and dominion, and every title that can be given, not only in the present age but also in the one to come" (Ephesians 1:20–22).

"Jesus is Lord" was not only the basic creed of the first-century church, it was its rallying battle cry. That's because the New Testament word for "Lord" comes from the Greek word *kurios*, which coincidentally was also the title bestowed upon the Roman emperors. In effect, the early church proclaimed that Jesus was above Caesar. Many were martyred because they refused to renounce Jesus as Lord. Given that background, we begin to sense how bold and powerful the following words of Paul must have been to the first generation of Christians:

> God, the blessed and only Ruler, the King of kings and Lord of lords, who alone is immortal and who lives in unapproachable light, whom no one has seen or can see. To him be honor and might forever. Amen. (1 Timothy 6:15–16)

Few pieces of art proclaim that Jesus is Lord more effectively than the *Sinai Pantocrator* icon (plate 4). Originally painted in the sixth century, the icon has been carefully preserved at the Monastery of St. Catherine in Sinai, Egypt, which interestingly sits at the foot of Mt. Sinai. The painter is unknown to us today but was most likely an Egyptian Christian. The Greek word *Pantocrator* means "Lord of All" or "Ruler of All." One of the most striking features of this icon is that Jesus' face appears oddly asymmetrical. The right side, with its penetrating eye and raised eyebrow depicts God's judgment. The left side, calm and inviting, portrays God's mercy. In his left hand, Christ is holding the Gospels, while his right hand is raised in blessing. Two fingers are raised symbolizing his dual nature as both God and man. The remaining three fingers are folded down, symbolizing the Trinity. Every time I look upon this icon, I am reminded that Jesus is indeed Lord of all, but I am also challenged as to whether Jesus is Lord of all of me.

"To the only God our Savior be glory, majesty, power and authority, through Jesus Christ our Lord, before all ages, now and forevermore! Amen" (Jude 25).

God Is All-Powerful

God not only has the authority to rule, he has the power to back it up. The psalmist writes, "Lift up your heads, O you gates; be lifted up, you ancient doors, that the King of glory may come in. Who is this King of glory? The Lord strong and mighty" (Psalm 24:7–8).

Theologians use the term *omnipotent* to describe God's almighty power. The Latin term *omni* means "all," and *potent* means "able to do and to have power." Therefore, omnipotence means "able to do all and to have all power." Ephesians 3:20 tells us that God is "able to do immeasurably more than all we ask or imagine." Our God is more than able to handle anything that comes our way; his power is unlimited. The angel who appeared to Mary proclaimed, "For nothing is impossible with God" (Luke 1:37). Jesus stated the same thing in the positive: "With God all things are possible" (Matthew 19:26, see also Genesis 18:14; Job 42:2; Jeremiah 32:17, 27). Nothing is too difficult or remotely challenging for our God. He can easily do anything and everything he wills to do. For starters, he created the universe—the heavens, the earth, the stars, the planets, the animals, and human beings—merely by speaking them into existence.

God's power is also evident in his ability to control and subdue nature. The questions God put to Job poetically underscore God's power over creation:

> Who shut up the sea behind doors when it burst forth from the womb, when I made the clouds its garment and wrapped it in thick darkness, when I fixed limits for it and set its doors and bars in place, when I said, "This far you may come and no farther; here is where your proud waves halt"?... Can you bind the beautiful Pleiades? Can you loose the cords of Orion? Can you bring forth the constellations in their seasons or lead out the Bear with its cubs?... Can you raise your voice to the clouds and cover yourself with a flood of water?... Who has the wisdom to count the clouds? Who can tip over the water jars of the heavens when the dust becomes hard and the clods of earth stick together?... Do you give the horse his strength or clothe his neck with a flowing mane?... Does the eagle soar at your command and build his nest on high? (Job 38:8–11, 31–32, 34, 37–38; 39:19, 27)

God's power was also demonstrated emphatically through Jesus Christ whose birth, death, and resurrection were astonishingly miraculous. And as if that weren't enough, Jesus also routinely cast out demons, healed the sick, and raised the dead. Jesus' power was not the result of "hocus-pocus" magic;

he possessed masterful knowledge of science and physics. Labeling him "the smartest man who ever lived," Dallas Willard writes,

> Jesus knew how to transform the molecular structure of water to make it wine. That knowledge also allowed him to take a few pieces of bread and some little fish and feed thousands of people.... He knew how to transform the tissues of the human body from sickness to health and from death to life. He knew how to suspend gravity, interrupt weather patterns, and eliminate unfruitful trees without saw or ax. He only needed a word.[5]

No wonder 1 Corinthians 1:24 proclaims Christ as "the power of God."

It's important to clarify that while God is all-powerful, he is not power hungry like we human beings tend to be. Instead, God shares power. He placed mankind in the garden and said, "Be fruitful and increase in number; fill the earth and subdue it. Rule over the fish of the sea and the birds of the air and over every living creature that moves on the ground" (Genesis 1:28). God also confers power and control by offering us free will, allowing us the prerogative to choose our own way. However, in sharing power, God's own power is never relinquished or diminished.

Right before Jesus healed two blind men, he asked them, "Do you believe that I am able to do this?" (Matthew 9:28). Apparently it's important to God that we acknowledge that he is indeed able. In the same way, every time we worship God, we affirm that he is all-powerful, that he is more than able to do anything beyond all we could ever imagine. "The Lord is robed in majesty and is armed with strength.... Splendor and majesty are before him; strength and glory are in his sanctuary" (Psalm 93:1; 96:6).

God Is Holy

God is morally perfect—the essence of purity. There is absolutely no evil in him. First John 1:5 proclaims that "God is light; in him there is no darkness at all." Because God is completely free from evil desires and intentions, he always does what is right. God's holiness is majestic and glorious, putting him, according to Exodus 15:11, clearly in a league of his own: "Who among the gods is like you, O Lord? Who is like you—majestic in holiness, awesome in glory, working wonders?" Because he is holy, it is impossible for God to ever be wrong or unfair. So we can be confident that his actions toward us are always right and that his dealings with us are always just.

Because God is holy, he hates sin. The prophet Habakkuk reminds us that God's eyes are "too pure to look on evil" and that he can't tolerate wrong-doing (Habakkuk 1:13). Throughout the Bible, God is outspoken in his intense hatred of sin. In Zechariah 8:17, for example, God says, "Do not plot evil against your neighbor, and do not love to swear falsely. I hate all this" (see also Proverbs 6:16–19). In his book *The Pursuit of Holiness*, Jerry Bridges says:

> Every time we sin, we are doing something God hates. He hates our lustful thoughts, our pride and jealousy, our outbursts of temper, and our rationalization that the end justifies the means. We need to be gripped by the fact that God hates all these things. We become so accustomed to our sins we sometimes lapse into a state of peaceful coexistence with them, but God never ceases to hate them.[6]

Indeed, human beings tend to be soft on sin. We try to make sin innocuous and less incriminating by referring to it as "bad judgment," an "unfortunate error," or a "moral indiscretion." God, on the other hand, cannot overlook any sin no matter how small or inconsequential it may seem to us; doing so would violate his character. That's why sin offends God. Joseph didn't allow himself to be seduced by Potiphar's wife because he didn't want to "sin against God" (Genesis 39:9).

God's holiness is one of the constant themes resonating throughout heaven. The apostle John reported seeing four creatures around the throne of God that never stop saying, "Holy, holy, holy is the Lord God Almighty, who was, and is, and is to come" (Revelation 4:8). So every time we praise God's holiness, we join the heavenly realms in worship.

"Exalt the Lord our God and worship at his holy mountain, for the Lord our God is holy" (Psalm 99:9).

God Is Good

God's moral perfection is manifested by his goodness. Psalm 106:1 is a phrase that's repeated throughout Scripture: "Give thanks to the Lord, for he is good; his love endures forever" (see also 2 Chronicles 5:13; Psalm 100:5; 107:1; 118:1; 136:1).

If God was sovereign and all-powerful, but not good, he'd be a tyrant. Instead, our God is exceedingly good. Psalm 31:19 reads, "How great is your goodness, which you have stored up for those who fear you."

Because God is infinitely, perfectly, and eternally good, his intentions toward us are always good; he is deeply committed to our well-being. Jesus was known as the "good shepherd" (John 10:14). He announced his purpose in coming to earth was to give us life "to the full" (John 10:10) and that our heavenly Father intends to give good gifts to those who ask (Matthew 7:11). So God wants the best for you and always has your best interests at heart. "'For I know the plans I have for you,' declares the Lord, 'plans to prosper you and not to harm you, plans to give you hope and a future'" (Jeremiah 29:11).

Not only are God's intentions toward us good, but so are his actions. The psalmist said to God, "You are good, and what you do is good" (Psalm 119:68). James states that God is the giver of all good things: "Every good and perfect gift is from above, coming down from the Father" (James 1:17). Paul adds that God "richly provides us with everything for our enjoyment" (1 Timothy 6:17). God even works on our behalf while we sleep: "It is vain for you to rise up early, to retire late, to eat the bread of painful labors; for He gives to His beloved even in his sleep" (Psalm 127:2 NASB).

Though God's intentions and actions toward us are good, we often doubt. We fear that God will abandon us or let us down. For example, we experience a few snags in a relationship and we conclude that we'll never experience the community and intimacy we long for. Or we experience conflict at church and we conclude that things will never work out for us in ministry. Or we bemoan our financial challenges as if they're insurmountable. Believing and acting as though God is always ready to pull the rug out from under us contradicts his character. The psalmist audaciously dares us to take advantage of God's good nature: "Taste and see that the Lord is good" (Psalm 34:8).

God is incapable of any evil deed. "When tempted, no one should say, 'God is tempting me.' For God cannot be tempted by evil, nor does he tempt anyone" (James 1:13). Instead, God persistently turns bad things into good.

Joseph was sold by his brothers into slavery, exiled in a foreign land, even imprisoned. But before it was all over, he became the most celebrated leader in Egypt, second only to Pharaoh in power and authority. His misfortune turned into fortune. Joseph later offered his brothers the following explanation: "You intended to harm me, but God intended it for good" (Genesis 50:20). Paul put it this way: "And we know that in all things God works for the good of those who love him, who have been called according to his purpose" (Romans 8:28).

Nothing is beyond God's power for good. As Dallas Willard points out, "Irredeemable harm does not befall those who willingly live in the hand of God."[7] Because God is good, we can leave the outcome of things up to him.

King David possessed an overwhelming confidence in the goodness of God, even amidst adversity. In the famous Twenty-third Psalm, he referred to God as his shepherd, whose goodness and mercy would follow him all the days of his life (Psalm 23:6 KJV). Even more emphatically he wrote, "I would have despaired unless I had believed that I would see the goodness of the Lord in the land of the living" (Psalm 27:13 NASB). No matter how hopeless your circumstances appear, be assured that God's goodness will prevail.

In C. S. Lewis's classic book *The Lion, the Witch, and the Wardrobe,* Mr. and Mrs. Beaver describe Aslan, the great Lion, to the children as one who will save Narnia from evil and danger. Little Susan questions whether it's safe to meet such an imposing figure.

> "Ooh!" said Susan, "I'd thought he was a man. Is he—quite safe? I shall feel rather nervous about meeting a lion."
>
> "That you will, dearie, and no mistake," said Mrs. Beaver; "if there's anyone who can appear before Aslan without their knees knocking, they're either braver than most or else just silly."
>
> "Then he isn't safe?" said Lucy.
>
> "Safe?" said Mr. Beaver; "don't you hear what Mrs. Beaver tells you? Who said anything about safe? 'Course he isn't safe. But he's good. He's the King, I tell you."[8]

"Give thanks to the Lord Almighty, for the Lord is good" (Jeremiah 33:11).

God Is Gracious

God's grace is an extension of his goodness to undeserving people. We are saved through grace (Romans 3:24). In love, God accepts us into his family because of his "glorious grace, which he has freely given us" through Christ (Ephesians 1:6). We've done nothing to merit God's blessings. He is gracious because that is his nature.

In defining "grace," Philip Yancey writes:

> Grace means there is nothing we can do to make God love us more—no amount of spiritual calisthenics and renunciations, no amount of knowledge gained from seminaries and divinity schools, no amount of crusading on behalf of righteous causes. And grace means there is nothing we can do to make God

> love us less—no amount of racism or pride or pornography or adultery or even murder. Grace means that God already loves us as much as an infinite God can possibly love.[9]

Jesus never used the word *grace* in his teaching. Instead, he told powerful stories illustrating God's grace. Three such stories are recorded in Luke 15. First there is the parable of the lost sheep: a shepherd has one hundred sheep, one gets lost, and the shepherd searches high and low for his missing sheep. Then there's the story of the lost coin: a woman has ten silver coins and loses one. She turns her whole house upside down looking for that missing coin. Finally, there is the well-known story of the prodigal son who demands an early inheritance only to squander it on loose living, but eventually comes to his senses, humbles himself, and returns home. In each case, extraordinary love and favor are shown for something or someone that no one else cares about. After all, who cares if one stupid sheep or one lousy coin gets lost? There are plenty of others. Who cares if some punk kid rebels and gets what's coming to him? That's just the point; God cares. His grace knows no limits. Where sin abounds, grace abounds more (Romans 5:20). God's grace is greater than our sinfulness.

These three parables reveal one more important thing about the heart of God: when what was lost becomes found, God is ecstatic with joy. The shepherd calls all his friends and neighbors together and says, "Rejoice with me; I have found my lost sheep" (Luke 15:6). The woman calls all her friends and neighbors together and says, "Rejoice with me; I have found my lost coin" (Luke 15:9). The heartsick father sees his prodigal son off in the distance and runs to meet him (Luke 15:20). To drive the point home, Jesus added, "In the same way, I tell you, there is rejoicing in the presence of the angels of God over one sinner who repents" (Luke 15:10).

Evidently, God enjoys being gracious. In fact, Isaiah says that God "longs to be gracious" to us (Isaiah 30:18). Noting that God didn't even spare his own son for us, Paul then asks, "How will he not also, along with him, graciously give us all things?" (Romans 8:32).

God's grace is extended to all people, not just the religious. For grace is nothing if not impartial. That's just the nature of grace; it is unmerited. The scandalous nature of grace lies in the fact that it is lavished extravagantly upon the best of us, the worst of us, and all the rest of us. Thus, grace can be downright baffling at times because it isn't "fair" from a purely human perspective. When good things happen to bad people, we scratch our heads and ask, "Why, Lord?" When your fellow artist works only half as hard as you do, and he or she gets all the opportunities and recognition, it doesn't seem fair, does it? Yet the same grace that seems to have been "wasted" on those so undeserving has also been affectionately tendered to you.

"Praise be to the God and Father of our Lord Jesus Christ, who has blessed us in the heavenly realms with every spiritual blessing in Christ" (Ephesians 1:3).

God Is Loving

Love is one of the most compelling aspects of God's character because it's such a vital human need. David wrote, "One thing God has spoken, two things have I heard: that you, O God, are strong, and that you, O Lord, are loving" (Psalm 62:11–12). However, Scripture reveals that God is not only loving, he defines love and embodies it. Love is not merely something God has, but something he is. First John 4:8 simply says, "God is love." So God's love doesn't depend on us, but instead flows freely and naturally out of the very essence of who God is.

God's love is also the ultimate manifestation of his goodness. God's love is excessive; he doesn't love us a little bit. Romans 5:5 asserts that God has "poured out his love into our hearts." The Bible says that God has lavished his love upon us (1 John 3:1) and shown us the "full extent of his love" (John 13:1). Paul advises all Christians to take in the "extravagant dimensions of Christ's love. Reach out and experience the breadth! Test its length! Plumb the depths! Rise to the heights!" (Ephesians 3:18–19 MSG). Writing in the fourteenth century, Julian of Norwich bids us "stand and gaze, eternally marveling at the supreme, surpassing, singleminded, incalculable love that God, who is goodness, has for us."[10]

Even if you don't "feel" it, God's love is always there. Paul wrote, "For I am convinced that neither death nor life, neither angels nor demons, neither the present nor the future, nor any powers, neither height nor depth, nor anything else in all creation, will be able to separate us from the love of God that is in Christ Jesus our Lord" (Romans 8:38–39). What made Paul absolutely certain of God's love? Was it because Paul was irresistibly lovable? No, it is because God is undeniably loving.

There is an astonishing amount of emotion and intensity behind God's love. Zephaniah 3:17 proclaims that God rejoices over us with singing. Imagine that! The God of all creation sings songs about you! However, God's love is not the syrupy kind of love so often exhibited in popular songs, novels, and movies. God's love is much more substantive, more than mere words. "God demonstrates his own love for us in this: While we were still sinners, Christ died for us" (Romans 5:8). Now it would be understandable, even noble, to give your life for someone important or famous, but Christ died for sinners—you and me—saying, "Greater love has no one than this, that he lay down his life for his friends" (John 15:13).

God's love is also unconditional; there is nothing we can do to earn it. In fact, it's simply astounding that a holy God would love sinners. Human beings tend to love each other for good reason—we find some quality in the other person that's attractive and worthy of our love. God, on the other hand, loves us even in our unloveliness.

God loves us not in spite of our sin, but with our sin. He sees all our faults, knows all our secret sins, yet he does not withhold love. Author J. I. Packer expounds on the incredulity of God's steadfast love:

> There is tremendous relief in knowing that His love to me is utterly realistic, based at every point on prior knowledge of the worst about me, so that no discovery now can disillusion him about me, in the way I am so often disillusioned about myself, and quench His determination to bless me. There is, certainly, great cause for humility in the thought that he sees all the twisted things about me that my fellow-men do not see ... and that He sees more corruption in me than that which I see in myself.... There is, however, equally great incentive to worship and love God in the thought that, for some unfathomable reason, He wants me as His friend, and desires to be my friend, and has given His Son to die for me in order to realise this purpose.[11]

A rich young man once approached Christ and asked him how to get into heaven. Jesus correctly perceived that one of this man's character defects was selfishness—that his love for money had hardened him to the needs of others. But instead of giving the man a merciless tongue lashing, the gospel writer tells us that Jesus "looked at him and loved him" (Mark 10:21). So you don't have to have your act together or have life all figured out for God to love you.

God loves us just as we are, but he doesn't let us stay there. God "disciplines those he loves" (Hebrews 12:6), meaning that he gently confronts our bad habits and dysfunction in order to rid us of such self-destructive behavior. If this pruning process ever causes you to doubt God's love, be assured that his "stockpiles of loyal love are immense" (Lamentations 3:32 MSG). The poet George Herbert reminds us that we can always rest on God's amazing love:

> My God, thou art all love.
> Not one poor minute scapes thy breast,
> But brings a favor from above;
> And in this love, more than in bed, I rest.[12]

"Because your love is better than life, my lips will glorify you" (Psalm 63:3).

God Is Compassionate

God's compassion is a manifestation of his love toward those who suffer or are in need. "The Lord is compassionate and gracious, slow to anger, abounding in love" (Psalm 103:8). As powerful as God is, it's simply astonishing how sensitive and tender he is to those in need. Isaiah 42:3 affirms that, "A bruised reed he will not break, and a smoldering wick he will not snuff out." God is full of loving-kindness.

Every day he walked the earth, Jesus gave us a picture of God's compassion in action. One time Jesus and his disciples came upon a funeral procession. A woman, already widowed, had lost her only son. Just seeing her evoked Jesus' deepest sympathies and Luke 7:13 reports that "his heart went out to her." On another occasion, Jesus saw a large crowd of people gathered to hear him teach and "he had compassion on them, because they were like sheep without a shepherd" (Mark 6:34).

When we hurt, God hurts. According to Isaiah 63:9, this is typical of God's relationship with his people: "In all their distress he too was distressed." For someone who is physically hurting, Psalm 41:3 contains these comforting words: "The Lord sustains them on their sickbed and restores them from their bed of illness" (TNIV). Other translations of that verse place God right by our bedside when we're ill:

> The Lord will strengthen him upon the bed of languishing: thou wilt make all his bed in his sickness. (KJV)

> Whenever we're sick and in bed, God becomes our nurse, nurses us back to health. (MSG)

When you couple God's great compassion with his awesome strength, it's no wonder Scripture often refers to God as our rock or refuge in times of trouble. "The Lord is a refuge for the oppressed, a stronghold in times of trouble" (Psalm 9:9). "The Lord is good, a refuge in times of trouble. He cares for those who trust in him" (Nahum 1:7). "Trust in the Lord forever, for the Lord, the Lord, is the Rock eternal" (Isaiah 26:4).

Even though sin offends God, Scripture teaches that his anger lasts for only a moment, being quickly overwhelmed by his great compassion. "With deep compassion I will bring you back," God says. "With everlasting kindness I will have compassion on you" (Isaiah 54:7–8).

"Praise be to the God and Father of our Lord Jesus Christ, the Father of compassion and the God of all comfort" (2 Corinthians 1:3).

God Is Merciful

Mercy is God's compassion toward sinners. "The Lord is full of compassion and mercy" (James 5:11). Far from begrudging, God delights to show mercy (Micah 7:18) and takes joy in exercising kindness (Jeremiah 9:24).

Though God is pure and holy, he is especially kind and merciful toward us sinners. "He saved us, not because of righteous things we had done, but because of his mercy" (Titus 3:5). Ephesians 2:4–5 adds that "because of his great love for us, God, who is rich in mercy, made us alive with Christ even when we were dead in transgressions." God is not obligated to pardon our sins. He does so out of sheer mercy (Romans 9:16). It's because of God's mercy that he is so patient with sinners, "not wanting anyone to perish, but everyone to come to repentance" (2 Peter 3:9). In fact, it's his kindness that leads us to repentance in the first place (Romans 2:4). Our God is a God of forgiveness (Nehemiah 9:17).

Central to Jesus' ministry was the forgiveness of sins. The Scriptures tell us that Jesus had "authority on earth to forgive sins" (Matthew 9:6). Jesus openly forgave sinners: a paralytic, an adulterous woman, the thief on the cross. Finally, he poured out his blood for the sins of all people (Matthew 26:28).

Though we fail him miserably, God never cuts us off or walks out on us (Nehemiah 9:31). Perhaps that's why "God, have mercy" is the most common prayer in the Bible and throughout history. However, the fact that we can ask anything of God rests upon the fact that he is merciful. As Daniel said to God,

"We do not make requests of you because we are righteous, but because of your great mercy" (Daniel 9:18).

"Praise be to the God and Father of our Lord Jesus Christ! In his great mercy he has given us new birth into a living hope through the resurrection of Jesus Christ from the dead" (1 Peter 1:3).

God Is Wise

Isaiah proclaims that our God is "wonderful in counsel and magnificent in wisdom" (Isaiah 28:29). Job says, "To God belong wisdom and power; counsel and understanding are his" (Job 12:13). Indeed, God alone possesses the knowledge, understanding, and power to always make right choices. He is "the only wise God" (Romans 16:27). Stephen Charnock wrote, "The resolves and ways of God are not mere will, but will guided by the reason and counsel of his own infinite understanding."[13]

Interestingly, Scripture often couples God's wisdom with his strength. "His wisdom is profound, his power is vast" (Job 9:4). "Great is our Lord and mighty in power; his understanding has no limit" (Psalm 147:5). Daniel 2:20 asserts that "wisdom and power are his." Thus, infinite power is ruled by infinite wisdom.[14]

If Jesus is truly Lord of our lives, we relinquish control to him. We don't lean on our own understanding, but instead look to him for all our marching orders. We seek his guidance in every area of our lives.

Much of God's wisdom and instruction is imparted through his Word. "All Scripture is God-breathed and is useful for teaching, rebuking, correcting and training in righteousness" (2 Timothy 3:16). Though sometimes regarded by the world as foolishness (1 Corinthians 1:18–31), God's wisdom has withstood the test of time and will continue to do so. "The grass withers and the flowers fall, but the word of our God stands forever" (Isaiah 40:8). God's wisdom was also manifested through Jesus Christ, who was hailed as Wonderful Counselor (Isaiah 9:6) and regarded as the "wisdom of God" (1 Corinthians 1:24). Indeed, the authority and profundity of Jesus' teaching constantly amazed his listeners (see Matthew 7:28–29). God's wisdom is also conveyed through the Holy Spirit, who readily guides us into truth (John 16:13).

Because God is infinitely and perfectly wise, he never makes a wrong decision; he always chooses the best means to achieve the best results. That's why

James describes God's wisdom as "first of all pure; then peace-loving, considerate, submissive, full of mercy and good fruit, impartial and sincere" (James 3:17).

Unlike human beings, God is never deceived or given to illusion. He always has a firm grasp on reality, viewing the world, and our lives in it, as they really are. That's why God's wisdom is true. It also explains why his wisdom is so far beyond us: "'My thoughts are not your thoughts, neither are your ways my ways,' declares the Lord. 'As the heavens are higher than the earth, so are my ways higher than your ways and my thoughts than your thoughts'" (Isaiah 55:8–9).

Because God's wisdom is true, we can trust his dealings with us. J. I. Packer writes:

> We should not, therefore, be too taken aback when unexpected and upsetting and discouraging things happen to us now. What do they mean? Why, simply that God in His wisdom means to make something of us which we have not attained yet, and is dealing with us accordingly.
>
> Perhaps He means to strengthen us in patience, good humour, compassion, humility, or meekness, by giving us some extra practice in exercising these graces under specially difficult conditions. Perhaps He has new lessons in self-denial and self-distrust to teach us. Perhaps He wishes to break us of complacency, or unreality, or undetected forms of pride and conceit. Perhaps His purpose is simply to draw us closer to Himself in conscious communion with Him; for it is often the case, as all the saints know, that fellowship with the Father and the Son is most vivid and sweet, and Christian joy is greatest, when the cross is heaviest.... Or perhaps God is preparing us for forms of service of which at present we have no inkling.[15]

"Oh, the depth of the riches of the wisdom and knowledge of God! How unsearchable his judgments, and his paths beyond tracing out! Who has known the mind of the Lord? Or who has been his counselor? Who has ever given to God, that God should repay him? For from him and through him and to him are all things. To him be the glory forever! Amen" (Romans 11:33–36).

God Is Faithful

God is completely reliable. He will never let you down. Deuteronomy 7:9 affirms that our God "is the faithful God, keeping his covenant of love to a thousand generations." God is not fickle or capricious. He does not vacillate back and forth like human beings do. "God is not a man, that he should lie, nor a son of man, that he should change his mind. Does he speak and then not act? Does he promise and not fulfill?" (Numbers 23:19).

Indeed, every aspect of God is faithful and true, including his attributes, his Word, and his promises. "Because of the Lord's great love we are not consumed, for his compassions never fail. They are new every morning; great is your faithfulness" (Lamentations 3:22–23).

Because God's promises never fail, he is completely trustworthy. Psalm 145:13 announces that "The Lord is faithful to all his promises." Right before he died, Joshua reminded the people of Israel of God's faithfulness: "Now I am about to go the way of all the earth. You know with all your heart and soul that not one of all the good promises the Lord your God gave you has failed. Every promise has been fulfilled; not one has failed" (Joshua 23:14).

God's loyalty is unwavering. Though we may wander, God remains faithful (2 Timothy 2:13). When we sin and make confession, "he is faithful and just and will forgive us our sins and purify us from all unrighteousness" (1 John 1:9).

God never abandons us when we struggle; he will never leave us or forsake us (Deuteronomy 31:6). Whenever we pray, he hears (Psalm 6:9). Whenever we face temptation, he is there, not allowing us to be tempted beyond what we can bear, but providing a way for us to stand up under it (1 Corinthians 10:13). "But the Lord is faithful, and he will strengthen and protect you from the evil one" (2 Thessalonians 3:3). When we experience growing pains in our quest for spiritual maturity, Paul reminds us that God is still at work: "The one who calls you is faithful and he will do it" (1 Thessalonians 5:24). Even during life's darkest moments, Jesus promised to always be with us (Matthew 28:20).

Praise God for his faithfulness: "I will sing of the Lord's great love forever; with my mouth I will make your faithfulness known through all generations. I will declare that your love stands firm forever, that you established your faithfulness in heaven itself" (Psalm 89:1–2).

FAITH: REMEMBERING WHO GOD IS

What about those times when all those wonderful attributes of God don't seem to mesh with reality? When God's power seems to be thwarted, his love withheld, or his goodness nonexistent? For centuries, theologians have struggled to explain why suffering occurs in a world supposedly ruled by God, and their answers usually involve dissertations on free will, sin, and redemption. However, it's clear that no one, not even a Christian, is immune to pain and suffering. Jesus said plainly, "In this world you will have trouble" (John 16:33). But on a personal level, how does one reconcile who God is with real life experience? In the scenario at the start of this chapter, Matty is so discouraged, she questions whether God really cares about her. Reading Scripture, it's obvious that Matty is in good company, for there are numerous passages that express similar frustrations about God. Here's a quick sampling from the psalmists:

> How long, O Lord? Will you forget me forever? How long will you hide your face from me? How long must I wrestle with my thoughts and every day have sorrow in my heart? How long will my enemy triumph over me? (Psalm 13:1–2)

> I am worn out calling for help; my throat is parched. My eyes fail, looking for my God. (Psalm 69:3)

> For I eat ashes as my food and mingle my drink with tears because of your great wrath, for you have taken me up and thrown me aside. (Psalm 102:9–10)

Apparently it's okay to tell God we're disappointed in him or to question his character. He can handle it; he is secure in his God-ness. In fact, it seems that questioning God is not only allowed but also encouraged, even if it results in whining and complaining against him. As Pastor Rob Bell writes:

> Central to the Christian experience is the art of questioning God. Not belligerent, arrogant questions that have no respect for our maker, but naked, honest, vulnerable, raw questions, arising out of the awe that comes from engaging the living God.[16]

Working through doubt is a necessary and healthy part of the spiritual journey. The psalmists cited above all cried out to God because they believed, in spite of their despair, that God was still just. They boldly questioned God in an effort to comprehend him.

Ironically, wrestling with doubt ultimately builds faith. At the height of his suffering, Job said, "Though he slay me, yet will I hope in him" (Job 13:15). When King Nebuchadnezzar threw Shadrach, Meshach, and Abednego into the fiery furnace, they boldly proclaimed that God was able to save them, but if he didn't they'd still never turn away from God. When their faith was tested, these Old Testament heroes didn't give up on God, but instead put their trust completely in him. Faith is confidence grounded in the reality of who God is, no matter the circumstances. "Now faith is being sure of what we hope for and certain of what we do not see" (Hebrews 11:1).

Though I've never suffered like Job, I, like all people, especially artists, have faced my fair share of adversity. At various times, I too have questioned God's goodness. But I keep coming back to a simple statement of faith often expressed during times of trouble: *God, you are still my God even when life is hard.*

My fellow artists, may your image of God be true, and when life is difficult, may you wrestle openly and honestly with who God is and discover that, in spite of circumstances, he is still sovereign, powerful, holy, good, gracious, loving, compassionate, merciful, wise, and faithful.

Follow-up Questions for Group Discussion

1. How is God's sovereignty manifested in your everyday life?
2. What does the phrase "God is able" mean to you?
3. What is the first thing that comes to mind when you think of God's holiness?
4. Have you ever doubted that God is good? Can you talk about it?
5. Can you share an example of God's grace in your life?
6. What evidence do you have of God's love for you?

7. Can you cite any other examples from the Bible illustrating the compassion of Christ?

8. What would God be like if he was all-powerful but not compassionate or merciful?

9. What factors contribute to God being "the only wise God"?

10. What does the fact that God is faithful mean to you personally?

Personal Action Steps

1. Write in your journal what you think of God after reading this chapter.

2. Over the next ten days, choose one of the attributes of God discussed in this chapter—a different one every day—and reread that particular section. Respond with praise however you feel led.

3. List the hymns or worship choruses you can recall that speak to each of the attributes highlighted in this chapter. Sing one as worship.

4. Select the attribute that you feel you have the least personal experience with. Ask God to reveal more of that specific attribute to you.

5. Create or perform something that highlights one of the attributes of God from this chapter and share it with your team.

1. Bathsheba Receiving David's Letter

Jan Steen

2. *The Incredulity of Saint Thomas*

Caravaggio

3. The Holy Trinity Icon

Andrei Rublev

4. Sinai Pantocrator Icon

chapter six
Who Am I?

> I am a Temple of the Holy Ghost, she said to herself, and was pleased with the phrase. It made her feel as if somebody had given her a present.
>
> From *A Temple of the Holy Ghost*
> by Flannery O'Connor

The following is based on a personal testimony that was shared at an Easter Sunday church service.[1]

"Hi, my name is Rachel. I've been attending Smith Avenue Bible Church for nine years and been part of the dance ministry for six. I've been asked to share part of my story this morning, and I hope you'll bear with me and excuse my nervousness. I've been on this platform hundreds of times, but public speaking is far scarier to me than dancing.

"When I was in high school, I always felt like the odd one out—second best—not good enough, pretty enough, skinny enough, or popular enough. I didn't fit in anywhere. In college, things got worse. I started restricting my eating, which is just a fancy way of saying I starved myself. Then I started purging—yet another euphemism for 'puking.' Then I started taking laxatives and working out like a fiend. Before I knew it, I was fighting a losing battle with anorexia, bulimia, and, underneath it all, depression. I spent years only eating 'safe' foods and avoiding others because they were bad. I sacrificed friendships for a gym membership. I consumed entire boxes of laxatives in one sitting. For ten years, I did this to myself.

"One time, about five years ago during an altar call here at church, I came forward sobbing, ready to 'give it to Jesus.' Things were a little better at first, but after a while I was back to binging and purging. I kept praying for God to heal me, but my life continued to spiral out of control. I even entertained thoughts of suicide.

"At that point, I started therapy and joined several support groups. My psychologist told me he believed I was clinically depressed and recommended medication, but I stubbornly refused. After two years of resisting medication, I finally gave in and added antidepressants to my daily regimen.

"I had 'given it up to Jesus' and I was on track to being healthy, and then things got worse. The voices from my past got louder, reminding me how disgusting I am—that I was a loser—ugly, fat, worthless, and that I was never going to get better. I decided I didn't need my meds anymore. After all, they obviously weren't working, and 'giving it up to Jesus' wasn't doing any good either.

"Then one night, just over three years ago, things got even worse. I was involved in a bad relationship and we had a horrible fight. Left with feelings of utter hopelessness, I attempted suicide by swallowing a bottle of pills. Instead of giving it up to Jesus, I simply gave up. I wanted nothing more than to sleep forever and put a stop to my pain and emptiness.

"At that point, things couldn't get much worse, and for once, they didn't. Giving up made me realize that it's not about giving *it* up to Jesus; it's about giving *me* up to Jesus. In all those years of praying, I had never given myself totally to God. I wouldn't say it was easier after I figured that out. My journey has been hard and I've been tempted often to give up. But what keeps me going is God's constant pursuit of my heart.

"Earlier I mentioned some of the negative thoughts I used to have about myself. I wish I could say that I never feel that way anymore, but sometimes those negative voices still haunt me. But what I do with those thoughts today is different. I don't just lay them at the cross and hope they go away. I'm learning over and over to lay myself at the cross, knowing that it is possible to be truly happy and that there is hope. It is a hope built on knowing that I am loved, that I am beautiful because I reflect God's beauty, and that no matter what I go through, I will never be left alone. I am totally amazed that, despite my failings and flaws, God not only loves me, he adores me."

Questions for Group Discussion

1. What are some of the external signs that indicated Rachel was suffering from anorexia and bulimia?

2. What factors contributed to Rachel's eating disorders?

3. Why do you suppose Rachel at first refused medication for her depression?

4. According to Rachel, what was the difference between "giving it up to Jesus" and giving herself to Jesus?

5. What's different about the way Rachel handles those negative voices now than in the past?

6. What are some of the benefits to sharing openly with each other about our personal struggles?

7. Are there any risks to sharing openly with each other about our personal struggles? If so, what are those risks?

8. How common do you think depression and eating disorders are among artists?

9. Is there anything about the artistic temperament that could make us susceptible to depression? If so, what?

10. How can the church help those suffering from anorexia, bulimia, and depression?

YOUR IDENTITY IN CHRIST

When I was a teenager, self-image was a hot topic of discussion. Strategies promoting healthy self-esteem were ubiquitous. A popular mantra during that era was, "I'm okay, you're okay," which was also the title of a trendy self-help book. And since we were all okay, that was supposedly ample reason for all of us to "believe in ourselves." However, none of us believed for a second that we were really okay, and the misguided loner who threatened to blow up the school certainly wasn't okay.

Even at our church youth group, we were taught to base our self-image on who we are in Christ, but none of us knew how to do that. And those of us who tried, I now realize, went about it the wrong way. We started with us; we attempted to define ourselves by looking within, and the results were always limited by our own self-perceptions. The appropriate starting point for discovering our true identity is always God, our Father Creator (Deuteronomy 32:6). Who I am in the context of a relationship with God is who I was meant to be. So who I am in relation to God is my truest sense of self.

To gain a better understanding of who God is, we began in the previous chapter by looking at the Trinity. To gain a clearer sense of who we are, we turn once again to Trinitarian theology and discover that we are children of God, disciples of Christ, and temples of the Holy Spirit.

You Are a Child of God

You are a child of the Most High God. "Yet to all who received him, to those who believed in his name, he gave the right to become children of God" (John 1:12). In his first epistle, John adds, "How great is the love the Father has lavished on us, that we should be called children of God!" (1 John 3:1).

In essence, you belong to God. Psalm 100:3 reads, "Know that the Lord is God. It is he who made us, and we are his; we are his people, the sheep of his pasture" (see also 1 Peter 2:9; 2 Corinthians 6:16). As a child of God, you have been adopted into God's family through Jesus Christ (Ephesians 1:5). Though you may have been rejected or abandoned by others, God always welcomes you with open arms. You belong—you have a unique place—in God's family. Even if your earthly father neglected you, God is a "father to the fatherless" (Psalm 68:5).

Membership in God's family has benefits and privileges. As Paul wrote: "Now if we are children, then we are heirs—heirs of God and co-heirs with Christ, if indeed we share in his sufferings in order that we may also share in his glory" (Romans 8:17). The first chapter of Ephesians features a brief summary of the benefits of being adopted into God's family: redemption, forgiveness, grace, worship, the Holy Spirit, and eternal life (vv. 6–14). Repeated throughout the preceding list, almost identically, is the phrase "to the praise of his glorious grace" or "his glory" (vv. 6, 12, 14). That same spirit of worship naturally wells up in all believers when reminded of the benefits of being a child of God.

Being a child of God is not a concept that's been easy for me to embrace. Given my personality and Midwestern work ethic, I know how to be a good soldier for Christ. But a child of God? That's where I have some growing to do. I know in my head that I'm a child of God, that I belong to him, and that I'm afforded benefits and privileges as a result, but I have a long way to go before that concept permeates my heart. However, what I've discovered so far is that being a child of God entails enjoying him, which for me means inviting him into times of recreation and rest in addition to my ministry work. To enjoy a game of tennis while cognizant of God's presence or commune with him over a good book or movie. To sense God's smile while doing those things reminds me that I am indeed a child of God.

You Are a Disciple of Christ

Jesus calls us to vibrant ongoing discipleship. A disciple is someone who is intentionally learning what it means to be like Christ and striving to put it into practice. Jesus said, "If you hold to my teaching, you are really my disciples" (John 8:31). A true disciple puts a high priority on spiritual growth, heeding the admonition of Ephesians 4:15 that we are to "grow up into him who is the Head, that is, Christ." In essence then, as a disciple of Christ, I am learning how to think and act as Christ would if Christ were living my life.

When Jesus says, "Follow me," he calls us to a life of commitment and sacrifice. Jesus said, "If anyone would come after me, he must deny himself and take up his cross daily and follow me" (Luke 9:23). True discipleship involves dying to self. Dallas Willard writes, "Being dead to self is the condition where the mere fact that I do not get what I want does not surprise or offend me and has no control over me."[2]

It takes effort to cultivate any relationship, in this case a relationship with God. The process of spiritual growth is sometimes arduous, other times easy, but it doesn't happen by itself. It entails intentionality, dedication, and perseverance. However, among the many rewards are joy (John 15:11), intimacy with Christ (John 14:21), and the freedom to be who God made you to be (John 8:32).

Finally, when Jesus invites you to be a disciple, it is a grand privilege. After all, he chose you because he thinks you have what it takes to eventually be like him. Jesus said, "My sheep listen to my voice; I know them, and they follow me" (John 10:27).

You Are a Temple of the Holy Spirit

Through the Holy Spirit, Christ dwells in all true believers, convicting us of sin, guiding us into truth, and empowering our lives (John 16:8, 13; Acts 1:8). By housing the Holy Spirit, our bodies become temples—holy, set apart for God's service (1 Corinthians 3:16). That means you and I carry God's spirit with us wherever we go. We are vessels of dynamic Holy Spirit activity, each of us a living temple of the living God (2 Corinthians 6:16). For that reason, we are to care for our bodies by adhering to healthy eating habits, exercising, and getting ample rest. Paul instructs us to honor God with our bodies (1 Corinthians 6:20) and to let Christ be exalted in our bodies (Philippians 1:20).

However, there are even deeper issues involved here. Much of the Bible's instruction on walking in the Spirit has to do with our physical bodies. Paul wrote:

> And if the Spirit ... is living in you, he who raised Christ from the dead will also give life to your mortal bodies through his Spirit, who lives in you. Therefore, brothers, we have an obligation—but it is not to the sinful nature, to live according to it. For if you live according to the sinful nature, you will die; but if by the Spirit you put to death the misdeeds of the body, you will live. (Romans 8:11–13)

Many of our addictions, compulsions, and bad habits are bodily behaviors. That's why Scripture implores us not to let sin reign in our bodies but to offer ourselves completely to God, to dedicate the various parts of our bodies to God as "instruments of righteousness" (Romans 6:12–13).

The point is this: what we allow "in us" determines our behavior. For example, if we tolerate lustful thoughts, they will produce bad habits, which in turn will lead to destructive patterns of lustful behavior. If, on the other hand, we let the Holy Spirit reign in us, we will not carry out the desires of the flesh (Galatians 5:16). Our actions will be motivated by love, joy, peace, patience, kindness, goodness, faithfulness, gentleness, and self-control (Galatians 5:22–23).

Dallas Willard writes:

> Nothing has power to tempt me or move me to wrong action that I have not *given* power by what I permit to be in me. And the most spiritually dangerous things in me are the little habits of thought, feeling, and action that I regard as "normal" because "everyone is like that" and it is "only human."[3]

Being a temple of the Holy Spirit means that we care for our bodies in such a way that it helps us know God better and follow Christ more consistently.

THE NEW YOU

As children of God, you and I have access to God. We can approach him "with freedom and confidence" (Ephesians 3:12). Having access to God also means that his attributes are readily available to shape us and work in our lives. As disciples of Christ, we become "partakers of the divine nature" (2 Peter 1:4 NASB). Some of God's attributes belong only to him. For example, only

God is omnipotent (all-powerful), omnipresent (ever-present), and omniscient (all-knowing). However, through the Holy Spirit, many of God's attributes, such as love, mercy, and kindness, are reproduced in us as we mature spiritually. To arrive, therefore, at a more complete picture of our identity in Christ, we must take into account the influence of God's character—the "new you" God calls you to be. To that end, we will now revisit the ten attributes of God presented in the previous chapter and examine who we are in light of who God is.

You will undoubtedly notice that personalizing each of God's attributes will incite within you a righteous restlessness—an earnest desire to change. You will not want to stay the same. That's because God is in the process of giving you a new heart and a new spirit (Ezekiel 36:26). According to the Bible, the essence of spiritual formation is the process of laying aside the old self and putting on the new:

> You were taught, with regard to your former way of life, to put off your old self, which is being corrupted by its deceitful desires; to be made new in the attitude of your minds; and to put on the new self, created to be like God in true righteousness and holiness. (Ephesians 4:22–24)

As we investigate further our identity in Christ, we will also consider specifically what it means to lay aside the old self and put on the new, in light of God's attributes.

Humbled by His Greatness

When we truly believe God is sovereign, we are naturally humbled by his greatness. "Submit yourselves, then, to God.... Humble yourselves, therefore, under God's mighty hand" (James 4:7; 1 Peter 5:6). The Old Testament admonition to "fear God" (i.e., Leviticus 25:17; Ecclesiastes 12:13; Proverbs 1:7) was never meant to scare us away from him. The original Hebrew word means "to stand in awe of" or "revere." It connotes the type of reverence befitting a superior being, a clarification that should produce within us, not a sappy and insipid view of God, but a healthy fear of God. After all, God is still God—the Almighty, the Creator of the universe, the one who holds eternity in his hands. We should rightly fear being alienated from such a God or displeasing him. Jesus said, "I tell you, my friends, do not be afraid of those who kill the body and after that can do no more. But I will show you whom you should fear: Fear him who, after the killing of the body, has power to throw you into hell. Yes, I tell you, fear him" (Luke 12:4–5).

Thus, a healthy fear of God breeds reverence. Psalm 33:8 reads, "Let all the earth fear the Lord; let all the people of the world revere him." Charles Spurgeon wrote, "There must ever be a holy fear mixed with the Christian's joy.... Fear, without joy, is torment; and joy, without holy fear, would be presumption."[4]

A healthy fear of God also breeds humility, which is listed by the prophet Micah as a basic requirement for godly character. "He has shown all you people what is good. And what does the Lord require of you? To act justly and to love mercy and to walk humbly with your God" (Micah 6:8 TNIV). Indeed, God has a special place in his heart for the humble: "For this is what the high and exalted One says—he who lives forever, whose name is holy: 'I live in a high and holy place, but also with those who are contrite and lowly in spirit, to revive the spirit of the lowly and to revive the heart of the contrite'" (Isaiah 57:15 TNIV).

Modern society tends to regard humility as weak and unsophisticated. However, God's brand of humility is far from demeaning. Jesus said, "For those who exalt themselves will be humbled, and those who humble themselves will be exalted" (Matthew 23:12 TNIV). James 4:10 adds, "Humble yourselves before the Lord, and he will lift you up." It's a paradox; we are exalted in humility. When we affirm our need for and utter dependence upon God, our stock, spiritually speaking, goes up. As Jesus said, "Blessed are the meek, for they will inherit the earth" (Matthew 5:5).

Have you ever noticed that most of our attempts to "act humble" are actually subtly self-serving? For example, when people praise us we may act all modest, but when they don't notice us we get upset and feel slighted. Authentic humility is never achieved by looking inward, but outward—beyond ourselves—to God. Godly humility allows us to swallow our pride and self-sufficiency. We can refrain from lying or propping ourselves up in order to look good. We can stop groping for attention or maneuvering for the approval of others. We can cease striving to prove ourselves or to be perfect. After all, God alone is perfect. True humility purges us of our defensiveness, arrogance, and self-righteousness, breaking down our self-serving facades and false pretense. The truly humble are real, open, and honest. They are free to be themselves in their most intimate relationships. Such humility results from encountering our Sovereign God and being truly humbled by his greatness.

Invested with His Power

As children of God, you and I have access to his unlimited power and strength. As David says, "The Lord gives strength to his people" (Psalm 29:11). Or to put it personally, "The Lord is my strength and my shield" (Psalm 28:7). After a lengthy description of God's mighty power, Isaiah proclaims that this power is readily available to us:

> He sits enthroned above the circle of the earth, and its people are like grasshoppers. He stretches out the heavens like a canopy, and spreads them out like a tent to live in.... Lift your eyes and look to the heavens: Who created all these? He who brings out the starry host one by one, and calls them each by name. Because of his great power and mighty strength, not one of them is missing.... The Lord is the everlasting God, the Creator of the ends of the earth.... (Here comes the clincher.) He gives strength to the weary and increases the power of the weak. (Isaiah 40:22, 26, 28–29, parenthesis mine)

Paul's prayer for the Ephesians affirms that God's power is ours for the asking: "I pray also that ... you may know ... his incomparably great power for us who believe.... I pray that out of his glorious riches he may strengthen you with power through his Spirit in your inner being" (Ephesians 1:18–19; 3:16).

God's power is available to work in us. "Now to him who is able to do immeasurably more than all we ask or imagine, according to his power that is at work *within us*" (Ephesians 3:20, emphasis mine). God is at work in you "to will and to act according to his good purpose" (Philippians 2:13) and to fulfill his purpose (Psalm 138:8). Jude 24 adds that God's power is also readily available to keep us from falling into sin.

God's strength attends to our fears and anxieties. The psalmist wrote, "When I am afraid, I will trust in you.... Even though I walk through the valley of the shadow of death, I will fear no evil, for you are with me.... The Lord is with me; I will not be afraid" (Psalm 56:3; 23:4; 118:6). Well over fifty times, Scripture says, "Fear not." Jesus said, "Do not let your hearts be troubled. Trust in God.... Peace I leave with you;... do not be afraid" (John 14:1, 27). Are there any more comforting words than those spoken by God through the prophet Isaiah? "So do not fear, for I am with you; do not be dismayed, for I am your God. I will strengthen you and help you; I will uphold you with my righteous right hand" (Isaiah 41:10).

Paul asserts that God's strength is manifested in our weakness: "Therefore I will boast all the more gladly about my weaknesses, so that Christ's power may rest on me. That is why, for Christ's sake, I delight in weaknesses, in insults, in hardships, in persecutions, in difficulties. For when I am weak, then I am strong" (2 Corinthians 12:9–10). We are invested with power from above. Paul encouraged the Ephesians to "be strong in the Lord and in his mighty power" (Ephesians 6:10). So whenever we feel overwhelmed, uncertain, or powerless, Psalm 105:4 exhorts us to "look to the Lord and his strength." Whenever we feel inadequate to do what God calls us to do, Habakkuk 3:19 reminds us that the Sovereign Lord is our strength; we can run like deer and scale the heights.

If I had to name one attribute of God that has been the most consistent theme throughout my life, it would have to be God's strength. Nothing has ever come easily for me including writing, leading, even parenting; everything has been hard work. For example, instead of being a music director at a modest-size church in a quiet pastoral setting out in the country, I served at a fast-paced megachurch. Instead of compliant children who do as they're told, God blessed us with two very strong-willed boys who challenged us at every turn. My wife and I even homeschooled them through high school. It seems as though the path of least resistance has never occurred to me.

I'm also a dreamer, a visionary, a pioneer of sorts. So whether launching new ministries or cowriting an original musical, I have often found myself out on a limb pleading for God to do the impossible or bless the improbable. In fact, my very first leadership challenge taught me to depend solely on God's power instead of my own. During college, I volunteered in the youth ministry at my church, and on one occasion organized an outreach concert at a local high school. With no funding and very little moral support from church leaders, my confidence started to wane. A few days before the concert, my soundman had to go out of town on an emergency, our equipment broke down, and we hit some snags in our rental agreement with the facility. At that point, I desperately dropped to my knees and cried out, "Lord, I'm in way over my head and I need your supernatural power to pull off this concert." At that point, I was reminded of Philippians 4:13: "I can do all things through Him who strengthens me" (NASB). From that day on, I have reminded myself of that truth, even sung it to myself, well over a thousand times. It rejuvenates me and gives me strength. The concert, by the way, went extremely well with dozens of decisions for Christ, but I will never forget the truth I learned that day in prayer; it has become the theme song of my life: God is able.

Dead to Sin

One of the most staggering tenets of the Christian faith is that through Christ, we have been made holy in our standing before God. As improbable as it sounds, "God made him who had no sin to be sin for us, so that in him we might become the righteousness of God" (2 Corinthians 5:21). Through his death on the cross, the totally sinless Christ presents desperately sinful human beings as holy to God. "But now he has reconciled you by Christ's physical body through death to present you holy in his sight, without blemish and free from accusation" (Colossians 1:22). Thus we've been redeemed; we are free from the penalty of sin. We are "dead to sin" (Romans 6:11, see also 1 Peter 2:24).

The righteousness that has been credited to us is not of our own doing. We have been made holy "through the sacrifice of the body of Jesus Christ" (Hebrews 10:10). Salvation may be free, but it was extremely costly to God (1 Corinthians 6:20). Christ paid for our pardon with his blood. "In him we have redemption through his blood, the forgiveness of sins" (Ephesians 1:7).

For a Christian to say, "I'm a sinner saved by grace," is not completely accurate. You are saved by grace, but in so doing, you are no longer a sinner—at least not in God's eyes. When God looks at you, he no longer sees those horribly ugly sins and those embarrassing failures from your past. Instead, he views you through the filter of the blood of Christ. Though our sins used to be as scarlet, they are now white as snow (Isaiah 1:18).

Righteousness is something that has been accomplished for us and, at the same time, something for which we are to strive. In Leviticus 11:44, God says, "I am the Lord your God; consecrate yourselves and be holy, because I am holy." According to 1 Thessalonians 4:7, godliness is part of our calling as Christ followers: "For God did not call us to be impure, but to live a holy life." In addition, 1 Peter 1:15 calls us to pursue holiness in every area of our lives: "But just as he who called you is holy, so be holy in all you do." God also invites us to aim for holiness in order to experience deeper fellowship with him: "Make every effort to live in peace with everyone and to be holy; without holiness no one will see the Lord" (Hebrews 12:14 TNIV).

Now the concept of holiness can be difficult to personalize because the word itself has become increasingly pejorative for us today. When we hear the word *holy*, we might imagine emaciated monks sitting cross-legged all day on a mountaintop or pale-faced old ladies in long plain dresses with their hair up in a bun. To most of us, a holy person is regarded as suppressed, boring, uptight, hypocritical, and prudish—a Goody Two-shoes. It's an affront to be labeled a "holy roller" or "holier than thou." So holiness is not something many of us aspire to. Yet, the Bible teaches that God "chose us in him before the creation of the world to be holy and blameless in his sight" (Ephesians 1:4).

Perhaps we need to redefine personal holiness. According to Richard Foster,

> Holiness means the ability to do what needs to be done when it needs to be done. It means being "response-able," able to respond appropriately to the demands of life. The word *virtue* ... means simply to function well. Virtue is good habits we can rely upon to make our life work.... So a holy life simply is a life that works.[5]

Holiness, therefore, has more to do with internals than externals. Though holiness is a lifelong process and not something we fully attain this side of heaven, it is clearly not a matter of following a list of "dos and don'ts." A "life that works" is free from the bad choices, the dysfunctional behavior, and the selfishness that characterizes sin. Instead, we are free to be who God truly made us to be.

Therefore, let us be "filled with the fruit of righteousness that comes through Jesus Christ—to the glory and praise of God" (Philippians 1:11).

Endowed with Goodness

Because God is good, he has endowed us with goodness, rendering us capable of good things. Paul's words to the Romans apply to all children of God: "I myself am convinced, my brothers, that you yourselves are full of goodness, complete in knowledge and competent to instruct one another" (Romans 15:14). Human beings tend to see the bad in each other and oftentimes only the bad. God, on the other hand, sees all the good in us. In our ongoing battle with sin and temptation we can often wonder whether we truly have it in us to obey God, especially if we're fighting a stubborn addiction. However, God knows the goodness we're capable of and beckons us to live up to that. Jesus was convinced that the woman caught in adultery was better than that. He told her, "Go now and leave your life of sin" (John 8:11) because he believed she was capable of good things.

God has delivered us not only from the penalty of sin but also from the power of sin. "For you were once darkness, but now you are light in the Lord. Live as children of light (for the fruit of the light consists in all goodness, righteousness and truth)" (Ephesians 5:8–9). We are "alive to God in Christ Jesus" (Romans 6:11). "God made you alive with Christ" (Colossians 2:13).

Whatever good is in us is the result of God working in our hearts. Even after we're saved God strives to keep us alive in Christ as he continues to deliver us from evil. Second Corinthians 1:10 states: "He has delivered us from such a deadly peril, and he will deliver us. On him we have set our hope that he will continue to deliver us." Jesus prayed, "Deliver us from evil" as part of the Lord's Prayer (Matthew 6:13 NASB). God's deliverance is a common theme throughout the Psalms: "From the Lord comes deliverance.... The Lord is my rock, my fortress and my deliverer.... You are my help and my deliverer; O Lord, do not delay" (Psalm 3:8; 18:2; 70:5). Thus, in the face of evil, Scripture teaches that we are victorious (1 Corinthians 15:57) and that we are overcomers (1 John 5:4–5). "We are more than conquerors through him who loved us" (Romans 8:37).

Because our God is a "God of deliverances" (Psalm 68:20 NASB), he offers us "divine power to demolish strongholds" (2 Corinthians 10:4). A stronghold is anything that has an unhealthy grip on us—a compulsion, addiction, or bad habit. Paul vowed never to be mastered by such things (1 Corinthians 6:12). Gerald May, in his book *Addiction and Grace*, describes further the spiritual aspects of deliverance:

> In my experience ... special miracles happen with uncommon frequency in the course of addictions. Without any evident reason, the weight of an addiction is lifted. "I was walking to the grocery store one day," said one alcoholic man, "and there, on the sidewalk, I discovered equanimity." He had suffered from alcoholism for many years.... Yet in a simple, wondrous moment, his life was transformed. He hasn't had a drink since....
>
> I can only call it deliverance. There is no physical, psychological, or social explanation for such sudden empowerments.... In many cases these people have struggled with their addictions for years. Then suddenly, with no warning, the

> power of the addiction is broken. To me, deliverance is like any other miraculous physical, emotional, or social healing.... In the case of addiction, healing takes the form of empowerment that enables people to modify addictive behavior.
>
> I am choosing my words carefully here. Deliverance *enables* a person to *make* a change in his or her behavior; in my experience deliverance does not *remove* the addiction and its underlying attachments. Something obviously happens to the systems of the brain when deliverance occurs; either the addicted systems are weakened or the ones seeking freedom are strengthened or both. But there is still a role for continued personal responsibility.... In none of these miraculous empowerments were people freed from having to remain intentional about avoiding a return to their old addictive behaviors. The real miracle was that avoidance became possible; the person could actually do it.[6]

The psalmist prayed, "Set me free from my prison, that I may praise your name. Then the righteous will gather about me because of your goodness to me" (Psalm 142:7). Notice that, in anticipation of God answering his prayer, the writer imagines the effect deliverance will have on him: he will be moved to worship; instead of loneliness and alienation, he will experience true community surrounded by godly people. And it's all because of God's goodness, which calls us to lay aside our attachments, bad habits, and addictions—those things that wage war against our souls (1 Peter 2:11). "Be at rest once more, O my soul, for the Lord has been good to you" (Psalm 116:7).

Blessed Abundantly

As children of the Most High God, we have been lavished with grace (Ephesians 1:7–8). First Corinthians 1:5 testifies that we have been "enriched in every way." Were you to write down all the ways God has blessed you—materially, physically, spiritually, relationally—the list would be long and impressive. "From the fullness of his grace we have all received one blessing after another" (John 1:16).

Though we are richly blessed, it is something of our human disposition to take for granted all we have. When we obsess over something we don't have, we quickly lapse into discontent. We're like a kid in a candy store who's worried about having enough candy, yet his dad owns the entire shop. Ephesians 1:3 declares that we have been blessed "with every spiritual blessing in Christ." Peter goes even further, stating that God "has given us *everything* we need for life and godliness" (2 Peter 1:3, emphasis mine). If we lack anything,

Jesus bids us, "Ask and it will be given to you; seek and you will find; knock and the door will be opened to you" (Matthew 7:7). So we can lay aside our jealousies and dissatisfaction because, as Paul reminds us, we are not poor, but rich especially in that which really matters: "For you know the grace of our Lord Jesus Christ, that though he was rich, yet for your sakes he became poor, so that you through his poverty might become rich" (2 Corinthians 8:9).

In addition to the blessings already mentioned, you have been graced with spiritual gifts and talents—those God-given qualities that allow you to do certain things well. If you're unaware of your spiritual gifts, I refer you to those listed in Romans 12:6–8 and 1 Corinthians 12:8–10. There are also many good books on spiritual gifts available from your Christian bookstore.

Also, as an artist, you have been blessed with talent. God graced you with the ability to create and/or perform, and it has undoubtedly played a major role in defining who you are. However, it's important to identify not only your artistic gifts but also your strengths as an artist. For example, if you're a dancer, but your strength is more in your communication skills than your technique, then play to your strength. Always work to improve your weaknesses, but never abandon your strengths. If you're unclear about your strengths as an artist, I suggest putting the question to people who know you well. Knowing your strengths and weaknesses is essential to the development of every artist.

In addition to your gifts and talents, you've been blessed with a unique personality. Some of you are driven and action oriented, others are laid back. Some are melancholy, others are sanguine. We are all complex combinations of various personality traits. There are some excellent tests you can take to help you identify your unique personality type (Myers-Briggs, Enneagram, etc.), but you can begin by simply asking yourself or someone who knows you, "What are my personal strengths?" Or to put it another way: "What are my positive personality traits?" Be careful to answer in terms of who you are, not what you do. For example, are you introverted or extroverted? A thinker or a feeler? Spontaneous or premeditated? Remember, there is no one like you. You are marvelously and wonderfully made (Psalm 139:14), and God desires that you be free to be the unique personality he created you to be.

All things considered, we are profusely blessed. Because our God is the most powerful being in the universe, exceedingly good and gracious, and because we're the apple of his eye (Psalm 17:8), we can lay aside our resentment when we don't get something we want. We need not grumble and complain, for we are indeed rich. As David put it, "The Lord is my shepherd, I shall not be in want" (Psalm 23:1).

Loved Unconditionally

God's love is global; he loves all people (John 3:16). However, God's love is also personal. Paul said, "I live by faith in the Son of God, who loved me and gave himself for me" (Galatians 2:20). God delights in you (Psalm 18:19). God cherishes you (Psalm 83:3). Isaiah 43:4 says that "you are precious and honored" in God's eyes. Jesus underscored how much God treasures us when he said, "Look at the birds of the air; they do not sow or reap or store away in barns, and yet your heavenly Father feeds them. Are you not much more valuable than they?" (Matthew 6:26).

Though Scripture affirms that God loves you, it doesn't mean anything unless you allow him to love you. In fact, letting God love you is more important than you loving him. In the book *Blue Like Jazz*, Donald Miller writes:

> And so I have come to understand that strength, inner strength, comes from receiving love as much as it comes from giving it. I think apart from the idea that I am a sinner and God forgives me, this is the greatest lesson I have ever learned. When you get it, it changes you. My friend Julie from Seattle told me that the main prayer she prays for her husband is that he will be able to receive love. And this is the prayer I pray for all my friends because it is the key to happiness. God's love will never change us if we don't accept it.[7]

How does one receive love? I have two suggestions. First, embrace fully your true identity as God's beloved child. Take your cue from the apostle John, who often referred to himself as the "disciple whom Jesus loved" (John 13:23; 19:26; 20:2; 21:7, 20). His self-esteem was not based on his talents, his appearance, or what he did for a living. His humble dignity emanated from the assurance that God loved him. You, too, are a disciple that Jesus loves; you are his beloved.

In his book *Life of the Beloved*, Henri Nouwen writes:

> We are the Beloved. We are intimately loved long before our parents, teachers, spouses, children and friends loved or wounded us. That's the truth of our lives. That's the truth I want you to claim for yourself. That's the truth spoken by the voice that says, "You are my Beloved.... I have called you by name, from the very

> beginning. You are mine and I am yours. You are my Beloved, on you my favor rests. I have molded you in the depths of the earth and knitted you together in your mother's womb. I have carved you in the palms of my hands and hidden you in the shadow of my embrace. I look at you with infinite tenderness and care for you with a care more intimate than that of a mother for her child. I have counted every hair on your head and guided you at every step. Wherever you go, I go with you, and wherever you rest, I keep watch. I will give you food that will satisfy all your hunger and drink that will quench all your thirst. I will not hide my face from you. You know me as your own as I know you as my own. You belong to me."[8]

Unfortunately, we all encounter negative voices ruthlessly determined to convince us that we don't measure up—that we are worthless. While it's true that you and I are unworthy of God's love, he never thinks of any of us as worthless. If Jesus thought we weren't worth it, he would have never given his life for us. Many people go through life with negative labels they picked up from childhood. "Ugly," "Stupid," and "Lazy" are cruel nicknames, heard every day on the school playground, that wound us as children and make us feel unlovable as adults. But you are not worthless and unlovable in the eyes of Almighty God. Deuteronomy 33:12 says, "Let the beloved of the Lord rest secure in him." You no longer have to feel insecure because God's love is real, faithful, and true. Zephaniah 3:17 states that the Lord "will quiet you with his love." So whenever those negative voices whisper that you're a worthless failure, let the Lord "quiet you with his love." Let God's love silence those hurtful voices from your past.

Second, identify at least one thing that God likes about you. If someone were to say, "I love you, but I really don't like you," that would totally negate their love, wouldn't it? God doesn't make such disclaimers. He loves you because he is a loving God, but he also likes you; he is very fond of you. You possess certain unique qualities that bring a smile to his face. Jesus was always quick to point out people's endearing traits. He commended the centurion for his faith, and he immortalized the poor widow because she gave all she had. So what exactly might God like about you? What part of your personality would you guess stands out in his mind? Or what specific character trait do you think he appreciates most?

I recently asked a class of college students to share one thing that they believe God likes about them. One young man said, "I think God likes my sense of humor." Another said, "I believe God likes my singing." A young woman added, "I bet God likes my passion and enthusiasm." When you identify something that God likes about you, you begin to personalize his love.

So God loves you. It's a fact, not a feeling. You can put to rest any thoughts that you're not good enough or that you're a loser. You can lay aside those nagging feelings of inferiority. You can stop living for the approval of others or seeking validation from false father figures. You matter more to God than you'll ever know.

Cared for Constantly

Because God is full of love and compassion, he cares for those in need. God "comforts us in all our troubles" (2 Corinthians 1:4). Whatever you're going through, God is neither oblivious nor disinterested; he cares deeply. Jesus cried out, "Blessed are those who mourn, for they will be comforted" (Matthew 5:4). Lamentations 3:22 insists that God's compassions "never fail," and the psalmist writes that God "daily bears our burdens" (Psalm 68:19). Thus, we are constantly cared for. God doesn't abandon us when difficulties arise. He said, "Never will I leave you; never will I forsake you" (Hebrews 13:5). "Fear not, for I have redeemed you; I have summoned you by name; you are mine. When you pass through the waters, I will be with you" (Isaiah 43:1–2). Rest assured you are never alone.

God invites us to look for him and find him amidst our pain and suffering. The Lord is near to the brokenhearted (Psalm 34:18). "Cast all your anxiety on him because he cares for you" (1 Peter 5:7). As a result of God's great compassion, we can seek refuge in him during any and every kind of adversity. "God is our refuge and strength, an ever-present help in trouble.... I will take refuge in the shadow of your wings until the disaster has passed" (Psalm 46:1; 57:1).

We need not fear the troubles of this day nor lose heart, for God is always there for us. So, as the psalmist asserts, we can be at peace: "I will lie down and sleep in peace, for you alone, O Lord, make me dwell in safety.... When I was upset and beside myself, you calmed me down and cheered me up" (Psalm 4:8 NIV; 94:19 MSG).

Forgiven Completely

Through Christ, our sins are forgiven (Acts 13:38). "In him we have redemption through his blood, the forgiveness of sins" (Ephesians 1:7). Therefore, we are free from the penalty of sin. "Christ redeemed us from that self-defeating, cursed life by absorbing it completely into himself" (Galatians 3:13 MSG).

We are completely and unequivocally forgiven. God declared, "For I will forgive their wickedness and will remember their sins no more" (Jeremiah 31:34 TNIV). "As far as the east is from the west, so far has he removed our transgressions from us" (Psalm 103:12). Thus, we are free from guilt and shame. We can be at peace with God for as far as he is concerned, the past is in the past. "Blessed is he whose transgressions are forgiven, whose sins are covered" (Psalm 32:1).

Forgiveness is available to all, but received only by those who repent. "If we confess our sins, he is faithful and just and will forgive us our sins and purify us from all unrighteousness" (1 John 1:9). Though we are clothed in righteousness and empowered to do good, that doesn't mean that we will never sin again. No one's perfect; no one's completely arrived. We will all fail. Therefore, confession and repentance are crucial components of the spiritual journey. Confession is openly and honestly admitting our sin; it is accompanied by remorse. Dallas Willard observes an alarming lack of sorrow and remorse among Christians today:

> It is common today to hear Christians talk of their "brokenness." But when you listen closely, you may discover that they are talking about their *wounds*, the things they have suffered, not about the evil that is in them.[9]

Repentance occurs when we declare our intention to turn away from sin, forsaking destructive fleshly desires for godly ones. In 2 Timothy 2:22, Paul advises that we flee from evil and instead "pursue righteousness, faith, love and peace, along with those who call on the Lord out of a pure heart."

David, an artist, repented of his adultery and penned the quintessential penitent's prayer:

> Have mercy on me, O God, according to your unfailing love; according to your great compassion blot out my transgressions. Wash away all my iniquity and cleanse me from my sin. For I know my transgressions, and my sin is always before me. Against you, you only, have I sinned and done what is evil in your sight.... Create in me a pure heart, O God, and renew a steadfast spirit within me. Do not cast me from your presence or take your Holy Spirit from me. Restore to me the joy of your salvation and grant me a willing spirit, to sustain me. (Psalm 51:1–4, 10–12)

No matter how often you and I fail, we should never give up trying to live for God. C. S. Lewis suggests:

> After each failure, ask forgiveness, pick yourself up, and try again. Very often what God first helps us toward is not the virtue itself but just this power of always trying again. For however important chastity (or courage, or truthfulness, or any other virtue) may be, this process trains us in habits of the soul which are more important still. It cures our illusions about ourselves and teaches us to depend on God. We learn, on the one hand, that we cannot trust ourselves even in our best moments, and, on the other, that we need not despair even in our worst, for our failures are forgiven.[10]

Guided by His Wisdom

Godly wisdom is the ability to make discerning choices and to distinguish right from wrong. In other words, it's the ability to see issues and circumstances from God's perspective. The book of Proverbs continually extols the value of wisdom: "Blessed are those who find wisdom, those who gain understanding, for she is more profitable than silver and yields better returns than gold. She is more precious than rubies; nothing you desire can compare with her" (Proverbs 3:13–15 TNIV).

God doesn't plop us down on this earth without guidance and direction. "For the Lord gives wisdom, and from his mouth come knowledge and understanding" (Proverbs 2:6). We don't have to walk aimlessly through life or lean on our own limited understanding and knowledge. As children of God, we have access to his perfect wisdom. The psalmist wrote, "You hold me by my right hand. You guide me with your counsel" (Psalm 73:23–24).

God's wisdom is ours for the asking. According to James 1:5, "If any of you lacks wisdom, you should ask God, who gives generously to all without finding fault, and it will be given to you" (TNIV).

We can acquire wisdom by asking for it, but we can also grow in wisdom by meditating on God's Word. "Let the word of Christ dwell in you richly as you teach and admonish one another with all wisdom" (Colossians 3:16). The psalmist discovered that he gained a surprising amount of wisdom simply by contemplating God's Word: "I have more insight than all my teachers, for I meditate on your statutes" (Psalm 119:99).

Worshiping God is the first step toward true wisdom. Psalm 111:10 insists, "The fear of the Lord is the beginning of wisdom," meaning that those who reverence God, who respect his wisdom and realize they need it, will grow in wisdom. Psalm 16:7 says it well: "I will praise the Lord, who counsels me."

Sustained by His Faithfulness

Because God is all-powerful, merciful, and good, he can be trusted. No matter what afflictions we face or calamities we encounter, God is faithful. "Let those who walk in the dark, who have no light, trust in the name of the Lord and rely on their God" (Isaiah 50:10 TNIV). As children of God, we are sustained by his faithfulness during times of adversity. We are no longer mired in hopelessness and despair, and we need not succumb to "doom and gloom" pessimism. Jesus said, "Do not let your hearts be troubled. Trust in God; trust also in me" (John 14:1). To trust is to be convinced that God is capable and ultimately dependable.

Throughout history and throughout each of our lives, God has proven himself faithful. His character is consistent and his presence persistent. His word is true and his promises reliable. Therefore, we can lay aside negativity, fear, and cynicism as did the psalmist: "When I am afraid, I put my trust in you. In God, whose word I praise—in God I trust and am not afraid. What can mere mortals do to me?" (Psalm 56:3–4 TNIV). Because God is faithful, we can stop worrying about the future. After all, Jesus said, "Who of you by worrying can add a single hour to his life?" (Matthew 6:27). Therefore, we can stop fretting and complaining when things don't go our way. We can also quit manipulating situations to our advantage. Instead, we can entrust ourselves to our faithful Creator (1 Peter 4:19).

Among God's many promises is the assurance that he hears and answers prayer. In Jeremiah 33:3, God says, "Call to me and I will answer you." Prayer then is a foundational act of trust because it assumes that God listens to and answers our supplications. That's why Philippians 4:6–7 says, "Do not be anxious about anything, but in everything, by prayer and petition, with thanksgiving, present your requests to God. And the peace of God, which transcends all understanding, will guard your hearts and your minds in Christ Jesus."

Whenever we put our trust in God, we are enveloped in that peace which passes all understanding. Isaiah announces that God "will keep in perfect peace those whose minds are steadfast, because they trust" in God. So "trust in the Lord forever, for the Lord, the Lord, is the Rock eternal" (Isaiah 26:3–4

TNIV). Indeed, God is our anchor during the storms of life. "But blessed are those who trust in the Lord, whose confidence is in him" (Jeremiah 17:7 TNIV).

HOPE: REMEMBERING WHO YOU ARE

What happens when you don't feel "clothed in righteousness," "endowed with goodness," or "cared for constantly"? It's important, first of all, to realize that our identity in Christ is something we possess and, at the same time, something we strive for. According to Rob Bell, "Your job is the relentless pursuit of who God has made you to be."[11] So when you're feeling weak and discouraged, remember who you are in Christ. When you succumb to sin, repent and renew your quest to become who God meant you to be. Again, Rob Bell puts it very succinctly: "The issue then isn't my beating myself up over all of the things I am not doing or the things I am doing poorly; the issue is my learning who this person is who God keeps insisting I *already am*."[12]

Our hope is not in how we feel about ourselves, but in who God says we already are. For most of us, our true identity calls out to us in powerful ways, begging to be taken seriously. At a party recently, a good friend introduced me not as an author or speaker, but as a composer. Not that I shun being an author or speaker, but I love writing music and my artistic side is the part of my identity that all too often gets lost in the shuffle. By introducing me as a composer, my friend spoke to something deep within me and awakened a vital part of who I really am. Buoyed by her affirmation, I spent several hours at the piano that week working on new songs. For the first time in a while, I felt like I was in the "sweet spot" of who I really am.

My fellow artist, as a child of God, disciple of Christ, and a temple of the Holy Spirit, may you heed the call to be who God says you already are: humbled by God's greatness, invested with his power, dead to sin, endowed with goodness, blessed abundantly, loved unconditionally, cared for constantly, forgiven completely, guided by his wisdom, and sustained by his faithfulness.

Follow-up Questions for Group Discussion

1. Explain the paradox that God exalts us in humility and how it differs from the world's tendency to only exalt those with money, power, and success.

2. What kinds of things could a team of Christian artists accomplish if they were convinced that they are fully invested with God's power?

3. What does it mean to be "clothed in the righteousness of Christ"?

4. How could knowing that one is endowed with God's goodness help in battling sin and temptation?

5. What are your strengths as an artist?

6. What prevents most people from personalizing God's love or feeling loved by God?

7. When in your life has the love of God been most apparent to you? What were the circumstances involved?

8. Why is it sometimes difficult to find God amidst our pain and suffering?

9. For Christians who live with constant guilt and shame, what kinds of obstacles prevent them from feeling completely forgiven?

10. How can one acquire godly wisdom?

Personal Action Steps

1. Summarize in your journal how you view yourself after reading this chapter.

2. Contemplate what it means to you personally to be a child of God, disciple of Christ, and a temple of the Holy Spirit.

3. Identify at least one personal trait that you suspect God likes about you.

4. Draw a picture of Deuteronomy 33:12: “Let the beloved of the Lord rest secure in him, for he shields him all day long, and the one the Lord loves rests between his shoulders.”

5. Psalm 136 is a history of God’s dealings with Israel that is laced with praise and thanksgiving. In a similar way, write your personal story as a tribute to God’s faithfulness and loving-kindness.

chapter seven

What Is God Inviting Me to Do?

When you encounter another person, when you have dealings with anyone at all, it is as if a question is being put to you. So you must think, What is the Lord asking of me in this moment, in this situation? If you confront insult or antagonism, your first impulse will be to respond in kind. But if you think, as it were, This is an emissary sent from the Lord, and some benefit is intended for me, first of all the occasion to demonstrate my faithfulness, the chance to show that I do in some small degree participate in the grace that saved me, you are free to act otherwise than as circumstances would seem to dictate. You are free to act by your own lights. You are freed at the same time of the impulse to hate or resent that person. He would probably laugh at the thought that the

> Lord sent him to you for your benefit (and his), but that is the perfection of the disguise, his own ignorance of it.
>
> From *Gilead* by Marilynne Robinson

Pete arrived home about 9:30 and was greeted at the door by his wife, Becky. "How did rehearsal go?" she asked.

"Pretty good," Pete replied as he set his Bible down and hung up his coat.

Becky followed him into the kitchen. "Did you have a full crew?"

"Yeah, pretty much." Pete opened the refrigerator and grabbed a Coke. "Any mail for me?"

"Just bills. So was there a full band? Did all the singers show up?"

Pete snatched a glass out of the cupboard and started to pour. "Yeah, as far as I could tell."

"So rehearsal went smoothly. No problems? No feedback? No dead microphones?"

Pete nodded, then turned away, pretending to be preoccupied with the brown foam ballooning over his glass.

"Pete," Becky exclaimed, turning very serious, "Brian called about 6:30."

"What did he want?" Pete asked, sounding rather uncomfortable.

"He called to tell you he canceled rehearsal tonight. He's sick."

"Oh." Pete pushed his glass away.

"Pete, where were you all night? Because you obviously weren't at church."

"I was driving around." Pete looked away.

"Driving around?" Becky asked incredulously.

"Yeah," Pete answered sheepishly.

"Okay. I'm going to ask straight out and I want an honest answer.... Pete ... are you having an affair?"

"No! Honest, Beck, I was driving around."

"Brian said you haven't been to rehearsal the last three weeks because you've been sick. In fact, he thinks he caught whatever he's got from you, and he hopes you're feeling better, by the way. Did you tell him you've been sick all this time?"

"Yes," Pete admitted, hanging his head.

Becky stood her ground. "Pete, what's going on?"

Pete sat down. He cleared his throat a couple times, then said, "Brian's been talking about taking the worship team on a missions trip."

"Really?" Becky looked puzzled. "What's wrong with that?"

"It's a missions trip—to the Dominican Republic!"

"I know. I've heard Brian talk about it and, honey, this sounds like a great experience. Why don't you want to go?"

"Beck, you know me—a whole week with all those people, rooming together, eating together, sharing together—and in a foreign country. I'll go crazy."

"Is that what this is about?" Becky asked, sounding relieved. "Honey, these people are your friends."

"I know, but I'm not like you. You love being with people. I don't. I'm not a 'people person.' When I signed up to do sound at church, I didn't think I'd be working with people."

"Pete, this is for a good cause."

Pete nodded. "Oh, I agree. I don't mind helping people; I just don't want to be with them."

Becky sat down and reached for Pete's hand. She smiled. "Honey, you're shy and that's okay; it doesn't mean you can't do this. Pray about it. If God wants you to go, then go. He'll give you the strength you need."

Pete let out a sigh and rolled his eyes. "I was afraid you were going to say that. If I pray about it, I know what God's going to say. He's going to want me to go. This is right up God's alley—helping people in third world countries."

Becky laughed and hugged her husband. "Then go."

"You're right. I'll call Brian first thing in the morning."

After embracing Pete, Becky cried out, "I'm so glad you're not having an affair!"

Pete smiled. "I may not be crazy about people, but I sure am crazy about you."

"Thanks." Becky chuckled. "I think there's a compliment in there somewhere. Let's go into town and get a piece of pie."

"Sounds good, but I ain't driving. I've done enough driving for one night."

Questions for Group Discussion

1. Would you recommend that Pete go on the mission trip to the Dominican Republic? Why or why not?

2. Can you relate to Pete's apprehension about the trip in any way? If so, how?

3. Given that Pete is introverted, what could his teammates do to make him feel more comfortable around them?

4. Pete's fear of relating to people made him unwilling to participate in what he knew was a good cause. What are some other fears that might keep someone from participating in a good cause like a missions trip?

5. What generally causes a person to become oblivious or insensitive to the needs of others?

6. What happens to a worship team that is so focused on task that it ignores the needs of people?

7. Whose job is it to try to meet the needs of your teammates?

8. What are some signs that a church or worship team is experiencing genuine community?

9. What sort of missions or outreach projects have you participated in?

10. What sort of missions or outreach projects could your team tackle in the future?

GOD IS GREAT, SO WHAT?

In high school, a friend of mine had an experience that still convicts me every time I recall it. She was talking on the phone one night, late into the evening, all the while doodling on a nearby message pad. By the time she hung up, this young enthusiastic Christ-follower had written, in beautiful calligraphy, the words "God is Great!" surrounded by pretty flowers and trees. The next morning she found her artwork hanging from her bathroom mirror with a message attached from her dad, who was not a believer at the time. His note read, "If God is so great, why can't he ever get you to do the dishes and help out around here?" My friend immediately realized that she had failed to do her chores before going to bed and, unfortunately, her negligence had become the norm rather than the exception. Her dad raised a valid point for all of us to consider. God is great—yes, but so what if it doesn't affect how we live?

Membership in God's family has its benefits and privileges, but they come with certain responsibilities. As the book of James clearly instructs: "Do not merely listen to the word, and so deceive yourselves. Do what it says. Those who listen to the word but do not do what it says are like people who look at their faces in a mirror and, after looking at themselves, go away and immediately forget what they look like" (James 1:22–24 TNIV). Jesus asked, "Why do you call me, 'Lord, Lord,' and do not do what I say?" (Luke 6:46).

After examining, in the last two chapters, who God is and who we are, we come now to our third vital question: What is God inviting me to do? In this chapter, we will survey the external behavior that results from knowing God and being who he meant us to be.

Before going any further, though, I need to stress that the sequence of these three questions is important. If you start at the wrong end of the equation, you'll end up in a much different place. For example, if your attempt at a self-concept excludes God and is the product of your own self-evaluation, the results will be limited at best, narcissistic at worst. In the same way, if your Christian experience is focused exclusively on keeping religious rules and regulations, you'll eventually become obnoxiously self-righteous or give up trying to be perfect out of sheer frustration. On the other hand, if your Christianity begins with knowing God and leads you then to discover and freely be who he made you to be, you will do what God wants you to do. Obedience, then, will be a more natural response; not that it will always be easy, but over time disobedience will seem more and more like foreign behavior. Instead of activities you *have* to do, obedience, acts of charity, and spiritual disciplines will be things you *want* to do. At that point, you will be "doing the will of God from your heart" (Ephesians 6:6). True fulfillment comes first from being who God made you to be, then doing what he calls you to do.

YOUR NEW LIFE

In addition to the "new you" we discussed in the previous chapter, God invites you into new life. "Now we look inside, and what we see is that anyone united with the Messiah gets a fresh start, is created new. The old life is gone; a new life burgeons!" (2 Corinthians 5:17 MSG). This new life is characterized by three continual interactions with the Trinity: worshiping God, abiding in Christ, and walking in the Spirit.

Worship God

While encountering God as he is presented in the Bible, it's quite natural to find him so compelling that one can't stop thinking about him. I hope you've been able to bask in the glory of every attribute of God discussed in this book. As our minds dwell increasingly upon God, we are drawn to love him more and more. At that point, we can't help but worship, for we can no longer contain our affection for God. Thus, worship is ultimately an expression of our love for God. When asked which is the most important commandment, Jesus replied, "Love the Lord your God with all your heart and with all your soul and with all your mind and with all your strength" (Mark 12:30). As Pedro Arrupe asserts, that which we love the most reflects our most unwavering loyalties:

> Nothing is more practical than finding God, that is, than falling in love in a quite absolute, final way. What you are in love with, what seizes your imagination,

> will affect everything. It will decide what will get you out of bed in the morning, what you will do with your evenings, how you will spend your weekends, what you read, who you know, what breaks your heart, and what amazes you with joy and gratitude. Fall in love, stay in love, and it will decide everything.[1]

By giving expression to our commitment and allegiance, true worship helps us to fall in love and stay in love with God.

Abide in Christ

To be a disciple of Christ is to bear fruit for his glory. In order to do that, we are invited to abide in Christ. Jesus said:

> "I am the true vine, and my Father is the gardener.... Remain in me, as I also remain in you. No branch can bear fruit by itself; it must remain in the vine. Neither can you bear fruit unless you remain in me.
>
> "I am the vine; you are the branches. If you remain in me and I in you, you will bear much fruit; apart from me you can do nothing." (John 15:1, 4–5 TNIV)

Jesus' method of discipleship was "hanging out" with his followers. For three years, he and his disciples shared meals, walked around the countryside, and healed people. They spent a lot of time together. In the process, Jesus showed them how to pray, read God's Word, and worship. Basically, he taught them how to effectively relate to God and to each other.

Jesus extends the same invitation to us today: "Learn from me," he says (Matthew 11:29). If you view spiritual disciplines like Bible reading, prayer, and worship as obligatory religious activities, you're missing the point. Instead, they're opportunities to "hang out" with Christ and to learn more about relating to God and others.

Walk in the Spirit

The goal of the Christian life is total, unequivocal surrender to the will of God in every area of our lives. That's how Jesus lived. He said, "For I have come down from heaven not to do my will but to do the will of him who sent me" (John 6:38). Jesus was completely abandoned to the supremacy of God in all things.

We may not always be able to do God's will, but we must at least desire to do so. For most of us, complete surrender to the Lord is a process. The Holy Spirit reveals areas of our lives that are out of sync with God and challenges us to submit our wills to his. Therefore, walking in the Spirit calls for moment-by-moment surrender to the will of God. "Since we live by the Spirit, let us keep in step with the Spirit" (Galatians 5:25). The Holy Spirit gives us the desire and the power to submit, but we must follow through. It is the Holy Spirit who whispers, "Look away," when tempted to lust with our eyes. Or "Hold your tongue," when tempted to gossip. Or "Forgive," when someone angers us. In each case we must be willing to say as did Christ, "Not my will, but yours be done" (Luke 22:42). The most urgent question we face then is not, Will God do what I want? but, Am I going to do what he wants?

BECOMING OTHERS-ORIENTED

God invites us to worship him, abide in Christ, and walk in the Spirit, not just for our benefit, but ultimately for the sake of others. Intrinsic to the Christian faith is this idea that we no longer live for ourselves, but for others (2 Corinthians 5:15). Rob Bell teaches:

> God doesn't choose people just so they'll feel good about themselves or secure in their standing with God or whatever else. God chooses people to be used to bless *other* people. Elected, predestined, chosen—whatever words people use for this reality, the point is never the person elected or chosen or predestined. The point is that person serving others, making their lives better.[2]

We are called to live out our faith in the context of community. As God's character is formed in us, we become increasingly others-oriented. All those attributes of God that we discovered in the last chapter as ours are ours to give away to others. With that in mind, we will now revisit the ten attributes of God we've been studying and examine what actions each one might inspire us to take. The following list, written as brief meditations, is by no means definitive. As you encounter the character of God, he may lead you to a slightly different course of action or one more specific to your situation. However, the actions God calls us to will be consummated, most often, on behalf of others.

Serve Others Selflessly

When we believe that God is sovereign and we are humbled by his greatness, we inevitably desire to serve others. God continually invites us to be subject to one another and to serve each other (Ephesians 5:21). Philippians 2:3–4 reads, "Do nothing out of selfish ambition or vain conceit, but in humility consider others better than yourselves. Each of you should look not only to your own interests, but also to the interests of others." Romans 15:2 adds, "We should all please our neighbors for their good, to build them up" (TNIV).

Jesus' life was a picture of selfless servanthood. He healed the sick and washed the disciples' feet. He fed hungry souls and hungry mouths. He set the captives free and gave his life for us. "For even the Son of Man did not come to be served, but to serve, and to give his life as a ransom for many" (Mark 10:45).

Jesus told a story about a king passing judgment on his people—separating the sheep from the goats—based on how faithful they were in serving others.

> Then the King will say to those on his right, "Come, you who are blessed by my Father; take your inheritance, the kingdom prepared for you since the creation of the world. For I was hungry and you gave me something to eat, I was thirsty and you gave me something to drink, I was a stranger and you invited me in, I needed clothes and you clothed me, I was sick and you looked after me, I was in prison and you came to visit me." (Matthew 25:34–36)

The good sheep were astonished and said in effect, "Lord, when did we see you in such desperate ways and minister to you?" The King answered, "I tell you the truth, whatever you did for one of the least of these brothers of mine, you did for me" (Matthew 25:37–40). The point of the story is clear: we serve God by serving others.

Because leading worship is an "up front" activity, artists must continually check their motives. There's always the danger of becoming self-serving even in our service. If we long to be admired or praised, or if we're starving for attention, the stage will be especially alluring. Remember, we are not on the platform for ourselves, but for God. Peter wrote, "If anyone serves, he should do it with the strength God provides, so that in all things God may be praised through Jesus Christ" (1 Peter 4:11).

Church artists are called, first of all, to serve their congregations. Artistic excellence is an important value, but should never distract worship leaders from their primary job—to facilitate worship for others. In a recent interview, Paul Baloche offered the following analogy:

> It's important to realize that when we're leading worship we're more like waiters. It's not our turn to sit down and eat our dinner. We may worship, but we

> actually have a role at that moment, and our job is to wait on others. We have to be willing to give up a little bit of our overwhelming connection with God and connect with Him through serving His people.[3]

Serving others is not limited to using our talents in corporate worship. God also invites us to serve those with whom we have regular contact—family, friends, and fellow artists. A good friend of mine, Sharon Sherbondy, modeled servanthood to her fellow artists in a way that I will never forget. Sharon is an excellent writer and actress, and was involved for many years in the drama ministry at our church. The Sundays when Sharon wasn't involved in drama, she arrived before the service specifically to pray for and encourage whoever had been cast for that weekend's script. I often saw Sharon waiting backstage after drama to congratulate the actors on a job well done. Sharon's faithful prayers and encouragement endeared her to all of us, but especially to her teammates. She exemplified true servanthood.

Pray Diligently for Others

Before Christ ascended into heaven he told his disciples, "But you will receive power when the Holy Spirit comes on you; and you will be my witnesses in Jerusalem, and in all Judea and Samaria, and to the ends of the earth" (Acts 1:8). Under the power of the Holy Spirit, Peter gave a powerful sermon and immediately three thousand people were saved. In addition, the disciples healed the sick and raised the dead. It's clear that God's power was not to be hoarded, but given away openly and freely.

One of the best ways to appropriate God's power on behalf of others is by praying for them. Paul prayed regularly for those in his charge (see Romans 1:9–10; Ephesians 1:16; Colossians 1:9; 2 Timothy 1:3) and commended a fellow named Epaphras for praying diligently for others (Colossians 4:12). Our most notable biblical heroes all knew, firsthand, the power of prayer.

Over the years, I have used a prayer list to remind me to pray for others. If you don't already use a prayer list and you'd like to try it, I suggest buying a small notebook and putting the days of the week at the top of the first seven pages. Then, for each day, list a few personal requests and five to ten names of people you'd like to pray for—family, friends, fellow artists at church, people you work with, those who don't know Christ yet, etc.

Having a prayer list also helps me be strategic in my prayers. Every day I pray for my wife, Sue, and our two sons, Micah and Joel. Instead of praying a general prayer like, "Lord bless my wife and kids," a prayer list enables me to pray something specific for them each day. For example, knowing that my boys need to make a living someday, I've been praying every Wednesday, for many years now, for God to guide them into meaningful careers.

If you'd like to take the prayer list idea even further, I have another suggestion. Some years back, I was convicted by how often I told someone, "I'll pray for you," and then didn't because I forgot. Breaking promises of such a serious nature should never be taken lightly. So I added a new section in my prayer journal under the heading, "People I promised to pray for." Having a place to record people's names has effectively solved my memory problem.

Help Reconcile Others to God

God doesn't want anyone to perish, but everyone to know his saving grace (2 Peter 3:9). And he enlists our help in reconciling others to himself (2 Corinthians 5:18). In defining this "ministry of reconciliation," Paul writes, "We are therefore Christ's ambassadors, as though God were making his appeal through us. We implore you on Christ's behalf: Be reconciled to God" (2 Corinthians 5:20).

Genuine worship, in and of itself, is highly evangelistic. Whenever Christ is lifted up, believers and unbelievers alike are drawn to him. Thus, David proclaimed: "He put a new song in my mouth, a hymn of praise to our God. Many will see and fear and put their trust in the Lord" (Psalm 40:3).

As lead worshipers, we help reconcile others to God on a corporate level every week, but why stop there? Why not make personal evangelism a priority for your worship ministry?

I served for many years in a church that was evangelistically aggressive; we were driven to reach seekers. As a result, each of our artists developed an evangelistic mindset. Often when the musicians gathered before a service, we'd ask if anyone had any "seeker friends" coming to church that day. Then we'd pray for those guests in attendance. One time I asked every team member to submit the name of one seeker in their life, and we prayed over our combined list for several months. On another occasion, I invited everyone to identify one non-Christian musician in their life with whom they could build a relationship. This last exercise was especially near and dear to my heart because I have a burden for all artists, especially those who don't know Christ yet. Who else is going to reach out to those unsaved artists if we don't?

I challenge you individually and as a worship team to take seriously God's call to help reconcile others to him. When you do, make sure you go beyond merely inviting unbelievers to a church service. Reconciling others to God is best done in the context of a relationship. So get to know the seekers in your life; build relationships with them. Love and accept them for who they are, whether they eventually come to Christ or not.

Do Good unto Others

If you believe that God is good and that you are capable of good things, you will naturally want to do good things for others. According to Ephesians 2:10, we are "God's workmanship, created in Christ Jesus to do good works, which God prepared in advance for us to do."

Sometimes God calls us to make dramatic career changes in order to do the good he has for us to do. A dentist friend of mine gave up a lucrative practice to serve on staff at his church. I have missionary friends who gave up the comfort and security of home to live and raise families in third world countries. God sometimes calls working mothers to be stay-at-home moms to focus on child rearing. It takes a great deal of courage to realign one's life to such callings.

We are called to do good in tangible ways, especially among the disenfranchised of society. "Speak up for those who cannot speak for themselves, for the rights of all who are destitute. Speak up and judge fairly; defend the rights of the poor and needy" (Proverbs 31:8–9). In Deuteronomy 15:11, God reminds us to be openhanded toward the poor and needy in our midst. The early church gave to anyone who had need (Acts 2:45). Are you giving money to the poor either directly or indirectly through organizations like World Vision? Are there any single moms or elderly people in your congregation who need financial assistance? Do you know a child of a single mom who has a birthday coming up?

God invites us to do good throughout our daily routines. "And let our people also learn to engage in good deeds to meet pressing needs, that they may not be unfruitful" (Titus 3:14 NASB). Unfortunately, we are often too busy or distracted to hear his leadings or follow through on them. Do you habitually act on promptings to call on someone who's sick, check in with an old friend, or write a note of encouragement? Paul prays that God may "fulfill every good purpose" of ours "and every act prompted by ... faith" (2 Thessalonians 1:11).

Whether the sacrifice is large or small, I challenge you to follow through on the good God calls you to do. "Let us not become weary in doing good, for at the proper time we will reap a harvest if we do not give up. Therefore, as we have opportunity, let us do good to all people, especially to those who belong to the family of believers" (Galatians 6:9–10).

David asked, "How can I repay the Lord for all his goodness to me?" (Psalm 116:12). One obvious answer to that question would simply be: do good unto others.

Extend Grace to Others

After all the grace God has lavished upon us, it's a shame how little grace we extend to each other. Somebody fails and we write them off. Someone else lets us down and we give them the cold shoulder. Another makes an innocent comment, yet we take offense. Instead of believing the best and giving others the benefit of the doubt, we can be very quick to judge or condemn. Unfortunately, Christians are often characterized as self-righteous, callous, and smug. The church, instead of being renowned as a wellspring of grace, is known for its petty bickering and intolerance. God extends his favor and goodwill to all, whether they deserve it or not, and invites us to do likewise. God's Word instructs us to "live in harmony with one another; be sympathetic, love as brothers, be compassionate and humble. Do not repay evil with evil or insult with insult, but with blessing" (1 Peter 3:8–9).

Every time we extend grace to others, we develop another layer of patience. We are called to bear the weaknesses and shortcomings of others, as they put up with ours (Romans 15:1). Also, when we believe the best about people, we are no longer so easily offended (1 Corinthians 13:6–7). According to Proverbs 19:11, "A person's wisdom yields patience; it is to one's glory to overlook an offense" (TNIV).

Extending grace also means that we accept people for who they are, warts and all. Romans 15:7 simply says, "Accept one another, then, just as Christ accepted you, in order to bring praise to God." Instead of being critical, Scripture encourages us to bear each other's imperfections "with all humility and gentleness, with patience, showing tolerance for one another in love"

(Ephesians 4:2 NASB). The Jewish philosopher Philo of Alexandria said, "Be kind, for everyone you meet is fighting a great battle."

Perhaps you're experiencing tension right now with a family member or someone at work or at church. Are you extending grace to that individual? Are you believing the best instead of assuming the worst? Or are you being overly critical, demanding, or controlling? Are you willing to give him or her a second chance? That's what extending grace is all about—blessing others, especially those who don't deserve it, because God has blessed us way beyond what we deserve.

Love Others Unconditionally

When you realize how much God loves you, you'll discover a greater capacity to love others. According to John (again our reigning expert on God's love), "since God so loved us, we also ought to love one another.... We love because he first loved us" (1 John 4:11, 19). Jesus said, "Love one another. As I have loved you, so you must love one another. By this everyone will know that you are my disciples, if you love one another" (John 13:34–35 TNIV).

Love is nothing if it is not acted upon, lived out, and demonstrated. First John 3:18 admonishes us to love "with actions and in truth." The Good Samaritan didn't set out to win a "Good Neighbor Award." He was simply going about his everyday business when he stumbled upon another man, of a different race, who had been beaten and robbed. He promptly cared for the victim and provided for his complete recovery. The lesson for us is crystal clear: love the people, regardless of race, color, or creed, that God brings into your life today.

It's easy to love our best friends or favorite relatives. The true test of character lies in how we treat those who are difficult to love—that overbearing relative, obnoxious coworker, or unruly neighbor. Jesus said, "If all you do is love the lovable, do you expect a bonus? Anybody can do that. If you simply say hello to those who greet you, do you expect a medal? Any run-of-the-mill sinner does that" (Matthew 5:46–47 MSG). Truth is, God loves *all* human beings; even the ones we dislike. And he commands us to love all people, even our enemies (Luke 6:27).

This is not to say that it's easy to love those who are difficult to love. At least, it isn't easy for me. My default mode of operation toward difficult people in my life is to withdraw from them, harbor anger against them, and constantly dwell on their faults. However, when I personalize God's love, I realize that what God thinks of me is also how he thinks of others. That's why Jesus said, "Love your neighbor as yourself" (Matthew 19:19; 22:39). The difficult people in my life are just as precious to God as I am, and he is merely asking me to show them the same kind of unmerited love that he has bestowed upon me. As Ephesians 5:1–2 teaches, "Be imitators of God, therefore, as dearly loved children and live a life of love, just as Christ loved us and gave himself up for us as a fragrant offering and sacrifice to God." Rob Bell says that how we love others is how we love God.[4] May love, therefore, be the compelling force in all we do and say (2 Corinthians 5:14).

Show Care and Compassion to Those in Need

Compassion means caring for those in need, to enter into their suffering, and meet them there. Our merciful and compassionate God invites us to "show mercy and compassion to one another" (Zechariah 7:9). Colossians 3:12 puts it this way: "Clothe yourselves with compassion." Or, as the New American Standard version reads, "Put on a heart of compassion."

If you've ever had your heart broken, experienced hardship, or suffered loss, you will naturally empathize with those in need. And if you've discovered God's comfort amidst your own adversity, you will be that much better equipped to comfort others who suffer. Second Corinthians 1:3–4 reads, "Praise be to the God and Father of our Lord Jesus Christ,... who comforts us in all our troubles, so that we can comfort those in any trouble with the comfort we ourselves have received from God."

Scripture directs us to weep with those who weep (Romans 12:15) and to "carry each other's burdens" (Galatians 6:2). Proverbs 11:25 promises that "whoever refreshes others will be refreshed" (TNIV). Is there anyone on your team, from your church, or in the neighborhood who's going through tough times? Can you call that person, or visit, or take that individual out to lunch? Do you know anyone in the hospital you could call on? How about bringing a meal to someone recuperating from surgery or illness?

"May our Lord Jesus Christ himself and God our Father, who loved us and by his grace gave us eternal encouragement and good hope, encourage your hearts and strengthen you in every good deed and word" (2 Thessalonians 2:16–17).

Forgive Those Who Offend Me

We all have people in our lives who have hurt us. Some we've forgiven, moved on, and maybe even forgotten the offense. Others come to mind, and a knot begins to form in the pit of our stomach. We realize that we haven't completely forgiven them or we thought we did, but anger and resentment keep creeping back in. Sometimes forgiving is easier said than done.

In spite of the challenges, Scripture commands us to forgive those who have wronged us. "Get rid of all bitterness, rage and anger, brawling and slander, along with every form of malice. Be kind and compassionate to one another, forgiving each other" (Ephesians 4:31–32). Jesus said, "Blessed are the merciful, for they will be shown mercy" (Matthew 5:7).

Forgiveness doesn't absolve someone who has hurt you; it takes the responsibility for justice off your shoulders and places it squarely on God who says, "It is mine to avenge; I will repay" (Deuteronomy 32:35).

Forgiveness frees us from the need to retaliate and spares us from being ravaged by bitterness and resentment. I have a couple relatives who carried lifelong grudges against each other to their graves. These two brothers got into a dispute while in their thirties and never spoke to each other again. Praying until the bitter end that the other one would "get what's coming to him," both men lived out their lives irascibly gloomy and ill-tempered. If you don't forgive others, anger will take root in you and eventually do more damage to your heart and soul than the original offense. So whenever you forgive someone who has wronged you, you actually set yourself free from the devastating control of bitterness and resentment.

Peter probably thought he would go to the head of the class by suggesting that people should forgive an offender seven times. Yet, Jesus placed the bar much higher: seventy times seven—a number implying infinity (Matthew 18:21–22 NASB). Remember that forgiveness is a process. Sometimes feelings of bitterness and resentment that you thought had been put to rest return. At that point, we must renew our commitment to the process. Gary Thomas concurs:

> The process of forgiveness involves overcoming negative emotions (such as resentment), thoughts (such as harsh judgments), and behaviors (such as revenge seeking) toward the person who did the wrong, and substitutes instead more positive emotions (such as wishing them well), thoughts (such as remembering that

> all of us have sinned), and behaviors (such as doing something to "bless" them). It is the "art of substitution": wishing well instead of wishing ill, blessing instead of cursing.[5]

Now you may be thinking, *I could never forgive so-and-so after what they did to me.* But what if God said that to us? What if God said, "You've sinned once too often. There's no way I could ever forgive you for that." Instead, the Bible exhorts us to "Bear with each other and forgive whatever grievances you may have against one another. Forgive as the Lord forgave you" (Colossians 3:13). As C. S. Lewis put it, "To be a Christian means to forgive the inexcusable, because God has forgiven the inexcusable in you."[6]

Help Others Discern God's Wisdom

As we worship God, abide in Christ, and walk in the Spirit, we grow in godly wisdom. God invites us to share that wisdom with others. We don't read the Bible or have devotions merely for our own good, but also for the sake of others—so we can be "thoroughly equipped for every good work" (2 Timothy 3:17). King Solomon asked for wisdom in leading his people (2 Chronicles 1:7–10). Manoah requested wisdom in raising his son, Samson (Judges 13:8). Whether it's a friend facing a difficult decision, a seeker wanting to know the plan of salvation, or your kid asking for advice, we all need to be prepared to offer godly wisdom. Proverbs 11:14 says, "Without good direction, people lose their way; the more wise counsel you follow, the better your chances" (MSG).

We learn God's wisdom by reading his Word regularly. However, offering godly wisdom involves more than just indiscriminately spouting Bible verses or Christian clichés. It involves sitting with a brother or sister and listening intently as spiritual problems and issues are unpacked. It entails prayer and discernment. These are the trademarks of spiritual friendship. True spiritual friends don't push their own agenda, or tell you what to do, or tell you what they think you want to hear. They help you hear God's voice, clarify his will, and discern his direction for your life. They help you discern how God is moving in your life and bring God's wisdom to bear on that work.

That's the type of friend God calls us to be to each other—one who sticks "closer than a brother" (Proverbs 18:24). "As iron sharpens iron, so one person sharpens another" (Proverbs 27:17 TNIV).

Prove Trustworthy and Reliable to Others

God has proven himself faithful in every way and invites us to be trustworthy and reliable to others. First Corinthians 4:1–2 describes a true servant as faithful and trustworthy. For that reason, we artists are called upon to faithfully steward our gifts and talents. In the parable of the talents, the master commended those who put what they were given to good use: "Well done, good and faithful servant! You have been faithful with a few things; I will put you in charge of many things. Come and share your master's happiness!" (Matthew 25:21, 23).

In addition to being faithful with our talents, we are to be trustworthy in our relationships. A trusted friend is someone you can count on; one who's "there" when needed, who can be trusted with your darkest secrets. Do you have friends like that? Or, more importantly, are you that kind of friend? Proverbs 17:9 reveals that "He who covers over an offense promotes love, but whoever repeats the matter separates close friends."

Jesus also taught that trustworthy people keep their word. They let their "Yes" be "Yes," and their "No," "No." Jesus said:

> Don't say anything you don't mean.... You only make things worse when you lay down a smoke screen of pious talk, saying, "I'll pray for you," and never doing it, or saying, "God be with you," and not meaning it. You don't make your words true by embellishing them with religious lace. In making your speech sound more religious, it becomes less true. Just say "yes" and "no." When you manipulate words to get your own way, you go wrong. (Matthew 5:33–37 MSG)

Do people regard you as a man or woman of your word? When you say you're going to do something by a certain time, do you do it? Are you a trustworthy employee, a reliable worker? According to Proverbs 28:20, "A faithful man will be richly blessed."

Faithfulness and dependability communicate loyalty and are learned first and demonstrated most within the family. That's why Scripture commands children to obey their parents (Ephesians 6:1–2) and for husband and wife to submit to one another (Ephesians 5:21–24). Wedding vows are a pledge of faithfulness, and Scripture specifically calls us men to love our wives as Christ loved the church (Ephesians 5:25). Remember, Jesus' idea of marital fidelity includes our thought lives: "You have heard that it was said, 'Do not commit adultery.' But I tell you that anyone who looks at a woman lustfully has already committed adultery with her in his heart" (Matthew 5:27–28). According to Christ, it is not enough not to commit adultery; we men shouldn't even look at a woman with lust in our hearts or indulge sexual fantasies. So for us husbands, being loyal means that we don't fix our gaze on other women whether they're at work, on television, or pictured in a magazine. We are to be faithful to our wives in every way.

"Many a man claims to have unfailing love, but a faithful man who can find?" (Proverbs 20:6).

LOVE: REMEMBERING OTHERS

Those of us involved in worship ministry carry out numerous tasks. Seems we're always busy planning, rehearsing, and preparing for church. We also invest a great deal of time and energy in the details of every service: transitions, equipment needs, lyric slides, etc. All these things are important, but I often wonder if our priorities are the same as God's. What if the way we treat each other as we go about the task of leading worship is just as important in God's eyes, if not more important, than the actual service? What if God prefers that we focus as much, if not more, on the people as on the task? What if God is more impressed with character than talent? In Amos 5:21–23, God expresses displeasure over the Israelites' religious celebrations:

> "I hate, I despise your religious feasts;
>   I cannot stand your assemblies.
> Even though you bring me burnt offerings and grain offerings,
>   I will not accept them.
> Though you bring choice fellowship offerings,
>   I will have no regard for them.
> Away with the noise of your songs!
>   I will not listen to the music of your harps."

On the outside the Israelites appeared to have a very slick worship service, but on the inside they were spiritually bankrupt. God was displeased and called for justice because the people neglected the needs of others; they lacked human courtesy; they treated each other unkindly and unfairly (v. 24). Worse yet, they neglected the poor (Amos 5:11–12).

Everything that God invites us to do on behalf of others can be summed up in one word: love. To truly love others, we must be aware and sensitive to their needs. In Mark 8:22–26, Jesus heals a blind man. He lays hands on him and asks, "Do you see anything?" The man answers, "I see people; they look like trees walking around." So Jesus lays his hands on the man a second time totally restoring his sight. The first thing that the blind man sees when he's healed is people—a little out of focus at the beginning, but then clearly.

May we all have our eyes and ears opened more to people. May we become increasingly sensitive to the needs of others and act on their behalf. Paul commends the church in Thessalonica because their love for each other was evident and growing (2 Thessalonians 1:3). May the same be said of you and your team. "Dear children, let us not love with words or tongue but with actions and in truth" (1 John 3:18).

IN SUMMARY

Should you wish to revisit the ten attributes of God we've been studying, the chart that follows not only provides a quick summary, but also consolidates the material for easy reference.

I trust the little devotional studies presented in the last three chapters inspire you to interact intellectually and emotionally with these and other attributes of God. I find that the deeper I go in worshiping God, the more reasons I find to worship him.

WHO IS GOD?	WHO AM I?	WHAT IS GOD INVITING ME TO DO?
God is infinitely, perfectly, and eternally…	As a child of God, disciple of Christ, and temple of the Holy Spirit, I am…	God continually invites me to worship him, abide in Christ, and walk in the Spirit, in order to…
… sovereign	… humbled by God's greatness	… serve others selflessly
… powerful	… invested with his power	… pray diligently for others
… holy	… dead to sin	… help reconcile others to God
… good	… endowed with goodness	… do good unto others
… gracious	… blessed abundantly	… extend grace to others
… loving	… loved unconditionally	… love others unconditionally
… compassionate	… cared for constantly	… show care and compassion to those in need
… merciful	… forgiven completely	… forgive those who offend me
… wise	… guided by his wisdom	… help others discern God's wisdom
… faithful	… sustained by his faithfulness	… prove trustworthy and reliable to others

Follow-up Questions for Group Discussion

1. What are some specific ways those on your ministry team can serve each other?

2. Do you think a prayer list has merit? Why or why not?

3. Are there any non-Christian artists for whom your team could pray regularly? Who are they?

4. Are there any needs within your team, the church, or community that your team could address? What are they and how can you help meet those needs?

5. Is there any way the artists on your team could do a better job of extending grace to each other during rehearsal or sound check? How?

6. What is the most vivid example of unconditional love that you've ever experienced?

7. Is there any hardship you've experienced that has given you greater empathy and understanding for those who suffer similar situations? If so, describe it.

8. What can make forgiving others difficult?

9. What practical steps can your team take to grow in the area of spiritual friendship?

10. Why is trust an essential part of true community?

Personal Action Steps

1. Create or express artistically any appreciation for the Trinity you've gained over the last three chapters.

2. Devote a half hour of prayer this week exclusively for others.

3. Are there any non-Christian artists in your life with whom you could build a friendship? Set up a time this week to get together with that person.

4. Is there anybody you need to forgive? Set up a time to call or meet with that individual.

5. Think about what practical steps you can take to engage more deeply with those close to you as their spiritual friend.

part three

Learning From Ancient Worship Leaders

> Remember the days of old; consider the generations long past. Ask your father and he will tell you, your elders, and they will explain to you.
>
> Deuteronomy 32:7

The Christian tradition offers a rich heritage of exemplary worship leaders from whom we today can learn a great deal. My hope is that learning from worship artists of the past will become a regular routine for the contemporary church. In the following chapters, we will scrutinize three examples of ancient worship leaders: the Levites, Asaph the psalmist, and the Byzantine artists who painted icons—known as iconographers.

"To him be glory in the church and in Christ Jesus throughout all generations, for ever and ever! Amen" (Ephesians 3:21).

chapter eight

The Levites

Erc said, "Where might you find a house with fifty and a hundred windows and all of them looking out onto Heaven?"
"King David's book of psalms," Brendan said.

From *Brendan* by Frederick Buechner

When Pastor Smith arrived at the church office Monday morning, Ida Mae was waiting outside his door. Ida Mae is eighty-four years old and never misses church. You can find her in the front row every Sunday. "Pastor, I need to talk to you," she said as the pastor walked up.

"Sure, Ida Mae," replied Pastor Smith. "Let's step into my office. It just so happens that my first appointment isn't due for another hour."

Ida Mae quietly sat across from the pastor with her hands folded firmly atop her old wooden cane.

"Can I get you some coffee?" the pastor offered.

"No thank you," answered Ida Mae glumly. "I didn't come here to socialize."

"Well then," said Pastor Smith, "what can I do for you?"

Ida Mae leaned forward, her eyes narrowed, and with pursed lips she blurted out, "Pastor, we didn't sing one single hymn yesterday."

"Yes, I know, Ida Mae, but since our last talk, I'm sure you've noticed that we've been using a lot more hymns."

"Well, you promised me at least one hymn every week," Ida Mae insisted. "I've been attending this church for over fifty years, mind you, and I don't think it's too much to ask for one hymn a week. It's bad enough that we have to sit through that other garbage you call music. You mean to tell me we can't have one worshipful moment in the whole service? And you know I'm not the only one who feels this way. There's a bunch of us who are fed up with how things are going around here lately."

"Now, now, Ida Mae," Pastor Smith said. "We've been all through this before. The majority of our parishioners love the worship here. I get no other complaints."

"That's because everybody else has left," quipped Ida Mae. "They're all going to Mainline Bible Church across the street."

"But our attendance is way up from last year."

Close to tears, Ida Mae said, "Well it's a crying shame that we cater to the world and use entertainment just to fill empty seats. I've had it, Pastor. I can't take it anymore. Either that new worship leader goes or I go."

"What have you got against Linda?" queried Pastor Smith. "She loves the Lord. Our congregation responds very well to her and the volunteers absolutely love her. She picks worship choruses with great lyrics. I'm very pleased with her work."

"Well, first of all," Ida Mae said, regaining her composure, "it's bad enough that you've put a woman in such a position of authority. You know this church has never had a female on staff before. Then you expect us to sing that gibberish. It's not even music. There's no melody. It's the same words over and over again, and it's so loud—"

Pastor Smith closed his eyes and put up his hand, signaling her to stop. He took a deep breath and then quietly, but firmly, said, "Ida Mae, I love you, sister, but I have to be honest with you and tell you that we as a church are going to stay the course. We've got nothing against hymns, but we'll be working in some of the new worship choruses as well. I'm also encouraging new forms of artistic expression like drama, dance, and video. I'm sorry if that offends you. It's never been my intention to alienate anyone. I certainly don't want you or anyone else to leave, but if you can't worship with a cheerful spirit here, then you might be happier at another church."

"You can't mean that," Ida Mae said incredulously. "After all I've given to this church, you'd kick me out just like that?"

"No one's kicking you out," Pastor Smith clarified. "You're always welcome here, Ida Mae. But, honestly, you seem so unhappy here."

Ida Mae stood up. "Well, if that's how you feel, Pastor, I hereby resign my membership here at the church."

"I'm sorry to hear that," Pastor Smith said.

As she headed for the door, Ida Mae turned and said, "From now on, my friends and I will be taking our tithes across the street."

Questions for Group Discussion

1. Do you think Pastor Smith handled this situation well? Why or why not?

2. Is there anything Pastor Smith should have done differently? If so, what?

3. In what ways did Pastor Smith exhibit support for his worship leader?

4. What advice do you have for Ida Mae and others who are offended by a particular style of worship?

5. Have you ever found it difficult to worship because of the style or quality of the music? How did you respond?

6. What kind of attitude should we artists adopt toward those like Ida Mae who oppose our style of worship?

7. What challenges might await a female worship leader or music director in a church like Pastor Smith's?

8. Many churches offer a contemporary and a traditional service at separate times. What are the advantages and disadvantages to that approach?

9. Some churches combine contemporary and traditional styles into one "blended" service. What are the advantages and disadvantages to that?

10. What is the best way for a church to navigate change?

THE LEVITES' CORE VALUES

Throughout the Old Testament, families from the tribe of Levi (the third son of the Jewish patriarch Jacob) performed various functions related to temple worship services. Though these functions varied over the course of time, the Levites generally served as helpers, custodians, and temple guards. However, the Levites were also in charge of leading the people in praise and/or providing music for worship services, especially during King David's reign. So, in essence, the Levites were ancient worship leaders; that was their calling (Deuteronomy 10:8; 21:5). In fact, 1 Chronicles 23:5 informs us that David appointed four thousand men from the tribe of Levi to worship the Lord with musical instruments (see also 1 Chronicles 16:4; 2 Chronicles 8:14). The glorious dedication of Solomon's temple provides a glimpse of the Levites in action: "The choir and orchestra of Levites that David had provided for singing and playing anthems to the praise and love of God were all there; across the courtyard the priests blew trumpets. All Israelites were on their feet" (2 Chronicles 7:6 MSG).

Throughout the Bible, the Levites are referred to most commonly as a tribe or family. They were a group, and like most worship ministries today, they functioned as a team. And like any successful team, the Levites had distinct core values. Let's examine those core values, gleaned from Scripture, and apply them to today's worship teams, bands, choirs, etc.

Unity

Unity in Christ is the cornerstone of an effective worship team. That's why Paul prayed: "May the God who gives endurance and encouragement give you a spirit of unity among yourselves as you follow Christ Jesus, so that with one heart and mouth you may glorify the God and Father of our Lord Jesus Christ" (Romans 15:5–6). Psalm 133 reveals that God manifests his fullest blessings where there is unity among worshipers. "How good and pleasant it is when God's people live together in unity!... For there the Lord bestows his blessing, even life forevermore" (Psalm 133:1, 3 TNIV). The Levites model two vital aspects of unity: solidarity and cooperation.

Stand Together in Christ

As you recall, when Moses descended from Mount Sinai, he walked in on his people carrying on and worshiping an idol they had created.

"Moses saw that the people were running wild and that Aaron had let them get out of control and so become a laughingstock to their enemies. So he stood at the entrance to the camp and said, 'Whoever is for the Lord, come to me.' And all the Levites rallied to him" (Exodus 32:25–26).

This was by far the Levites' finest hour. When all others had forsaken the Lord, the Levites took a stand for God *together*. Their solidarity was based on their commitment to God.

In the same way, your team's unity is based on the fact that you are all brothers and sisters in Christ. You share a common purpose, to lead others in worship, but Jesus Christ is your reason for being—he's your bond of unity. Paul writes, "God is building a home. He's using us all—irrespective of how we got here—in what he is building. He used the apostles and prophets for the foundation. Now he's using you, fitting you in brick by brick, stone by stone, with Christ Jesus as the cornerstone that holds all the parts together. We see it taking shape day after day—a holy temple built by God, all of us built into it, a temple in which God is quite at home" (Ephesians 2:20–22 MSG).

The worship team is the most visible example of unity that your church sees every week. In fact, your team's most lasting impression may not be its talent, but its unity. That was certainly the case with a church I visited in downtown Chicago. The worship leader had average piano and vocal skills. The band and worship team reflected the ethnic diversity of the congregation, but otherwise there was nothing remarkable or "flashy" about the musicians. Yet, the worship time was extraordinarily rich; the room felt "electric." I concluded that it was the Holy Spirit at work, but when I talked to the worship team members afterward, I found out why. These artists possessed a deep love for each other; they were a genuine community, unshakably unified. For example, when I asked whether they considered invitations to lead worship at other churches, one female singer said, "Yes, but we don't accept unless we can all go. We just love doing ministry together."

Unity doesn't come easily; it takes dedication and hard work. That's why Paul says, "Make every effort to keep the unity of the Spirit through the bond of peace" (Ephesians 4:3). Unity is the personal responsibility of every team member. I know of several ministries that require members to sign a covenant outlining rehearsal demands and various spiritual guidelines. Whether your team adopts that practice or not, all teammates should agree to the following basic tenets of unity:

1. I commit to resolve relational conflict expediently in a spirit of humility, deference, and grace (Matthew 18:15–17).
2. I pledge to watch my tongue—to refrain from gossip and slander (Proverbs 10:19; 15:1; James 1:26; 3:3–12).
3. I promise to believe the best of others, especially my leaders (1 Corinthians 13:6–7; James 4:11).
4. I covenant to guard my heart against jealousy, resentment, and bitterness (Galatians 5:26; Ephesians 4:31–32; James 5:9; 1 Peter 2:1).
5. I purpose to accept those who are different from me, to celebrate the uniqueness of others, and not to judge them (Romans 15:7; Ephesians 4:2).

Cooperate Fully with Your Pastor

Scripture makes a deliberate distinction between priests and Levites. In ancient Israel, the priests were authorized ministers who officiated over religious rites and services. God instructed Moses to appoint priests from among the descendants of Aaron: "Have Aaron your brother brought to you from among the Israelites, along with his sons ... so they may serve me as priests" (Exodus 28:1). The Levites, on the other hand, were called to assist the priests. Numbers 3:6–7 outlines God's design: "Bring the tribe of Levi and present them to Aaron the priest to assist him. They are to perform duties for him and for the whole community at the Tent of Meeting by doing the work of the tabernacle" (see also 1 Chronicles 23:28–31). The Levites therefore played a collaborative, yet subservient, role. Interestingly, the priest-Levite relationship parallels today's alliance between pastor and worship leader.

Numbers 18:2 states that the Levites were invited to join the priests in ministry. In the same way, ministry is a joint venture between pastor and artist. In fact, the relationship between the senior pastor and the artists is one of the most pivotal relationships in the church—one that is certainly on public display at every service. In fact, whenever I visit a church, I can usually tell just by listening and observing body language whether or not the pastor and worship leaders work well together. When the relationship is healthy, both parties are on the same page; they cooperate with each other; there is mutual respect and appreciation.

Sadly, when there is miscommunication or constant conflict between church leaders and artists, worship is hindered. On one occasion, a church sought my help in resolving a rift that had developed between their pastor and the arts teams. Bad blood between the two sides had become painfully obvious. Misunderstandings and miscommunication had resulted in hurt feelings, suspicion, and a lack of trust. After meeting with both sides, I offered a few suggestions, one of which was directed to the artists. I challenged them to offer their pastor a definitive vote of confidence, since their support had been called into question. As you can imagine, this caused a great deal of soul searching, but a few days later the programming team leaders walked into the pastor's office and expressed their full support of his leadership, which firmly planted all involved on the road to reconciliation.

My fellow artists, your pastor needs to know you're behind him or her—that you're willing to cooperate and work together. Always work *with* your pastor and *for* your pastor, not against him or her. The Levites' worst moment is recorded in Numbers 16. One of their leaders, Korah, was jealous of Moses and Aaron and started to defy their authority. He formed a faction of 250 whiners and complainers, all opposed to Moses. However, God stepped in and struck the perpetrators dead. Obviously, in God's eyes, it's a serious offense to undermine a leader. So, even if you and your pastor disagree on some issues, always avoid negativity, cynicism, and grumbling. Instead, be loyal, encouraging, and as helpful as you can possibly be. In 1 Thessalonians 5:12–13, Paul wrote, "Now we ask you, brothers, to respect those who work hard among you, who are over you in the Lord and who admonish you. Hold them in the highest regard in love because of their work. Live in peace with each other."

In Numbers 18:6, God says to the priests, "I myself have selected your fellow Levites from among the Israelites as a *gift* to you, dedicated to the Lord to do the work at the Tent of Meeting" (emphasis mine). Can your pastor honestly say that you've been a gift from God? Or have you been a hindrance or an obstacle? Does your worship team have an adversarial attitude toward those in leadership? In an effort to better cooperate, I suggest you ask your pastor the following five questions:

1. Is there anything we (or I) can do to increase our effectiveness as worship leaders?
2. Is there anything we're currently doing that you feel hampers our ability to facilitate worship?
3. Is there anything we're doing that makes it difficult for you to work with us?
4. What can we do on our part to work more effectively with you?
5. How can we be praying for you?

Accountability

First Chronicles 25:6 reveals that the Levites "were under the supervision of their fathers for the music of the temple of the Lord, with cymbals, lyres and harps, for the ministry at the house of God. Asaph, Jeduthun and Heman were under the supervision of the king." In other words, everyone was accountable to someone else. The rank and file were subject to their fathers who, in turn, answered to the king.

I have a friend (whom I'll call Wayne) who had one of those dramatic conversions. A rock musician heavily addicted to drugs and alcohol, Wayne found Christ, and started playing drums in the worship band at his church. I discipled Wayne for a year, and nearly every time we met I'd ask him how his battle with addiction was going. There were times when he reported a relapse, but for the most part he stayed on the straight and narrow. One time, toward the end of one of our meetings, he said, "Thanks for always checking up on me about my drinking. I'm kinda surprised that none of my other church friends ever brings it up." Though Wayne was heavily involved at church and had a lot of Christian friends, he didn't have much accountability in his life.

Accountability is sharing the appropriate details regarding your moral choices with godly friends who are committed to challenging and encouraging you. You could divulge to one person or to a small group; however, accountability works only when all involved are committed to it. Ever since the garden of Eden, human beings have tried to hide from God and from each other when we sin. Hiding forces us to live in denial about our own depravity. And by putting repentance on hold, hiding only encourages more sin.

Scripture encourages us to bring that which is hidden into the light (Ephesians 5:11). James 5:16 says, "Therefore confess your sins to each other and pray for each other so that you may be healed." Secret sins and addictions always lose their power over us when we bring them out into the open. For that reason, no one makes progress in overcoming sin, addiction, or dysfunctional behavior without accountability.

Acquiring accountability requires three vital steps:

1. Initiate accountable relationships.
2. Ask challenging questions.
3. Respond honestly.

Initiate Accountable Relationships

If you currently have no accountability, you may have to take the initiative for such relationships. If you wait for someone to approach you, that may never happen. I realize that making the first move often makes you feel vulnerable, but don't let pride deprive you of deep spiritual friendships. Besides, maintaining your reputation is not as important as growing in character. So when you've identified a potential accountability partner, simply approach that person and ask, "Can you keep me accountable in a certain area of my life?" Every time I've asked this of someone, I've been surprised at how receptive the other person was. In fact, most people I've approached have admitted their own need in the same area and asked me to hold them accountable in specific ways as well. When we invite others into our struggles, it often opens the door for them to share with us as well.

Ask Challenging Questions

Sometime ago, a young man I was discipling asked me to keep him accountable in his ongoing struggle with lust. So for the first few weeks we met, I asked, "How are you doing with lust?" He replied, "Pretty good," and we moved on. I soon realized that I was not serving him well; I needed to be tougher. He was depending on me to hold him accountable, so I tried asking more specific questions: "Have you looked at any pornography this week? Do you have a clear conscience about your sex life? Have you and your girlfriend violated any boundaries in your physical relationship lately?" My young friend confessed to some failures, we discussed some strategies for dealing with temptation, and then prayed together. Asking challenging questions enabled us to deal openly and honestly with his issue.

In any accountable relationship, it's imperative to ask tough questions. Always avoid vague, general, or easy-to-answer questions. Every duo or group should adopt its own set of questions. As an example, the following questions have been commonly used with many of the men's groups in which I've participated:

1. Did you read your Bible and pray every day this past week?
2. Have you spent quality time with your wife, kids, and/or friends this week?
3. Have you told any half-truths or lies to present yourself to others in a more favorable light?
4. Did you lose your temper this week?
5. Have you had any lustful thoughts this week or exposed yourself to pornography, whether in a magazine, a movie, or online?

Respond Honestly

Accountability won't accomplish anything if those involved are not committed to telling the truth. One men's group uses questions like the ones posted above, and then at the very end they ask, "Have you lied to us in answering any of the previous questions?" If you ever sense that your accountability partner is not shooting straight with you, probe gently but firmly. Without digressing into the Spanish Inquisition, invite your partner to be totally honest. Above all, accountability relationships should be marked by genuine care and concern. When somebody fails, don't scold or lecture. Instead, encourage and pray for that person. Galatians 6:1 says, "Brothers and sisters, if someone is caught in a sin, you who live by the Spirit should restore that person gently" (TNIV).

Worship as a Spiritual Discipline

Numbers 1:50 informs us that the Levites were appointed, or set apart, for ministry. They took their calling seriously and trained rigorously for it (see 1 Chronicles 25:7). However, worship was not merely a task performed on weekends but also a spiritual discipline that infused their lives every day. In fact, the Levites were instructed to "stand every morning to thank and praise the Lord. They were to do the same in the evening" (1 Chronicles 23:30). There are two important lessons we can learn from the Levites regarding the spiritual discipline of worship:

1. The value of immersing yourself in the Psalms.
2. What it means to bring a sacrifice of praise.

Immerse Yourself in the Psalms

We know very little about the style of music the Levites employed or the instruments they played. But we do know that their hymnal was the book of Psalms, which the Hebrews referred to as "The Book of Praises."

The Psalter is a virtual textbook on the rich language of praise. If you're unfamiliar with it, you may at first find this language unusual. For example, words like *exalted*, *magnify*, and *ascribe* are not words we use every day, but they convey an appropriate sense of reverence and awe. "Be exalted, O God, above the heavens; let your glory be over all the earth" (Psalm 57:5). "O magnify the Lord with me" (Psalm 34:3 NASB). "Ascribe to the Lord glory and strength. Ascribe to the Lord the glory due his name" (Psalm 29:1–2).

The Psalms offer a wealth of words and phrases especially suitable for worship. In Acts chapter 4, Peter and John are interrogated by the religious authorities, threatened, and released. We pick up the story in verses 23–24: "On their release, Peter and John went back to their own people and reported all that the chief priests and elders had said to them. When they heard this, they raised their voices together in prayer to God." Notice, in verse 24 that their prayer begins with worship drawn from the Psalms: "Sovereign Lord, . . . you made the heaven and the earth and the sea, and everything in them." That line is actually a quote from Psalm 146:6. Dallas Willard points out the value of learning the worship language of Psalms:

> Still today the Old Testament book of Psalms gives great power for faith and life. This is simply because it preserves a conceptually rich language about God and our relationships to him. If you bury yourself in Psalms, you emerge knowing God and understanding life.[1]

The Psalter is also a prayer book, offering a wide variety of prayers for all occasions. When Jonah was stuck in the belly of the whale, he cried out to God. His prayer was a hodgepodge of phrases borrowed from the Psalms (see Jonah 2:2–9). When you can't find the right words for worship or prayer, do what believers have done for centuries—turn to a psalm.

To quote from the Psalms in a moment of crisis obviously shows that Peter, John, and Jonah were intimately acquainted with this beautiful book of praise. They even had large portions of it memorized. In the same way, I recommend that all lead worshipers immerse themselves in the book of Psalms. Read it regularly, worship in its unique language, pray its heartfelt prayers, and memorize any passages you find especially meaningful.

When reading the Psalms, it's important to take a different approach than you would most other books of the Bible. Philip Yancy points out that Psalms is more like a "sampling of spiritual journals, much like personal letters to God," and should be read as if you're looking "over the shoulder" of the writer. Instead of "pronouncements from on high, delivered with full apostolic authority, on matters of faith and practice," the Psalms are "personal prayers in the form of poetry, written by a variety of people—peasants, kings, professional musicians, rank amateurs—in wildly fluctuating moods." Whereas most of Scripture is God's word to human beings, the Psalms represent our words to God. Explaining further, Yancey writes:

> Psalms gives examples of "ordinary" people struggling mightily to align what they believe about God with what they actually experience. Sometimes the authors are vindictive, sometimes self-righteous, sometimes paranoid, sometimes petty.
>
> Do not misunderstand me: I do not believe Psalms to be any less valuable, or less inspired, than Paul's letters or the Gospels. Nevertheless, the psalms do use an inherently different approach, not so much representing God to the people as the people representing themselves to God.[2]

Bring a Sacrifice of Praise

The Levites were directly involved in preparing the sacrifices for temple worship. According to Numbers 16:9, their job was to "stand before the community and minister to them," which is probably in reference to them assisting the priests by slaughtering the sacrifices.[3] In 2 Chronicles 30:15–17, we learn that it was the Levites' job to kill the lambs for the Passover ceremony. So the Levites understood, perhaps better than anyone else, the sacrificial nature of worship.

Interestingly, the first time the word *worship* is found in the Bible, it's in connection with sacrifice. God tested Abraham by commanding him to sacrifice his son Isaac. While trekking up the mountain toward the place of sacrifice, Abraham told his servants to stay behind while he and Isaac continued onward. Abraham said, "We will worship and then we will come back to you" (Genesis 22:5). Abraham was asked to put everything that was near and dear to him on the altar as an act of worship.

Worship always costs something. At the very least, it requires an effort of one's time and energy. As Hebrews 13:15 stresses, worship is a "sacrifice of praise" that we offer to God. In various parts of the world, some Christians travel great distances and even risk their lives to gather for worship.

Leading others in worship requires not only a great deal of time and energy, but also a surrendering of one's talent and artistic skill. This depth of commitment is perhaps why King Jehoshaphat gave the Levites in his service the following admonition: "You must serve faithfully and wholeheartedly in the fear of the Lord" (2 Chronicles 19:9). My fellow artists, don't be dismayed when leading worship turns arduous; sometimes ministry takes a lot of plain old hard work. Also, don't be alarmed when leading worship necessitates that you surrender control of your talent or abandon your need for recognition, artistic gratification, or even appreciation. God gave you your artistic gifts in the first place; you can trust him with your talent. "Therefore, my dear brothers and sisters, stand firm. Let nothing move you. Always give yourselves fully to the work of the Lord, because you know that your labor in the Lord is not in vain" (1 Corinthians 15:58 TNIV).

There may also be times when you don't feel like worshiping because you're downcast, lonely, or angry. You may even be depressed. The Bible cites many examples of those who worshiped amidst great hardship or in spite of desperate need: the leper (Matthew 8:2), the ruler whose daughter died (Matthew 9:18), the woman whose daughter was demon-possessed (Matthew 15:22–25), David after the loss of his son (2 Samuel 12:20), Paul and Silas in prison (Acts 16:23–25). None of these worshipers were in denial about their grief. But through worship, they found God amidst their pain and suffering.

Job lost all his sheep, livestock, camels, workers, and even his children. In anguish, "Job got to his feet, ripped his robe, shaved his head, then fell to the ground and worshiped: Naked I came from my mother's womb, naked I'll return to the womb of the earth. God gives, God takes. God's name be ever blessed" (Job 1:20–21 MSG). Though understandably distraught, Job knew that no matter what happens, God is still God; he is still worthy of our deepest devotion and highest praise (Revelation 4:11). The prophet Habakkuk agrees: "Though the fig tree does not bud and there are no grapes on the vines, though the olive crop fails and the fields produce no food, though there are no sheep in the pen and no cattle in the stalls, yet I will rejoice in the Lord, I will be joyful in God my Savior. The Sovereign Lord is my strength; he makes my feet like the feet of a deer, he enables me to go on the heights" (Habakkuk 3:17–19).

Worship helps us view this present life in the context of God's ultimate reality. For that reason, God invites you to bring all your despair and disappointment to him as a sacrifice of praise. "The sacrifices of God are a broken spirit; a broken and contrite heart, O God, you will not despise" (Psalm 51:17).

Intimacy with God

The Levites were well versed in their Bible, the Torah, to the point that they were even capable of teaching it. Second Chronicles 17:8–9 reveals that the Levites "taught throughout Judah, taking with them the Book of the Law of the Lord; they went around to all the towns of Judah and taught the people" (see also Nehemiah 8:7). The Levites were experts in the Torah, having spent their lives reading it and praying over it. However, their expertise was more than mere head knowledge. God's Word led them into deeper intimacy with the Almighty. In Ezekiel 44:15, God invites the Levites to "come near to minister before me." Thus, intimacy with God was a high priority for this team of worship leaders.

Unfortunately, many of us today get so busy doing church work that we're left with little or no time to spend with the Lord. There's a scenario I've seen played out in churches dozens of times. A new volunteer or staff member joins the worship ministry. Let's say his name is Bob, a guitar player. Bob joined the worship band thinking that it would not only be fun but spiritually uplifting. Having always struggled with spiritual discipline, Bob thought, *Now that I'm on the worship team that should keep me motivated to pray and have devotions.* At first, Bob was very consistent. He'd get up at six and have his devotions first thing in the morning. Soon, though, there were numerous late-night rehearsals and early-morning breakfast meetings. Within two weeks, Bob was neither praying nor reading the Bible. He was so busy at church, he no longer had time to be with God.

Protect Your Time with the Lord

It probably doesn't surprise anyone that one of Jesus Christ's highest priorities was spending time alone with his heavenly Father. Luke tells us that Jesus would often slip away into the wilderness to pray (Luke 5:16). What may shock us, though, is the urgency with which he protected those times of solitude, especially amidst the hectic pace of ministry.

One time, after a full day of teaching, ministering, and healing, Matthew reports the following: "Immediately Jesus made the disciples get into the boat and go on ahead of him to the other side, while he dismissed the crowd. After he had dismissed them, he went up on a mountainside by himself to pray" (Matthew 14:22–23). In spite of how busy he was, in spite of all the demands people were making of him, Christ *immediately* sent everyone away so he could fellowship with the Father.

Did the disciples understand this quirky habit Jesus had of withdrawing from the fray to fellowship with the Father? Probably not, judging from Matthew's description. He writes that Jesus *made* them go away. The disciples must have thought Jesus was crazy to retire from the public eye as their ministry was gaining momentum. This was certainly not the right time for Jesus to go off by himself. Yet, in Christ's mind there was no better time to steal away and pray. If the Son of God needed to make room in his life regularly for solitude, how much more so do we? Jesus knew that activity for God can never replace time with God.

On another occasion, Jesus sent the disciples out on a little missionary trip. When they returned, "The apostles gathered around Jesus and reported to him all they had done and taught. Then, because so many people were coming and going that they did not even have a chance to eat, he said to them, 'Come with me by yourselves to a quiet place and get some rest.' So they went away by themselves in a boat to a solitary place" (Mark 6:30–32).

My fellow artists, protect your personal time with the Lord. Whether you schedule your quiet time daily or weekly, treat it like any other priority appointment. Within reason, don't schedule anything that would conflict with the time you've set aside for your devotions. I try not to schedule early-morning appointments because I'm already "booked" at that time. That's when I meet with the Lord. Just as you exert healthy boundaries to protect your marriage or your family, do so to protect your personal time with God.

Don't Let Guilt Keep You Away from God

Some of you immediately associate the words quiet time or devotions with guilt. Like Bob, you too have tried to have regular devotions in the past but weren't able to be consistent, so you feel embarrassed or ashamed anytime someone brings up the subject. You may even believe that God is holding a serious grudge against you because of your lack of discipline. So you begin your quiet time with these words, "Oh, God, I'm such a no-good, worthless wretch. I'm sorry and I'll never miss another quiet time again." Friends, I invite you to jump off that vicious cycle. That guilt trip is not from God anyway. It's from the Evil One, the one who constantly accuses and criticizes us. The Lord doesn't say to us, "Hey, you undisciplined ingrates, you better have your devotions or I'll strike you dead." God is not like that. We are his beloved children, so instead he says, "Come to me. Let's talk. I want to be close to you." The Lord is inviting you into intimacy with him. He's drawing you near because he loves you and wants to spend time with you.

So if you've had trouble being consistent with personal devotions, don't waste time dwelling on the past. Get right back into the routine. As Hosea says, "Press on to know the Lord" (Hosea 6:3 NASB). When it comes to the spiritual life, it's not how many times you fall or fail, but how often you get back up and try. "If you seek him, he'll make sure you find him" (1 Chronicles 28:9 MSG).

Character Growth

The ultimate test of character is how one responds to change. Over the course of time, the role the Levites played in leading worship underwent various changes. Let's examine these changes in detail and glean all we can about how to handle change in our own lives.

After the Israelites escaped Pharaoh and were delivered from exile in Egypt, they wandered in the desert for forty years. During this time, the Levites were put in charge of the tabernacle, or Tent of Meeting, which is where the people met for worship. The Levites' duties included transporting the tabernacle, setting it up, and taking care of it (see Numbers 4, especially vv. 4, 25, 31). However, when Solomon's temple was built, it became the permanent place of worship so there was no longer any need to transport the tabernacle (1 Chronicles 23:25–26). So the Levites were given new ministry responsibilities, which included, among other things, maintaining the temple's courtyards, furniture, and utensils (1 Chronicles 23:28–29).

Be Open to Your Role Changing

The lesson for us is this: be open to the possibility that your ministry role might change over time. In fact, change is as much a part of ministry as it is a part of life. Ironically, it's one of the few constants. Thus, change is inevitable, especially in a growing church, but it's not always a bad thing. During thirty years of church work, my role changed, sometimes dramatically, sometimes subtly, about every two years. For what it's worth, here are a few things I've learned along the way concerning change.

How to Respond to Change

First, change is not always as bad as it first appears. I used to feel threatened by every change that came along. I would overly dramatize the consequences and predict nothing but doom and gloom. Yet, in all my years of church work, not a single change lived up to my negative expectations. More often than not, the change was for the good. So don't view change as a castastrophe. It's rarely as devastating as you might fear.

My second bit of advice is to hold on to your role lightly. Those who fear losing their place in the ministry usually are victims of their own insecurity. If you lose your position, it doesn't mean you no longer matter. Your value and identity, as a child of God, is so much greater than any task you perform. Evidently the Levites didn't clutch their positions tightly. When it came time to divvy up responsibilities, they were in the habit of casting lots. "They drew names at random to see who would do what. Nobody, whether young or old, teacher or student, was given preference or advantage over another" (1 Chronicles 25:8 MSG). I'm not suggesting that you draw straws next Sunday to determine who sings, plays drums, or mixes sound. However, in the case of the Levites, it demonstrates an openhandedness concerning the use of one's gifts and talents.

Third, I suggest you allow yourself to grieve over the inevitable losses that change brings. I learned this lesson through personal experience. As a leader, I've always been well aware of the need to delegate, but it was rarely without some pain. For example, turning over a musical ensemble to someone else to lead was always difficult, though not because I distrusted the new leader. On the contrary, I knew the group would be in better, more capable hands, but I knew I'd miss working with the people in that ensemble. Though I knew change was for the best, I couldn't help grieving the loss of those relationships. Whenever change occurs, you gain something and you lose something. It's okay to grieve your losses.

Last, after you've grieved, move on to whatever new adventure God has for you. In Isaiah 43:18–19, God says, "Forget the former things; do not dwell on the past. See, I am doing a new thing!" So when your current role comes to an end, look for and embrace whatever new adventure God has for you.

The Aging Artist

When you're old, it doesn't mean you're done ministering. The Levites, for example, never really retired; they just moved on to their next assignment. Numbers 8:25 says that the Levites were to stop working at age fifty, but that didn't mean that they stopped ministering. Verse 26 continues, "They may assist their brothers in performing their duties at the Tent of Meeting, but they themselves must not do the work." So even though the older Levites were exempt from heavy lifting, they still hung around and made themselves available to help, mentor, and encourage the younger generation.

Following the Levites' example, I'd like to propose an idea for how the church should handle the aging artist. I'll direct separate remarks to each group. First, to the artist: be open to becoming a mentor of younger artists. The wise artist realizes that his or her art will someday go out of style. Skills might decline. When it's time to exit the stage, so to speak, do so graciously. When it's time for the next generation to take over, get behind them. Don't badmouth them; don't criticize their style of worship; don't complain that their music "sounds like noise." It may sound that way to you because their musical style is different from yours—not right or wrong, just different. Instead of judging the next generation's music as inferior or ungodly, pray for them. Make yourself available to them. Extend unconditional love and grace to your younger brothers and sisters in the Lord. I have several relationships with worship leaders in their twenties that started out by me simply asking, "How can I be praying for you?" That question has opened the door for many rewarding mentoring relationships.

In his old age, King David deeply desired to build a temple, but God told him that he wanted Solomon, David's son, to build it. Instead of pouting or complaining, David threw his total support behind the next generation's efforts. He even started to stockpile supplies and mobilize workers so they'd be available when needed (1 Chronicles 22:14–15). You may not be singing solos in church anymore, but you can still make yourself available to serve the next generation of worshipers in whatever way they need. Just because you're getting older, it doesn't mean you've outlived your usefulness.

To the church I would say: consider mobilizing some of your aging artists into strategic mentoring roles. Truth is, you need the "oldsters" around. They bring stability, perspective, and the wisdom of their years to your ministry. In the first-century church, it was common for older believers to train and encourage younger ones (Titus 2:4–6). Today's church is in dire need of veteran believers who can help disciple young people. When I taught at Wheaton College, I heard many students express a longing for someone older to mentor them.

Speechwriter Peggy Noonan worked for CBS News in the 1970s, and in her book *What I Saw at the Revolution* she notes that at the time, CBS kept its aging journalists on the payroll as a reminder of the newsroom's glory days. After all, these older reporters embodied the values that made the newscast great. CBS eventually terminated that practice. Eighteen months after Peggy Noonan left the station, she received a note containing these sad words from ex-coworker Andy Rooney: "CBS has not been a good place to be.... They got rid of some dead wood but a company, like a forest, needs some of it. And they got rid of a lot of wood that wasn't dead, too."[4]

Like corporate America, churches too have been guilty of getting rid of "dead wood" that wasn't really dead. That doesn't mean that you have to put eighty-year-old Aunt Mame up front for a solo, but consider other meaningful roles, even nonartistic ones, that an older person could play, like praying, teaching, or mentoring.

When I was the music director at Willow Creek Community Church, we had an eighty-something-year-old man named Bob Carbaugh playing in the church orchestra. By his own admission, Bob's musical skills were not what they used to be, but we valued him more for who he was than how he played. Bob was one of the most fascinating people I had ever met. In the early 1940s, he worked for a church in Pearl Harbor, Hawaii, and he was there that infamous day it was bombed. He later taught at Moody Bible Institute, where he also directed various choral groups and pioneered their reputable piano-tuning department. Bob had been a Christian and had been in music ministry longer than some of our players had been alive. Very often between services or after rehearsals, I'd see three or four young people huddled around Bob, picking his brain about life, music, and ministry. One time Bob asked me if I thought he should quit playing because of his age, but I assured him he was welcome to play as long as he wanted to. Besides, he sat in the back of the second violin section and he would drop out here and there if a passage was too difficult, so his playing never hurt us. I strongly believe that we modeled inclusiveness every time our congregation saw this old white-haired gentleman playing his heart out in a rock orchestra.

Follow-up Questions for Group Discussion

1. What are some core values that you and your teammates could adopt for your ministry?

2. Why is unity important for a worship team?

3. What are the most common causes of division for any worship ministry?

4. Do you have any guidelines to add to the unity covenant suggested in this chapter?

5. Why is accountability important for a believer?

6. Do you agree that those involved in worship ministry should be well versed in the Psalms? Why or why not?

7. What does the term "sacrifice of praise" mean to you personally?

8. How can busy people involved in church work keep their relationship with God vital and vibrant?

9. Do you have any further advice for anyone going through a season of change in his or her life?

10. What might a dedicated mentoring ministry look like in your church?

Personal Action Steps

1. Set up a meeting with your pastor this week to discuss the effectiveness of your working relationship or to ask the questions posed in this chapter.

2. If you don't have accountability in your life, ask the Lord to show you someone who could meet that need, and approach that person this week about entering into an accountable relationship with you.

3. If you have accountability in your life, consider adopting a set of regular questions, like the ones outlined in this chapter, that would serve your needs.

4. Are you spending as much personal time with the Lord as you'd like? If not, consider ways to improve in this area.

5. Consider any changes you're presently experiencing or have experienced in the past. What have you learned from this chapter that can help you navigate life's inevitable seasons of change?

chapter nine

The weight of this sad time we must obey;
Speak what we feel, not what we ought to say.

From *King Lear* by William Shakespeare

Cory reluctantly pops in the DVD from last week's service and starts to watch. *What am I looking for again?* he wonders. *Oh yeah, stage presence*, he remembers, wondering what that has to do with leading worship.

Pastor Rich had told him he needed to work on his stage presence. "You're a good worship leader with a lot of potential, but you're not connecting with the congregation."

"What do you mean?" asked Cory somewhat defensively. "People tell me all the time how great the worship is whenever I lead."

"I don't doubt that, but I hear otherwise from people who aren't willing to say it to your face."

Cory was stunned and hurt to think that people were talking about him behind his back.

"Look, Cory, you're a great guitar player and your heart's in the right place, but your communication skills need some work."

"So what are people saying about me?" queried Cory.

"It's not just other people," the pastor said. "I've been telling you for some time now that you need to engage more with the congregation. You've got your eyes buried in your music stand a lot, and when you make comments between songs, you sound nervous. It's not always clear what you're trying to say, and sometimes it even sounds like you're mumbling. Honestly, you look a little stiff up there. You need to relax, smile more, have fun."

"I'm not Christopher," snapped Cory, referring to the previous worship leader. "That happy-go-lucky stuff doesn't feel authentic to me. That just isn't me."

"We both know you've got some pretty big shoes to fill, but no one's asking you to be Christopher. In fact, that's just my point—we want you to be yourself up on the platform."

"I *am* being myself," protested Cory, "but apparently that's not good enough."

"Cory, I can tell this is hard for you, but believe me, no one wants you to succeed more than I do. You're doing a good job, but there's room for improvement and I'm more than willing to help you any way I can. But if you fight me on this, there will be repercussions."

Obviously softened, Cory cleared his throat and said, "Well, then, I'd like to take you up on your offer to help me. Where do we start?"

"Good," replied Pastor Rich, sounding relieved. "The first thing I'd suggest is that you sit down and look at the DVD from last week's service. Then let's meet in a couple days and discuss what you observe."

With that conversation fresh in his mind, Cory begins to review the service over his lunch break. He pulls out pen and paper and gets ready to record his reactions. As the first song starts, Cory is glued to the monitor, but after five minutes, he turns off the DVD. He has seen enough. "They're right," he admitted out loud. "I do look stiff and uncomfortable. I'm looking down the whole time and when I talk, my voice trails off like I'm mumbling."

Humbled, but rejuvenated, Cory wrote down his first observation: *I guess there's more to leading worship than just singing and playing guitar.*

Questions for Group Discussion

1. Do you think Pastor Rich handled this situation well? Why or why not?

2. How would you evaluate Cory's response?

3. Why do you suppose Cory was defensive at first?

4. Do you think acquiring good "stage presence" is necessary for lead worshipers? Why or why not?

5. What does it mean for a worship leader to "connect with the congregation"?

6. What advice do you have for worship leaders about speaking between songs?

7. How can worship leaders get accurate feedback regarding their effectiveness?

8. Cory didn't agree with his pastor's assessment of his worship leadership until he saw himself on DVD. Why do you suppose he was unaware of his deficiencies?

9. Do you believe it's valuable for a worship team to watch themselves on tape or DVD? Why or why not?

10. Why do you think Cory's realization (that leading worship is more than just singing and playing guitar) was such a revelation to him?

ENROLLING IN THE ASAPH SCHOOL OF WORSHIP LEADING

The name Asaph may not be a household word, but the man's been impacting worshipers for 3,000 years. Asaph was a Levite, a musician, who helped lead King David's choir. He started out sounding the cymbals before the ark of the covenant (1 Chronicles 15:14–19) and eventually became one of the leaders in charge of music for the temple services (1 Chronicles 25:1–9). However, Asaph is best known as a psalmist. You've probably noticed his name under the heading of several psalms, specifically Psalms 50 and 73–83. Because all twelve of these psalms are attributed to Asaph, we can assume that he wrote most, if not all, of them. Some scholars believe, for example, that Psalm 83 was written by a descendant because it describes events that took place after Asaph's time. Other scholars contend that, in such instances, Asaph was speaking prophetically. After all, 2 Chronicles 29:30 informs us that Asaph was a "seer"—someone who predicts the future.

Many valuable insights are gained by studying the psalms of Asaph. He was a contemporary of David, who wrote the majority of the psalms. While similar insights can be gleaned from David, Asaph's perspective is unique because he was a full-time worship leader. Unlike David, who went on to become king, Asaph, as far as we know, remained a worship leader his entire life.

Though this book is intended for all church artists, this chapter may hold special appeal for those who are paid specifically to lead worship or who, paid or not, are leading the worship ministry at their church. Having said that, though, I believe we can all learn a great deal from Asaph about what it means to be a worshiping artist.

Offer Your Congregation a Balanced Vision of God

As an exercise, I recently read the psalms of Asaph and listed all the attributes and characteristics of God referenced in each psalm. I was struck, first of all, by Asaph's comprehensiveness. Though he wrote only twelve psalms, Asaph managed to present a balanced picture of God. Personally, I tend to gravitate toward the "feel good" attributes of God, like his love, mercy, and grace. Asaph presents such attributes, but isn't afraid to remind us about God's justice and judgment or his anger over sin. In Psalm 78:65, for example, Asaph describes God as a drunken warrior waking up from a hangover and unleashing his anger on his enemies. That's in stark contrast to other verses in the Bible that describe God as "slow to anger" (Psalm 103:8). However, this is not a contradiction, but a paradox. Apparently, it takes a lot to provoke God's anger, but when incited, his anger comes down hard. As displayed throughout Scripture, sin is what angers God. So his is a holy anger, aimed at steering us away from the destructiveness of sin.

Asaph graphically reveals God's grief over sin. In Psalm 81, an obviously brokenhearted God pleads for Israel to return to him:

> "Hear, O my people, and I will warn you—
> if you would but listen to me, O Israel! . . .
> If my people would but listen to me,
> if Israel would follow my ways,
> how quickly would I subdue their enemies
> and turn my hand against their foes!"
> Psalm 81:8, 13–14

In reviewing Asaph's psalms, I also couldn't help but notice that Asaph had a big God. His most common theme was God's power and strength. In Psalm 50, he wrote:

> The Mighty One, God, the Lord,
> speaks and summons the earth
> from the rising of the sun to the place where it sets. . . .
> "For every animal of the forest is mine,
> and the cattle on a thousand hills.
> I know every bird in the mountains,
> and the creatures of the field are mine."
> Psalm 50:1, 10–11

My favorite example is from Psalm 76:4: "You are resplendent with light, more majestic than mountains rich with game." Indeed, Asaph had a highly exalted, transcendent view of God.

Like Asaph, your job as a lead worshiper is to offer your congregation a well-rounded vision of God. Christianity breeds a mysterious mix of familiarity and reverence toward God. On one hand, we have been granted "the Spirit of sonship," allowing us to address God as "Abba, Father," the Hebrew equivalent of "Dad" or "Daddy" (Romans 8:15). On the other hand, we are to approach God with reverence. Another psalmist wrote, "In reverence will I bow down toward your holy temple" (Psalm 5:7). Hebrews 12:28–29 reads: "Therefore, since we are receiving a kingdom that cannot be shaken, let us be thankful, and so worship God acceptably with reverence and awe, for our 'God is a consuming fire.'" As Robert W. Bailey contends, "We cannot worship rightly until we recapture, as the principal element in worship, the overwhelming sense of awe and reverence in the presence of God. God's greatness, love, and compassion call forth our praise and adoration."[1]

The worship artist must offer the congregation a balanced view of God. We must strive to present the full range of God's attributes, not necessarily all in one service, but definitely over time. At the same time, we must always present a biblically accurate picture of God. For that reason, we should pay close attention to the lyrical content of our music. Avoid lyrics that misrepresent God. No matter how much you love a certain song, if it inaccurately portrays God, don't use it. If you have doubts about the theological integrity of any artistic expression, run it by your pastor or elders for approval.

Leverage the Power of Corporate Worship

Though private worship is an important spiritual discipline, corporate worship offers an even broader experience. There is nothing like corporate worship. When people come together to praise God, we experience the power and blessing of community, a dynamic so unique it simply can't be replicated when we're alone, by ourselves. Even a live recording of a worship event is never as good as being there. While it's true that I can sing, pray, and read Scripture when alone, doing those things with others inimitably amplifies the experience. For that reason, corporate worship should never be neglected, but should always remain an essential part of every believer's regular routine. The writer of Hebrews agrees: "Let us not give up meeting together, as some are in the habit of doing, but let us encourage one another—and all the more as you see the Day approaching" (Hebrews 10:25).

The worshiping artist must never lose sight of the communal aspect of leading worship. Early in my songwriting career, I received a rejection letter from a publisher explaining that they were looking exclusively for praise songs addressed to God from a personal point of view. For example, "I bless your name, O Lord." I didn't think much of it at the time, but have since noticed a disturbing trend within the worship movement: corporate individualism replacing corporate worship. I've sat through worship services in which every song, even the prayers, were presented in the first person singular. It was as if the worship leader forgot he was leading a community of people into God's presence and praying as their spokesperson. I could have had the same experience by myself at home or at the park. While there's nothing inherently wrong with personalizing worship, we should always be careful, when leading worship, not to diminish the power of togetherness, which lies in the fact that *we* declare God's worth; we pray, "*Our* Father who is in Heaven" (Matthew 6:9 NASB, emphasis mine). "For it is *we* ... who worship by the Spirit of God, who glory in Christ Jesus" (Philippians 3:3, emphasis mine).

Asaph led worship with the congregation clearly in mind. In Psalm 79:13 he wrote, "Then we your people, the sheep of your pasture, will praise you forever; from generation to generation we will recount your praise." Even Asaph's prayers were corporate in nature: "Do not hold against us the sins of the fathers; may your mercy come quickly to meet us, for we are in desperate need" (Psalm 79:8).

I've observed a few worship leaders who lead almost entirely with their eyes closed. When I asked one such leader why, he said, "Well, I'm just up there to worship. I really don't care what anybody else is doing." I agree that worship should always be the top priority, but the worship leader's job is to call others to worship and point them toward God. When leaders withdraw into their own little world, they alienate themselves from the congregation. Instead of being drawn into worship, the congregation feels left out, like they're watching someone else's private worship.

I challenge all worship leaders not only to be mindful of the congregation but also to leverage the power of community during corporate worship. At one church I visited, a drama sketch was presented not as a performance, but as a story in which the congregation participated. The topic of the pastor's sermon was shame, so the drama presented, in "reader's theater" style, the story of the woman caught in adultery. When it came time in the narrative for Jesus to say, "Your sins are forgiven; go and sin no more," the congregation was prompted to speak those words. Though this approach doesn't work for every drama sketch, in this case it was extremely poignant to hear a room full of people repeating those powerful words. It was as if we were saying them to each other. On another occasion, a worship leader instructed his congregation to turn and sing to each other reminders of God's goodness and glory. Those who were suffering or going through difficulty were especially encouraged.

As a worship leader, when you stand in front of the congregation, remember, you're not addressing an audience, you're leading a community. Such a distinction was modeled not only by Asaph but by another notorious psalmist as well. David wrote, "I will declare your name to my people; in the assembly I will praise you.... Glorify the Lord with me; let us exalt his name together" (Psalm 22:22; 34:3 TNIV).

Give Us Fresh Words to Sing

Whether you write music, poetry, or prose, or you want to better understand those who do, there is much we can learn about good writing by studying the psalms of Asaph. Such learning will also prove valuable to those responsible for selecting music and other elements for corporate worship.

First, Asaph had a way with words. Though he was a successful songwriter, we have no idea what his music sounded like. It's not his music that has come down to us through the ages; it's his words that have withstood the test of time. He obviously was a highly gifted wordsmith. When referring to God, for example, he often relied on lofty language. Note his description of God parting the Red Sea:

> Your ways, O God, are holy.
>   What god is so great as our God?
> You are the God who performs miracles;
>   you display your power among the peoples.
> With your mighty arm you redeemed your people,
>   the descendants of Jacob and Joseph.
>
> The waters saw you, O God,
>   the waters saw you and writhed;
>   the very depths were convulsed.

The clouds poured down water,
    the skies resounded with thunder;
    your arrows flashed back and forth.
Your thunder was heard in the whirlwind,
    your lightning lit up the world;
    the earth trembled and quaked.
Your path led through the sea,
    your way through the mighty waters,
    though your footprints were not seen.

You led your people like a flock
    by the hand of Moses and Aaron.
Psalm 77:13–20

However, my favorite Asaph line is from Psalm 81:10 (NASB): "I, the Lord, am your God, who brought you up from the land of Egypt; Open your mouth wide and I will fill it."

Second, Asaph's writing was fresh and creative. Among other skills, he displayed a knack for clever analogy. In Psalm 80:8–16, Asaph likens Israel to a vine that God uprooted from Egypt and transplanted in the land of Canaan. Then he affectionately asks God to "look down from heaven and ... watch over this vine" (v. 14). Earlier in this same psalm, Asaph refers poetically to Israel's sufferings as "the bread of tears" (v. 5).

Asaph also made ample use of refrains—recurring phrases or sections. Psalm 80 repeats the phrase "make your face shine upon us" to good effect (vv. 3, 7, 19). In the same way, a good song has a memorable "hook" or chorus, something musically or lyrically that pulls you in and that you remember long after you've heard it. Such praise songs work especially well for worship.

Third, Asaph's writings clearly show that he was a man of great spiritual depth. When searching for answers to life's most difficult questions, he turned to God (Psalm 73:16–17). He walked close to the Lord. In Psalm 73:23–24 he wrote, "Yet I am always with you; you hold me by my right hand. You guide me with your counsel, and afterward you will take me into glory." Being an avid worshiper, Asaph spent time meditating on God's wondrous deeds (Psalm 77:11–12). Asaph was a man of substance and his art reflected that.

Generally, I'm enthused about the quality of the arts found in most churches today, but we must continue to strive for excellence, as did Asaph. With that in mind, my advice to writers, especially those who write praise music, is this: give us fresh words to sing, words of depth and substance. That same advice applies to those who program worship services. Worn-out phrases and predictable rhymes such as "Jesus changed my heart / Gave me a brand new start" should be avoided. Instead, the church needs creative new expressions of deepening faith. In my opinion, we could use more songs that acknowledge the struggles of the Christian life, that don't minimize pain, but give voice to it. We could use more songs that address sin and temptation or encourage us in the faith. We could also use more songs that illustrate the teachings of Christ or other tenets of doctrine, like redemption, the church, or the Trinity. We have a number of songs about God's love, but what about some of his other attributes, like God's sovereignty, wisdom, or justice? And how about more songs that emphasize loving others or blessing the poor, needy, and oppressed? Writing songs for the church is a high and noble calling. My fellow artists, let's continue to strive for art that is relevant, excellent, and substantive.

Connect Your Art with Your Heart

Asaph not only had a big God, he had a big heart. He was a man with intense feelings. And like many great artists, his work reflects a wide range of emotions. He could erupt with exuberant praise, as in Psalm 81: "Sing for joy to God our strength; shout aloud to the God of Jacob! Begin the music, strike the tambourine, play the melodious harp and lyre" (vv. 1–2). However, Asaph was also no stranger to depression, anguish, and heartache. Charles Spurgeon described Asaph as a man of "exercised mind, and [who] often touched the minor key; he was thoughtful, contemplative, believing, but withal there was a dash of sadness about him."[2] In Psalm 77 Asaph wrote:

> I found myself in trouble and went looking for my Lord;
>   my life was an open wound that wouldn't heal.
> When friends said, "Everything will turn out all right,"
>   I didn't believe a word they said.
> I remember God—and shake my head.
>   I bow my head—then wring my hands.
> I'm awake all night—not a wink of sleep;
>   I can't even say what's bothering me.
> I go over the days one by one,
>   I ponder the years gone by.

> I strum my lute all through the night,
> wondering how to get my life together.
> Psalm 77:2–6 MSG

Like Asaph, great artists are in touch with their emotions—the negative as well as the positive—they allow those emotions to breathe life into their art. They're able to connect their art with their hearts. Proverbs 4:23 says, "Watch over your heart with all diligence, For from it flow the springs of life" (NASB). Your art, your best work, comes from deep within and very often reflects your own personal journey. That's why Colossians 3:16 invites us to "Let the word of Christ dwell in you richly as you teach and admonish one another with all wisdom, and as you sing psalms, hymns and spiritual songs with gratitude in your hearts to God." Notice the connection between one's heart (where Christ dwells) and one's art (in this case psalms, hymns, and spiritual songs). A heart that abides in Christ produces Spirit-filled art. In the same way, Asaph's poetry reveals a heart that was on fire for God and yearned for God: "As for me, I will declare this forever; I will sing praise to the God of Jacob.... It is good to be near God. I have made the Sovereign Lord my refuge; I will tell of all your deeds" (Psalm 75:9; 73:28).

Get in Touch with Your Feelings

In order to effectively connect your art with your heart, you need to stay abreast of your innermost thoughts and feelings. However, getting in touch with feelings can sometimes be painful. After all, it hurts to feel hurt; it's painful to feel sad. Even positive emotions, like hope or joy, can be bittersweet because they're fleeting. When they're gone, we're left aching for more. Feelings force us to face reality, which as we all know, can be harsh at times. For that reason, Paul says all creation "groans" for the fullness of joy that awaits us in heaven. "We know that the whole creation has been groaning as in the pains of childbirth right up to the present time. Not only so, but we ourselves, who have the firstfruits of the Spirit, groan inwardly as we wait eagerly for our adoption as sons, the redemption of our bodies" (Romans 8:22–23).

Though it often seems easier to avoid, deaden, or escape our emotions, such attempts only sever us from reality. Though difficult, we're better off embracing and listening to our feelings. Authors of the book *The Cry of the Soul* contend that feelings can potentially put us in touch with God:

> The presence of disruptive emotions that feel irrational or out of control is not necessarily a sign of disease, sin, or trauma. Instead, it may be the signal that the heart is struggling with God. Therefore, we must view the ups and downs of our emotional life not as a problem to be resolved, but as a cry to be heard.... Emotions open the door to asking hard questions: Does life make sense? Is there any real purpose to my pain? Why must every relationship end? Is God good? If we are to understand ourselves honestly—and, more importantly, know God—we must listen to our emotions.... Ignoring our emotions is turning our back on reality; listening to our emotions ushers us into reality. And reality is where we meet God.[3]

Getting in touch with our emotions helps us better understand God. After all, how can we understand God's anger or jealousy if we continually suppress those feelings? Perhaps those so-called "negative" emotions aren't so negative after all.

In order to stay in touch with your inner thoughts and feelings, you need time alone—by yourself. This is different from the type of meditation that seeks to empty the mind. Artistic solitude is an opportunity to get quiet and still—to ruminate over thoughts and feelings, and to ponder what God's doing in your life. As Asaph demonstrates, such inner awareness adds depth to your art. In addition, when you connect your art with your heart, you create and communicate with greater authenticity and passion.

Create and Communicate Authentically

As we've observed, Asaph was honest about his feelings, even the negative ones. He wrestled often with God and, in various psalms, even questioned and openly doubted God. In Psalm 77, for example, he asked:

> Will the Lord walk off and leave us for good?
> Will he never smile again?
> Is his love worn threadbare?
> Has his salvation promise burned out?
> Has God forgotten his manners?
> Has he angrily stalked off and left us?
> "Just my luck," I said. "The High God goes out of business
> just the moment I need him."
>
> Psalm 77:7–9 MSG

Asaph honestly faced his own shortcomings as well. In Psalm 73:3, he admitted feelings of jealousy: "For I envied the arrogant when I saw the prosperity of the wicked." A willingness to "go there"—to be real, vulnerable, and transparent with ourselves, with God, and with others is not only a valuable asset for an artist, it is a sign of spiritual health. As Brennan Manning writes:

> Feelings that are not expressed cannot be fixed. For example, suppressed anger leads to resentment; repressed resentment leads to guilty self-flagellation; guilt leads to depression. Repressed persons are often depressed persons. An integral life implies creative listening to our emotions, taking responsibility for them, and courageously expressing them.[4]

Getting in touch with your inner thoughts and feelings is not only cathartic, it helps an artist create and communicate authentically. As Nancy Beach notes, honesty and authenticity go hand in hand for the church artist:

> There can be no authenticity without honesty. People who sit in our churches on Sunday morning are waiting to see if we will simply tell them the truth—the truth about life, about struggle and pain, about the mess in this world, and about our own shaky experiences. They also need to hear the truth about ultimate hope. But first we must admit that we understand trouble, that none of us is exempt from trials and temptation, and that we know life is difficult. If Christians sugarcoat the truth or try to hide, escaping the reality of what everyone else clearly sees, we will be perceived as out of touch. Church is not the place for pretense or platitudes. It's the place for telling the truth.[5]

Create and Communicate with Passion

Renee Grant-Williams is a vocal coach who is often hired by the country music industry to work with up-and-coming singers. In her book *Voice Power*, she describes her experience with one such client:

> Some time ago, a young singer walked into my Nashville voice studio for a consultation—and I must say, he looked great. He was tall, handsome, had the perfect chin dimple, and melted into his jeans. He really looked like a "singin'" star.
>
> But the high-wattage smile and winning manner couldn't disguise his frustration. He had been in Nashville three years and didn't understand why none of the record labels had signed him to a major record deal. Just looking at him, I was pretty surprised myself.
>
> So, I asked to hear him sing. He had a fine natural voice. He sang in tune and his rhythm was good. It was all very pleasant, but before long, I found myself drifting off—adding items to my grocery list. He was *not* holding my attention.
>
> Now that is a serious problem for a singer. Mr. Dimple had a good voice and

> he looked good, but this guy could have been arrested for loitering in front of a band. There was definitely something missing . . .
>
> That same summer, a management firm brought me another young singer who made a completely different impression. He was friendly and sincere looking—like someone you would trust with your X rays or who might help you get your car running again. No movie star dimple. No flowing locks. And the jeans? Not bad, but you could see that wrestling with his weight might be an ongoing concern. Nothing about him hinted that he could be a major country star, although the management team that sent him was a good one and they certainly believed in him. I, however, didn't get it.
>
> As soon as I heard him sing, though, I *did* get it. He didn't have the perfect voice. Or the loudest voice. Or the best tone in the world. But I couldn't stop listening. When he sang, I felt completely and totally engaged. I was hanging on every word. *There* was the mystery ingredient absent in Mr. Dimple.
>
> So what ever happened to Joe Bob Dimple? I think he's somewhere back home in Fresno growing raisins now. But the other singer? He went on to sell more records than any recording artist of the entire past century. It was Garth Brooks.[6]

Some artists, like Garth Brooks, are born with "it"—the ability to communicate effectively. They can hold an audience in the palm of their hand. Even if you don't come by it naturally, you can still become an effective communicator.

As a church music director, I spent a great deal of time preparing vocalists to sing, which included helping them communicate effectively. One singer put it crudely, but accurately, when she asked, "How can I do a better job of selling this song?"

Facial expression is the most important part of communication. Musicians, for example, with no facial expression or with their heads buried in their music stands don't draw anyone into worship. This applies not only to musicians. I recently attended a church service where a gifted dancer interpreted an upbeat and spirited worship song. Her choreography fit the music well, but her face was solemn and stern throughout. It was as though she put all her time and energy into where her feet should go and forgot about her face. Remember, your face, especially your eyes and your smile, plays a major role in effective communication.

Make sure your facial expression fits the mood and/or lyrics. Too often I have seen worship team members smiling while singing about Jesus suffering on the cross. Such contradiction makes lead worshipers appear oblivious and insensitive. Also, make sure your eyes are directed appropriately. On more than one occasion, a singer has asked, "What exactly should I be looking at during worship?" That's a good question because your focus could change from one line to another, so it's important to clarify to whom you're singing. It makes no sense to sing, "I love you, Lord" while looking out at the congregation or, even worse, at fellow worship team members. Generally speaking, if a lyric is meant to build up the body or is about God, feel free to establish eye contact with the congregation in order to draw them in. If the words are directed to God, I recommend singing to a point slightly above the congregation.

Another question often put to me by worship artists is, "How can I avoid looking stiff while leading worship?" Unfortunately, church musicians are notorious for standing rigidly "at attention" on the platform with their arms down at their sides, like the somber guards at Buckingham Palace. Not wanting to draw undo attention to ourselves, we sometimes swing the pendulum too far the other way and fail to give the gospel message the passionate communication it deserves.

That brings us to the real issue behind connecting one's art with one's heart: how can a church artist create and communicate with passion? In the movie *Walk the Line*, the actor portraying Johnny Cash auditions for a local record producer. Less than a minute into his first song, an old gospel song by the then popular Jimmie Davis, the producer is obviously unimpressed. He motions for Johnny and his band to stop and asks if he brought anything else to sing. Johnny is taken aback. The producer explains, "I don't record material that doesn't sell, Mr. Cash, and Gospel like that doesn't sell."

Johnny presses further, "Was it the Gospel or the way I sing it?"

"Both," replied the producer.

"What's wrong with the way I sing it?" asked Johnny.

"I don't believe you," he replied.

Johnny looks like he's about to pick a fight. "You saying I don't believe in God?"

The producer clarifies. "You know exactly what I'm telling you. We've already heard that song a hundred times just like that, just like how you sang it."

"Well you didn't let us bring it home," Johnny said defensively.

The producer laughs incredulously. "Bring it home? All right, let's bring it home. If you was hit by a truck and you were lying out in that gutter dying, and you had to sing one song people would remember before you're dirt — one song that would let God know what you felt about your time here on earth, one song that would sum you up, you're telling me that's the song you'd sing? That same Jimmie Davis tune we hear on the radio all day? About your peace within and how it's real and how you're gonna shout it? Or would you sing something different? Something real, something you felt because I'm telling you right now, that's the kind of song people want to hear. That's the kind of song that truly saves people."[7]

Johnny then proceeds to sing a song he wrote and, unlike the Jimmie Davis tune, he sings it with passion. Later that day, he walks out of the studio with a record deal.

In order to create and communicate effectively, artists must get in touch with their passions. Asaph was obviously passionate about God. In Psalm 73:25, he wrote, "Whom have I in heaven but You? And besides You, I desire nothing on earth" (NASB). Asaph also spoke out passionately on behalf of the poor and oppressed (Psalm 72:4, 12–14; 74:21). Psalm 82 is an ardent plea for social justice.

How about you? What are you passionate about? If you had twenty-four hours to live, and you were given the opportunity to say something to the world, what would you say? How would you say it?

If you're a singer, for example, I recommend getting in touch with how you feel about the lyrics you sing. What lines or phrases of the song speak powerfully to you? How does the message of the song affect you? Why is this message important? The lyrics won't come alive for others until they've come alive in you.

After identifying your passions, you must then convince others you really believe what you're saying. Again, if you're a singer, try speaking the words aloud. Or summarize the message of the song in a few sentences. Don't just sing notes; always sing *to* someone. Imagine someone in your life who needs to hear that message. Speak the words as if you were saying them to a friend.

When I walk vocalists through such exercises, their sense of urgency is usually awakened. They automatically emphasize certain words or phrases as they recite the lyrics. They use facial expressions and hand gestures that fit the words. Truth is, when people feel strongly about something, they rarely speak in a monotone or stand rigid and motionless. They emote in ways that fit their personalities and temperaments. I encourage singers to incorporate those same facial expressions, inflections, and gestures into their singing. That way they'll communicate in a style that's natural and comfortable to them.

My fellow artists, we have the most important message in the world. Let's communicate it with passion.

Be a Worship Leader at Home

Scripture mentions Asaph's family a number of times (1 Chronicles 6:39; 25:1–2, 9; 2 Chronicles 29:13). The family was apparently very musical and served in the worship ministry (1 Chronicles 25:1–9). However, one particular passage offers a close look at Asaph the devoted family man. In Psalm 78, we see him telling his children about the glory of God:

> I will open my mouth in parables,
>   I will utter hidden things, things from of old—
> what we have heard and known,
>   what our fathers have told us.
> We will not hide them from their children;
>   we will tell the next generation
> the praiseworthy deeds of the Lord,
>   his power, and the wonders he has done....
> so the next generation would know them,
>   even the children yet to be born,
>   and they in turn would tell their children.
>
> Psalm 78:2–4, 6

Asaph was not only a worship leader at church, he was also one at home. We too must make worship a family priority. That doesn't necessarily mean that you have to gather the children around the piano and sing, although I commend families that do that. Don't feel obligated to duplicate church at home. In fact, you don't have to sing to lead your family in worship. Though Asaph was a trained and gifted singer, a professional worship leader, he resorted to the spoken word when telling his children about the Lord. Hebrew families were adamant about proclaiming God's greatness and faithfulness to the next generation. Their feasts, like Passover, were commemorations of God's miracles on their behalf. Hebrew parents were given the responsibility of teaching their children about the Lord as they went about their everyday activities: "These commandments that I give you today are to be upon your hearts. Impress them on your children. Talk about them when you sit at home and when you walk along the road, when you lie down and when you get up" (Deuteronomy 6:6–7).

As our boys were growing up, one of our family themes was gratitude. We opened Christmas presents one at a time and expressed appreciation before moving on to the next gift. Sue made the boys write "Thank you" notes for all gifts. Our attitude of gratitude stemmed from the fact that God had blessed us beyond our wildest dreams. When we were starting out in ministry, and finances were extremely tight, someone helped us buy our home, other people gave us furniture, and someone gave us an expensive television. One family bought us a new car and another let us spend a week at their vacation home. Still another family gave us a vacation in Florida. Each time, Sue and I used the opportunity to point out God's goodness and grace to our sons.

Many churches today offer age-segregated programs simultaneously, presenting fewer opportunities for families to worship together—all the more reason to look for such opportunities in the home. Prayer before meals is an obvious example. As long as you're thanking God for his provision, why not praise him for any one of his glorious attributes? Identify the seven names or attributes of God that are most meaningful to your family, assign one for each day of the week, and highlight it during mealtime prayers. Some families pop in a worship CD while driving. Those who spend a lot of time outdoors have ample opportunity to note God's beauty and grandeur in creation. Camping, for example, can be a family worship experience, as can a drive through the country or a day at the beach. Celebrate a much-needed answer to prayer by throwing a party or going out to eat. As the worship leader in your home, always look for opportunities to point your children toward God.

A Few Words to Pastors about Leading Artists

A couple months ago, a pastor called me asking for advice. Weeks before, he had dismissed his worship leader due to moral failure. The whole ordeal had been gut-wrenching for all involved. "I don't ever want to go through that again," he said. However, his last words, before hanging up the phone, were very revealing. He said with a great deal of frustration, "I don't know the first thing about leading artists." On many occasions, I've heard pastors admit that leading their more artistically minded staff members leaves them baffled and befuddled.

Unfortunately, most leadership books are geared to "type A" personalities and offer good advice on leading other type A personalities. The problem is most artists don't fit that mold. The artistic temperament is unique and demands a different approach.

Asaph inadvertently offers some thoughts on the subject of leadership from an artist's perspective. First Chronicles 25:2 informs us that Asaph "prophesied under the king's supervision." Hence, Asaph worked for and reported to King David. Given the tension we often see today between worship leader and pastor, one can't help but wonder what kind of working relationship Asaph and David had. Based on a couple verses at the end of Psalm 78, it appears the two men worked well together. While recounting God's faithfulness to Israel throughout history, Asaph presents the emergence of King David as further proof of God's goodness:

> He chose David his servant
> and took him from the sheep pens;
> from tending the sheep he brought him
> to be the shepherd of his people Jacob,
> of Israel his inheritance.
> And David shepherded them with integrity of heart;
> with skillful hands he led them.
>
> Psalm 78:70–72

Obviously, Asaph deeply respected his boss. In paying tribute to the king, Asaph noted David's three most prominent strengths: he had a shepherd's heart, he was a man of integrity, and he was a good leader. By examining how these strengths might play out in today's pastor–worship leader relationship, we inevitably arrive at the three most important things a worship leader needs from a pastor: encouragement, godly leadership, and sermon information.

Encourage Your Worship Leader

What Asaph seems to have admired most about David was his shepherd's heart. A true shepherd genuinely cares about people, is sensitive to their needs, and actively ministers to them. When shepherding artists, the most important thing you can do is encourage them. The most common complaint I hear from worship leaders is that they don't feel encouraged by their superiors. In fact, many are walking around downright discouraged. Any encouragement from you, the pastor, goes a long way and means more to your worship leader than you may realize.

I don't have to remind you that encouragement is biblical. First Thessalonians 5:11 says it straight out, "Therefore encourage one another and build each other up." Artists need encouragement. We thrive on it. And instead of doing it once in a while, Hebrews 3:13 tells us to make encouragement a regular ritual. It says, "Encourage one another daily."

We all receive encouragement differently. Some of us like to hear it spoken, while others appreciate notes. Some need it more often than others. Some of us are encouraged whenever we're asked to participate in a meaningful ministry opportunity. For example, if you encourage your worship ministry to tackle a recording project, it communicates that you think they're good enough to make a worship CD.

Pastors should ask their worship leaders the following question: How do you best receive encouragement? Put another way: What is the most effective way for me to encourage you? Learning how to encourage your worship leader will help you shepherd him or her more effectively.

Lead with Integrity

David was a man of integrity. He wrote, "I will be careful to lead a blameless life.... I will walk in my house with blameless heart" (Psalm 101:2). Integrity to David was more than just wishful thinking; it was a value he lived out. When God made a covenant with Solomon, God said, "If you walk before me in integrity of heart and uprightness, as David your father did,... I will establish your royal throne over Israel forever" (1 Kings 9:4–5).

There are a growing number of young worship leaders today who need such a godly example to emulate. Pastors can play a huge mentoring role in the lives of their worship leaders. In fact, most pastors are already mentoring their worship leaders whether they realize it or not. Worship leaders observe their pastor's example—learning what to do or what not to do by watching how the pastor leads and navigates the challenges of ministry. Your worship leader is noticing how you deal with people and respond to criticism, even how you treat your spouse and kids.

Rest assured that no one expects a pastor to be perfect. If you're open, honest, and humble about your failures and shortcomings, it will endear you to those you lead. They will appreciate that you're still growing spiritually, emotionally, and relationally, and that you're serious about dealing with your "stuff." Integrity is not so much about being perfect, but about being real and authentic.

Provide Sermon Information in a Timely Fashion

Asaph reported that David "guided the people wisely and well" (Psalm 78:72 MSG). Wisdom—making wise decisions—is essential for any leader. For the most part, David sought God's wisdom before taking action (see 1 Samuel 23:2, 4, 10–12; 2 Samuel 5:19, 23). He was wise, assertive, and courageously decisive.

Today there are many who advocate running a church like a business, and there is certainly merit to being well organized and strategic. However, the Bible has always coupled decisiveness with spiritual discernment. For example, the early church habitually prayed and fasted to discern God's will (Acts 1:24; 13:2). In the same way, the church today must always proceed prayerfully when facing decisions. Like Asaph, most artists love working under Spirit-led leaders. It's a joy to follow a leader who's obviously following God.

According to Asaph, David led skillfully. While commanding armies, he learned how to prepare soldiers for battle. In the same way, pastors can help their artists prepare to lead worship by providing sermon information in a timely manner. I realize this can be a sore subject at times. Sometimes pastors feel like we're nagging if we ask for information about upcoming sermons. However, in order for us to do our jobs well, we need as much information as the pastor can give us. In order to find great songs to fit the message, or to incorporate various art forms creatively, we need as much lead time as we can get. We not only have to find great material for the service, we have to rehearse it with volunteers. We understand that pastors are under a lot of pressure, but the more information we receive, the better we'll be able to serve the congregation. Even if the information is sketchy, it's better than nothing.

If you haven't already discussed this with your worship leader, I suggest you ask how much lead time is needed regarding sermon information. If the timetable is completely unrealistic, strike a compromise. A conversation like that would insure a good working relationship with the worship leader.

Though artists are notoriously wary of authority, when they find a leader they trust and respect, they are extremely loyal. When leading artists, encourage them, lead with integrity, and provide sermon information in a timely fashion, and I guarantee the artists will flourish and blossom. They will give back tenfold and the arts will be unleashed at the church in a powerful way.

A WORSHIP LEADER'S LEGACY

Asaph honored God with his life as well as his art. No wonder God used him in such a mighty way. His legacy is characterized by a serious dedication to God, to his family, and to the ministry of worship. Before leaving our study of Asaph, it's only fitting that we each ask ourselves: What kind of legacy am I leaving? Does my art reflect spiritual growth and depth? Does my worship leading reflect a close connection to God?

Tomorrow's legacies are built on today's choices. Asaph became a man of spiritual depth and substance because he intentionally walked in that direction. My fellow artists, may you continue to make right choices and find that when you reach the end of your life you leave behind a rich spiritual legacy.

Follow-up Questions for Group Discussion

1. Psalm 2:11 states that we are to “rejoice with trembling” before God. How can worship leaders balance familiarity and reverence of God in corporate worship?

2. Can you think of any praise songs that, in your opinion, misrepresent God?

3. What do you think are the benefits of corporate worship?

4. What are some ways worship leaders can emphasize the power of community during corporate worship?

5. What makes a worship song excellent?

6. What characterizes excellence in other expressions of worship, like instrumental music, drama, dance, painting, poetry, video, sound, etc.?

7. Why is authenticity an important value to the worshiping artist?

8. If you had twenty-four hours to live and you were given the opportunity to say something to the world, what would you say? How would you say it?

9. How can a worship leader impart an appreciation for worship to his or her family?

10. Do you have any more suggestions to pastors about how to lead artists? If so, what are they?

Personal Action Steps

1. Read through the psalms of Asaph (Psalms 50 and 73–83). List the attributes of God that are cited, the main themes, or any other impressions.

2. Journal about what you're feeling in this moment or any thoughts or emotions you've been experiencing lately.

3. Just for the fun of it, create an artistic expression that is unconventional in its approach, style, or topic.

4. Psalm 78 is a record of God's faithfulness to the nation of Israel. In a similar way, write your family history as a tribute to God's mercy and grace.

5. Identify your pastor's top three personal and/or ministry strengths. How can you help your pastor play to his or her strengths?

chapter ten

The Iconographers

> Such if there be, who loves so long, so well;
> Let him our sad, our tender story tell;
> The well-sung woes will soothe my pensive ghost;
> He best can paint 'em, who shall feel 'em most.
>
> From "Eloisa to Abelard" by Alexander Pope

Mikayla is sitting behind the baptistery all by herself. It's the only place one can truly be alone during a church service. The pastor is not more than fifty feet away, but he's on the other side of the wall, so she can barely hear him. It sounds like he's praying, perhaps wrapping up the service. *Good,* she thinks, *this nightmare is mercifully coming to an end.* Mikayla had put a lot of hard work into this service, but things didn't go as planned. Now she feels it was all for nothing.

Three weeks ago, the music director at the church approached Mikayla with an intriguing idea. He had just written a new worship chorus and wondered if she could put some video footage behind it. Mikayla is a very talented graphic artist—expressionism is her favorite style—and has produced some wonderful videos for the church in the past. She loved the new worship song and immediately began work on the project. It was all she could think about for three weeks. She took a couple days off from work and shot some great footage at the beach and a nearby forest preserve. She even painted a few scenes that mixed in well with the video shots. The plan was to perform the song live on Sunday morning, so the music director gave her a "scratch track" with "click." Everything was synching up nicely and the project was going smoothly.

On Sunday morning before the service, they ran through the video with the live music for the first time. There were a few false starts because the drummer didn't have the click in his headphones, but that was quickly fixed. After the first run-through, it was completely silent in the sanctuary. Everyone was deeply moved. The music director acknowledged Mikayla and said, "I can't ever remember being so moved by a piece of art, and this is only rehearsal! Just wait until the service. Our congregation is in for a real treat this morning."

When the service started, Mikayla sat near the back, affording her a panoramic view of the video, the musicians, and, most importantly, the congregation. She eagerly anticipated their response. She was so excited she had difficulty focusing on all that led up to the video—the prelude, the first song, and the welcome. Then the music director introduced his new praise chorus and explained that worship was going to be enhanced by an outstanding video presentation. However, not long into the song, Mikayla sensed something was wrong. The music was slightly off with the video. Mikayla looked back at the sound engineer trying to get his attention, but he didn't see her. Then she glanced up front and saw the drummer fidgeting with his headset. *Something's wrong*, she thought. *I bet the drummer can't hear the click.* She looked back at the soundman again. *Why doesn't anybody stop this?* The singers had their eyes closed. They were caught up in worship. Besides, they all had their backs to the screen. Mikayla got up out of her seat and went back to the soundboard. "The video is off," she shouted. "They're not together!"

"I know," agreed the sound engineer. "They're off by about a beat, but there's nothing we can do from back here."

"Let's stop this train wreck and start over," demanded Mikayla.

"I don't feel comfortable making that call," the sound engineer whispered trying to avoid a scene. "Besides, I really don't think it's that noticeable."

"It's horrible and it's getting worse," Mikayla exclaimed.

"Well, we let it go this long, we might as well let it finish out," he replied.

Mikayla couldn't bear to watch anymore. She was crushed. She ran out of the sanctuary and took a hard left down the hallway. She didn't want to see or speak to anyone. She just wanted to be alone.

When the song ended, that same hush that occurred at rehearsal came over the congregation. Then they erupted with applause; they loved it.

Meanwhile, backstage behind the baptistery, Mikayla sat with her head in her hands. She was too angry to cry. She was mad at the music director for insisting the song be performed live, and she blamed the soundman for the technical glitch. However, she was mostly upset with herself. "What did I knock myself out for? All that hard work went down the drain."

After the service, Mikayla's friends tried to cheer her up, but she was inconsolable. They assured her that the video presentation wasn't nearly as bad as she thought, but she didn't believe them. *They're just saying that to make me feel better.*

She went home depressed. For the next two weeks, she kept replaying the "train wreck," as she referred to it, over and over in her mind. She couldn't get past it. "I'll never do anything artistic for a church again," she vowed. "It's just too much work with too little return."

Questions for Group Discussion

1. Why do you suppose Mikayla took the technical breakdown so hard?

2. Mikayla's anger is understandable, but do you believe it is justified? Why or why not?

3. What are some indications that Mikayla is a perfectionist?

4. How would you advise a perfectionist when it comes to handling personal mistakes and failure?

5. How would you advise a perfectionist on responding to the mistakes and failures of others?

6. Is there any way this technical glitch could have been avoided? If so, how?

7. What would you do or say to encourage Mikayla?

8. Do you agree with Mikayla that worship had been ruined by the technical breakdown in the video? Why or why not?

9. Is there any way one can prepare emotionally and/or spiritually for the kind of disappointment that Mikayla experienced?

10. Do you think Mikayla will follow through on her promise never to do anything artistic for a church ever again? Why or why not?

WHO ARE THE ICONOGRAPHERS?

As a student of the arts, I've always appreciated not only every form of art, like music, dance, theater, film, literature, and the visual arts, but also the artists behind those various disciplines. In college, as my music history professor lectured on the fusion of Italian, French, and German influences in the music of J. S. Bach, my mind was preoccupied with how Bach was able to teach school, oversee the music at two churches simultaneously, father twenty children, and write a brand-new cantata every month. I'm just as fascinated by the art makers as I am their art.

I've recently stumbled across a group of artists that deserve special attention not only for their artistry but also for the high priority they give to their spiritual lives. These artists are called "iconographers." They create religious icons.

What's an Icon?

Long before they were cute little pictures on your computer screen, icons were a type of sacred painting that flourished during the time of the Byzantine Empire, from the fourth century to the fifteenth century. In spite of being out of vogue for some time, icons are making a comeback throughout the world today, even among evangelicals.

Stylistically, icons may look a little strange to us in the West. The figures look stiff and the shapes appear odd or disproportionate. The perspective is sometimes reversed so the viewer is drawn in instead of remaining on the outside looking in. As a result, the figures appear to be moving toward you instead of away from you.

Indeed, these "pictures" are not meant to be realistic. Instead, they're meant to communicate theological truths in a highly stylized visual language. The Church Council of 869–870 stated that "what the Gospel proclaims to us by words, the icon also proclaims and renders present for us by color."[1] That's why iconographers speak of "writing" an icon instead of "painting" or "drawing" one. They are writing the text of a specific aspect of salvation, using images rather than words. Furthermore, icons are not meant to be "touching" or sentimental, but instead demand that we respond, as viewers, with our minds as much as with our emotions. That's why icons are sometimes called "the thinking person's art."

Historically, icons have been highly controversial at times. During the eighth and ninth centuries bitter disputes arose over whether an icon constituted the kind of "graven image" that Scripture condemns in Exodus 20:4 (KJV) and Leviticus 26:1 (KJV). Those opposed to icons were called "iconoclasts." In 725, Emperor Leo III ordered all icons to be removed from churches and destroyed. Also during this period, iconographers were imprisoned and tortured.

Playing into the controversy over icons was the misperception that they were objects of worship. Sadly, that same misconception exists even today. The truth is, Orthodox Christians do not worship icons; they deeply venerate them. Because icons are windows into the spiritual realm, theology in visual form, Eastern Christians hold them in high regard, but they are not idols.

RULES FOR THE ICON PAINTER

Exceeding my interest in icons has been my fascination with the artists who create them. They possess a depth of spirituality that I for one find very humbling. When an iconographer writes an icon, he or she submits not only to certain artistic guidelines but also to certain spiritual disciplines as well. Those spiritual practices have been captured simply, but powerfully, in a list of nine rules that originated perhaps as early as the thirteenth century and have been refined and handed down through the centuries.[2] I'd like to present those nine rules to you and offer some suggestions as to how we, as artists in the church, can apply them to our lives today. Iconographers come from a different faith tradition than evangelicals and Protestants, so I'm not suggesting that we adopt all their philosophies. However, as you will discover, icon painters are dedicated worship leaders, and I believe there is much we can learn from them.

1. Before starting work, make the sign of the cross; pray in silence, and pardon your enemies.

An iconographer knows that creating a bridge between the worshiper and the heavenly world is an awesome responsibility. It's important to get it right, so before doing anything else, the artist prays earnestly for God's blessing. The Eastern Orthodox Church puts a great deal of stock in meditation, silence, and solitude. This is no quick catch-prayer, thrown hastily heavenward while on the run. It is deep, unhurried, heartfelt prayer. There is as much, if not more, time devoted to listening and waiting on God as there is to speaking words of intercession and supplication.

Bathe Your Work in Prayer

Edward M. Bounds in his book *Purpose in Prayer*, gives a very insightful quote on prayer:

> There can be no substitute, no rival for prayer; it stands alone as the great spiritual force, and this force must be imminent and acting.... Many persons believe in the efficacy of prayer, but not many pray. Prayer is the easiest and hardest of all things; the simplest and the sublimest; the weakest and the most powerful; its results lie outside the range of human possibilities—they are limited only by the omnipotence of God.
>
> Few Christians have anything but a vague idea of the power of prayer; fewer still have any experience of the power. The Church seems almost wholly unaware of the power God puts into her hand; this spiritual carte blanche on the infinite resources of God's wisdom and power is rarely, if ever, used—never used to the full measure of honoring God.... Prayer is our most formidable weapon, but the one in which we are the least skilled, the most averse to its use.[3]

How about you? Before you write a song, create a painting, or mix sound, do you bathe your work in prayer? Before you sing or play, do you pray over the lyrics? Do you engage in prayer regularly or is it spotty? Do you hurry through prayer or are you fully present?

Pardon Your Enemies

In rule number one, the iconographer is also exhorted to pardon enemies. One may wonder what that has to do with creating art, but if you consider how distracting and oppressive broken relationships can be, it makes sense. For many of us, it's hard to think clearly if we're bogged down by bitterness and resentment.

In addition, an artist is no stranger to criticism. We've all received our fair share of "bad reviews." Forgiving those who have said hurtful things to us regarding our talent can be difficult, especially for those who experienced such rejection and failure early in life. I know a young girl, an aspiring actress, who was told by her own father that she'd never be pretty enough or thin enough to be in movies.

Some people get labels that they can't seem to shake. I know a few musicians who were labeled as "poor sight readers." As a result, whenever they're called upon to sight-read a new piece of music, they clam up. I know a number of people who were told that they're not creative, so that's how they see themselves.

Because many artists are sensitive by nature, the wounds left by rejection and failure can run deep. At one of the first churches I served, there was a young woman who had a beautiful voice, but her deep-seated insecurity held her back. She constantly cut herself down, especially during rehearsal. As soon as she finished singing, she'd rattle off four or five criticisms about her voice before I had a chance to say anything. Then I learned a little about her past. As a child, she loved to sing. When she asked her parents if she could take lessons, they scoffed at the idea. "Why should we bother?" they asked. "You're never going to amount to anything anyway." Those are harsh words for a young person to hear.

Artists in the church may also experience rejection and failure. For example, you auditioned for the worship team and didn't make it. Or you keep getting passed over for lead roles in drama sketches or plays. Or you've been asked to step down from a ministry position you've held for years. We tend to vilify those who are merely doing their jobs when they make such decisions. Whether it's our ministry leader, the pastor, or a congregation member, we all too often turn our critics into Public Enemy Number One. However, when we pardon such leaders and others who have rejected our work, we free ourselves from the oppression of bitterness.

Have you ever experienced rejection as an artist? Have you forgiven those who said hurtful things regarding your talent?

2. Work with care on every detail of your icon, as if you were working in front of the Lord himself.

Evidently, iconographers take their work very seriously. To them, church work is God's work, and he deserves our best. So they take great care with every detail. This is not the pursuit of a self-absorbed perfectionism, but the offering of one's imperfect best for the glory of God. These painters do their work wholeheartedly as unto the Lord, and not merely for the approval of others (Ephesians 6:7).

Pay Attention to Details . . .

Artists have an eye (or ear) for detail, a quality that nonartists sometimes find tedious. A friend of mine, who has exquisite taste in design, was asked her opinion on the layout of her church's newsletter. When she gently criticized the colors chosen, her pastor promptly rebuked her. "I'm sure you're the only one who cares about such things, let alone notices," he said. What nonartists don't understand is that our attention to detail does make a difference. Those attending my friend's church may not be as informed as she is, but a newsletter that is pleasing to the eye will be noticed, while one not done well will be met with indifference.

A worship leader recently reported that a group of volunteer artists at his church took responsibility for tastefully decorating the rented gymnasium in which they meet. The results were stunning. Nonartists, who never voiced displeasure before, commented that the church now felt "warmer, friendlier, and more joyful."

Attention to detail takes time and effort. In my years of church work, I remember having to rehearse the last few lines of a drama sketch over and over in order to get it, as we artists are fond of saying, "just right." With an especially poignant ending, it's the "little things" that become big things, like a calculated pause in the actors' dialogue, a sensitive rubato in the music, or the timing of the lights fading out. When such details are coordinated, a special moment is created. Nonartists might not be able to discern when it's not done well, but they're certainly moved emotionally when it's done right.

Even if no one else notices, most artists are convinced that God deserves their best. The story is told of an artist who was working on the ceiling of a large cathedral. Perched on scaffolding high above the floor, the artist labored for hours on a small detail barely visible from below. A visiting tourist noticed the artist slaving away and called out, "Why are you exerting so much effort on details that no one else will ever see?" Without missing a brushstroke, the busy artist replied, "Because God sees."

Unlike the cathedral artist, most of the time our attention to detail does not go unnoticed. A choir or worship team that crescendos or phrases together is pleasant to the ear. Sound technicians that aren't satisfied until they find the right EQ or effect are to be applauded. Making sure the slides for the lyrics are correct and that there are smooth transitions between songs makes worship less distracting. So, my fellow artists, you are not crazy for attending to detail in your work.

... But Don't Obsess Over the Details

I know a church worship band that prides itself on playing every song "just like the CD." They go to great lengths to duplicate every detail of the original recording—down to the exact keyboard voicings and guitar riffs. When the pastor, or anyone else, suggests making changes, like shortening the song or lowering the key to better fit the congregation, the musicians vehemently resist. Coincidentally, at this church, the congregation doesn't sing much during worship. Services resemble worship concerts because the musicians are more obsessed with musical nuance than leading their flock in worship. A rigid obsession with details can cause one to miss what's truly important.

Beware of perfectionism. A young music director confided to me that he was angry and upset by all the "little things" that went wrong every Sunday. He described his singers as having "horrible intonation," his band as a "mediocre garage band," and his drama team as a bunch of "schlock amateurs." He was embarrassed and wanted to quit. When he invited me to watch a service and make suggestions, I was hardly looking forward to it. However, what I observed was so much better artistically than I expected. Yes, I heard some intonation problems, some wrong notes in the band, and some overacting on the part of the drama team, but none of those things was so blatant that it detracted from the overall effectiveness of the service. It also helped that the artists on that platform worshiped with such an infectious spirit of joy and thanksgiving that it covered a multitude of musical sins. No wonder the church was packed to standing room only, and the congregation worshiped loudly and enthusiastically. Much like Mikayla in our opening scenario, my friend had become so obsessed with a few negative details that he failed to see all the good things that were happening at his church. Indeed, how you respond to mistakes and failings indicates how healthy or unhealthy you are in regard to perfectionism.

In *The Heart of the Artist*, I suggested that the pursuit of excellence is a much healthier and more productive alternative to pursuing perfection. The perfectionist fears failure, loathes criticism, and dwells on mistakes. Those who pursue excellence have realistic expectations. They anticipate success because their goal is simply to do the best they can with what they have. As a result, they welcome criticism and learn from mistakes.

These two different approaches were effectively played out in the 1980 movie *Chariots of Fire*. The main character, Eric Liddel, is motivated by a love for running. That's what God created him to do. "God made me fast," he says, "and when I run I feel his pleasure." By contrast, his rival, Harold Abrahams, is driven by insecurity and fear. "If I can't win, I won't run" is his motto. As a result, he is constantly out to prove himself because he never feels he's good enough. Eric Liddel joyfully pursued excellence, while Harold Abrahams was mired in perfectionism.

How does one attend to detail without becoming obsessed with it? I believe iconographers have the right idea. They labor as if "in front of the Lord himself." Their persistent sense of God's presence keeps bringing them back to the heart of worship, which is not our art, but the Lord Jesus Christ. Keeping their eyes on the Lord also helps to minimize perfectionism by reminding them that only God is perfect. So whenever you lead worship, don't let an obsession with detail distract you from worshiping God.

3. During work, pray in order to strengthen yourself physically and spiritually; avoid, above all, useless words and keep silence.

It's no accident that prayer is mentioned several times in relation to the spiritual practices of icon painters. Not only do they pray before they start a project, they pray during it as well, petitioning the Lord for strength to finish what they start. Summing up the importance of prayer to the creative process, contemporary iconographer Nicholas Tsai, from San Francisco, told me in an email, "When you paint an icon, you pray."

Pray for Strength amidst the Rigors of Ministry

Most congregation members have no idea how much work goes into the average church service. After one such service that featured a forty-piece orchestra playing thirty minutes of worship music, a gentleman from the congregation commented to me that the music had greatly contributed to his worship experience. Apparently not knowing that I was employed full time for the church overseeing multiple teams and services, he then asked me, "So what do you do for work the rest of the week?" When I explained that I spent the entire week planning and arranging music, and that all the other musicians put in a great deal of time preparing and rehearsing, he exclaimed, "Wow! I thought you all just got together a few minutes before the service and started playing." Bless his heart; he just didn't know any better.

The truth is, arts ministry is hard work. Whether it's weekly services, a holiday program, or a special event, church artists often invest huge amounts of time and energy. When ministry becomes taxing, we artists are more susceptible to negativity and cynicism. The rules for icon painters suggest instead that we pray for strength and perseverance.

Be Prepared Spiritually for the Rigors of Ministry

Early in my ministry, I used to dread Christmas and Easter, the two busiest times of the church year. By Christmas day I was too exhausted to celebrate and Holy Week was one big blur. My soul was parched and I sure didn't feel close to God. Then early one Advent season, I found a verse that changed my whole approach to the Christmas season. Jesus was born amidst a whirlwind of activity. Mary and Joseph had been traveling, they frantically found a place to stay, Mary gave birth, and they entertained visiting shepherds. The busiest person in the Christmas story is Mary. Yet we are told that Mary "treasured up all these things and pondered them in her heart" (Luke 2:19). In spite of the hectic pace, Mary withdrew to meditate on God's activity in her life. Following Mary's example, I began to withdraw at some point before the onset of the Christmas and Easter rush to ponder the spiritual significance of the season. The suggestion, in rule number three, for iconographers to avoid "useless words" and observe silence is a good way for us to "treasure and ponder" the significance of the season.

Over time, preparing for Christmas and Easter meant more to me than an increased workload, extended meetings, and late-night rehearsals. It meant preparing my heart and soul for these two holiest days of the year. As a result, I stopped dreading them and actually enjoyed them.

Times of spiritual preparation for Christmas and Easter are automatically built into the church calendar. Historically, Christians have used Advent to prepare for Christmas and Lent to prepare for Easter. During Advent, which is four weeks long, we prepare for the coming of God's greatest gift of grace to humankind: his Son, our Savior. Lent, which is forty days before Easter (not counting Sundays), is characterized by self-examination and fasting. In both cases, we prepare our hearts so we don't miss the significance of the holy days. If your church doesn't observe Lent or Advent, there are many helpful resources available at your Christian bookstore or even online to assist you in preparing spiritually for these two glorious holidays.

4. Pray in particular to the saint whose face you are painting. Keep your mind from distractions and the saint will be close to you.

For Eastern Orthodox and Roman Catholic believers, praying to saints has its scriptural justification in the book of Hebrews. After presenting an impressive list of Old Testament heroes of the faith, the writer of Hebrews begins chapter 12 with these words: "Therefore, since we are surrounded by such a great cloud of witnesses, let us throw off everything that hinders and the sin that so easily entangles, and let us run with perseverance the race marked out for us" (v. 1). Since believers who have gone before us are apparently observing our lives, some Christians are compelled to talk to them through prayer. While Protestants and many who read this book may be uncomfortable with this practice and question the biblical grounds suggested, in the case of iconographers, it helps them concentrate on what they're painting. The result is a deep familiarity with their subject that is never lost on even the most casual observer.

Know Your Subject Thoroughly

Some time ago, my wife and I attended a service that featured a drama sketch set in Iraq during the war. A U.S. soldier was portrayed writing a letter home during the holidays. Because our younger son was stationed with the Marines in Iraq at the time, we were immediately drawn in. However, it quickly became obvious that whoever wrote the sketch had no understanding of what it was like having a loved one overseas and certainly no knowledge of military life. Whenever you communicate through the arts, make sure you know your subject well.

If your subject is God, as is the case when leading worship, take the time to know him intimately—not just cerebrally, but from firsthand experience. For example, if the subject is God's holiness, look up verses and meditate on that topic. Challenge yourself to experience God's holiness in a personal way. Even if you work "behind the scenes" in the technical area, be sure you know the theme of next week's worship service. Or better yet, take the lyrics of the hymns or worship choruses home and meditate on them before the service. Don't let the task of making art cause you to lose sight of the message behind your art.

Guard against Pride

One of the artist's most common distractions is pride. However, iconographers realize that worship leading is never about them, and they go to great lengths to subdue ego. They adopt John the Baptist's reference to Jesus as their own motto: "He must increase, but I must decrease" (John 3:30 NASB). As a result, their personality takes a backseat to the biblical character or event they're depicting. They refrain from injecting too much of themselves into their work so as not to become the focus of worship. That's why they never sign their names to their work as that would call undo attention to themselves.

Icon painters are not interested in "doing their own thing." Instead, they meticulously follow strict guidelines as to style, subject, and form. These rules, governing everything from color choices to facial features, have been handed down through the centuries. So iconographers are not concerned with being innovative, which explains why icons depicting the same subject, even those painted centuries apart, look alike. Instead of imposing their personality or even creativity into their work, icon artists strive to be faithful to an artistic tradition. Western artists may find this approach terribly limiting, but keep in mind that an iconographer's mission is not to create a "masterpiece" for a prestigious art gallery. In fact, iconographers would be mortified to see their work hanging in museums today because their art was meant to facilitate worship. Icons are meant to be hanging in people's homes or in churches. Iconographers don't measure success by the size of their audience or the scope of their influence, but by their faithfulness to God. This self-effacing mindset raises the following questions for us today: Do you need a large audience to be satisfied as an artist? Do you need to be noticed to be content? Is the Audience of One enough of an audience for you?

Like icon painters, church artists must vigilantly guard against pride. Not only is it inappropriate in God's presence, it impedes relationships and obstructs ministry. Labeling pride "the complete anti-God state of mind," C. S. Lewis contends that

> Pride is competitive by its very nature.... It is Pride which has been the chief cause of misery in every nation and every family since the world began. Other vices may sometimes bring people together: you may find good fellowship and jokes and friendliness among drunken people or unchaste people. But Pride

> always means enmity—it *is* enmity. And not only enmity between man and man, but enmity to God.... As long as you are proud you cannot know God. A proud man is always looking down on things and people: and, of course, as long as you are looking down, you cannot see something that is above you.[4]

A friend of mine with a checkered past recently described a holy moment that he experienced during worship at church. "God broke through to me," he said choking back tears, "and it was as if the Lord was speaking directly to me, telling me that he loves me and that he forgives everything I've ever done in my life." Since I'm familiar with the arts program at my friend's church, I asked him who the worship leader was that particular night. He squinted and thought for a bit, then he said, "I don't remember." I can't think of a higher compliment bestowed upon a worship team. Worship is not about us, it's about God.

5. When you have to choose a color, stretch out your hand interiorly to the Lord and ask his counsel.

Prayer is mentioned yet again, and one can't help but be impressed with the persistence with which icon painters prayed. Unlike many of us who pray quick one-liners and then forget about it, iconographers persevered in prayer. The Bible illustrates prayer in the most tenacious of terms. The Old Testament calls it "wrestling" (Genesis 32:22–30) and describes it as strenuous and exhausting (Exodus 17:11–13). The New Testament uses the term "struggle" (Romans 15:30) and describes prayer as "laboring earnestly" (Colossians 4:12 NASB). We are to be devoted to prayer (Colossians 4:2), "faithful" (Romans 12:12) and "fervent" in it (James 5:16 KJV). Jesus used the Parable of the Persistent Widow to teach his disciples "that they should always pray and not give up" (Luke 18:1). So once more, the iconographer is admonished to pray, but in this case, it's a specific kind of prayer—the prayer for artistic wisdom.

Call on God to Help You Create or Perform

As any creative person will attest, the artistic process involves dozens of decisions. To the iconographer, no decision is too small or insignificant for prayer. So whether you create and/or perform, be sure to seek God's wisdom. By the way, whenever I discuss performing in conjunction with worship, I'm not equating ministry with entertainment. I'm using the word in its most literal sense. For example, musicians play and/or sing, actors act, dancers dance. By nature, some art has to be *performed* to communicate its message. Therefore it is wise for worship teams to pray for God to help them play and sing "skillfully" (Psalm 33:3).

Whenever you pray for God's help, live like you expect an answer. Years ago, I was convicted of my lack of faith in this regard. Whenever I started writing a song, I would pray for God's help. Then I'd get these great ideas while shaving or driving, but I'd never write them down because I was in a hurry to get to work. I forgot more good ideas than I could remember, so I started carrying a little notepad around to capture lyrics and melodies. I even kept the notebook at my bedside in case inspiration struck during the night. I know many creative types who carry a small digital recorder around to collect and store new ideas.

The Artist's Prayer

Psalm 90:17 reads, "May the favor of the Lord our God rest upon us; establish the work of our hands for us—yes, establish the work of our hands." The New American Standard version renders that last line: "confirm the work of our hands."

There is a simple prayer I have often recited based on this verse: *Lord, bless the work of my hands.* I call this "The Artist's Prayer" because many artists use their hands to play, build, write, or paint, but it could be easily adapted for singers, dancers, and actors. Throughout the artistic process, ask the Lord to bless the fruit of your labor.

6. Do not be jealous of your neighbor's work; his success is your success too.

I recently heard a pastor define envy as resenting God for his goodness toward others while ignoring God's goodness in my own life. Indeed, jealousy causes us to focus on what we don't have instead of all God has given us. In *The Heart of the Artist*, I devoted an entire chapter to the subject of jealousy, so I'd like to take this opportunity to broaden our discussion and examine how all sin, not just jealousy, hinders art and ministry.

Beware the Consequences of Sin

Because God is holy, his presence is incompatible with sin. Scripture teaches that the Lord is intimate with the upright (Proverbs 3:32 NASB) and reveals himself to those who keep his commandments (John 14:21). Jesus said, "Blessed are the pure in heart, for they will see God" (Matthew 5:8). Sin, therefore, alienates us from God. As John Ortberg writes, "Every choice to sin—no matter how small—diminishes my capacity to experience God."[5] When the Israelites rebelled, God told them, in Joshua 7:12, "I will not be with you anymore unless you destroy whatever among you is devoted to destruction." A. W. Tozer asserts that sin creates "moral incompatibility between God and man. God is not far away in distance, but He seems to be because He is far away in character."[6]

Sin also deprives us of inner peace. That's why Peter says, "Dear friends, I urge you, as aliens and strangers in the world, to abstain from sinful desires, which war against your soul" (1 Peter 2:11). Sin hinders prayer, dulls our ears to God's voice, and obstructs his fullest blessing upon our lives (Psalm 66:18; 1 Peter 3:7). God's love is unconditional; there is nothing you could ever do that would make him stop loving you. However, his blessings are contingent upon our obedience. "No good thing does he withhold" from those who walk in his way (Psalm 84:11). According to Jonah 2:8, "Those who cling to worthless idols forfeit the grace that could be theirs." Sin stifles our receptivity to grace because it takes our eyes (and ears) off God.

Sin also greatly impedes our fruitfulness in ministry. In 1 Thessalonians 1:5, Paul says, "Our gospel came to you not simply with words, but also with power, with the Holy Spirit and with deep conviction. You know how we lived among you for your sake." On many occasions, I've used this verse as a prayer before speaking, performing, or leading: *Lord, help me to minister in your power, with your anointing, and with passion and conviction. And help me to live what I preach.*

Sin sabotages every facet of that prayer. The power of God resides in each of us like a treasure in jars of clay (2 Corinthians 4:7), but sin forces God to be less inclined to manifest his power in us. Moral compromise quenches the Holy Spirit, thus diminishing our anointing (Ephesians 4:30 MSG; 1 Thessalonians 5:19). Sin robs us of passion and conviction by draining us of strength and vitality. David wrote, "My bones have no soundness because of my sin. My guilt has overwhelmed me like a burden too heavy to bear.... My pain is ever with me" (Psalm 38:3–4, 17). Sin tarnishes our godly example and undermines our spiritual authority. In Colossians 1:10, Paul admonishes us to walk in a manner worthy of the Lord and to "please him in every way."

Shortly after David committed adultery, we learn that David's son Amnon raped his half-sister Tamar. When word of this reached David, Scripture tells us that he was angry (2 Samuel 13:21). But he didn't discipline his son. How could he? Chastisement is rarely taken seriously from someone who's recently committed adultery and murder. You can't effectively call others to live a life that you yourself aren't living.

According to 2 Timothy 2:21, God calls all of us who minister in his name to forsake sin and become instruments "for noble purposes, made holy, useful to the Master and prepared to do any good work." Isaiah 52:11 puts it best: "Come out ... and be pure, you who carry the vessels of the Lord."

Early in life, I learned a valuable lesson about the consequences of sin. Two days after I graduated from college, I stuffed all my possessions into the trunk of my Ford Maverick and moved halfway across the country to start my first ministry assignment as a youth pastor in a Baptist church. I rented an apartment in town and was enjoying the freedom and autonomy of being out on my own. One day, as I was listening to my stereo cranked as high as it would go, I heard a knock at my door. Thinking it was the neighbors gathered with pitchforks and torches to demand I turn down my music, I lowered the volume on the stereo and nonchalantly walked over to open the door. Instead of a horde of angry villagers, there was a young college-age girl at my door, wearing the skimpiest bikini I had ever seen. She introduced herself by explaining that she lived in the apartment directly below mine, and asked if she could borrow some milk. I obliged and she was on her way. However, that was not the last time she paid me a visit. Apparently, her apartment lacked many necessities that she needed to borrow from me every weekend, each time appearing at my door with her female form in various stages of exposure. What I didn't know at the time was that this girl was an exotic dancer who worked at one of the local strip joints.

Being new in town, I was lonely and looking for love. And at an age when a young man's hormones normally rage out of control, I was definitely vulnerable to temptation. Now I'm not proud of this, but I must admit that the thought of doing something stupid with this woman crossed my mind. I found myself thinking, *This girl is practically throwing herself at me. I could have some real fun here and why not? No one would know. No one would ever find out.*

Another thing I didn't know at the time was that, beneath her flirtatious exterior, this girl was genuinely seeking God. She had recently befriended another young woman in our building who had been witnessing to this Buxom Bikini Babe about the saving grace of Jesus Christ.

Fortunately, I didn't follow through on my carnal thoughts; I didn't do anything stupid with the exotic dancer. She eventually accepted Christ and turned her life around. And the gal who witnessed to her and led her to Christ, the one who lived in our building, eventually became my wife. So the story has a happy ending, but it could just as easily have ended sadly. For I know that if I had committed an indiscretion, my seeking neighbor from the apartment below would never have found Christ. She knew I worked for a church, so any duplicity on my part would certainly have been a stumbling block to her finding God. I am also convinced that if I had sinned with this woman, I would have never married the wonderful woman who is my wife today because she undoubtedly would have learned about my moral failure and written me off as a hypocrite. So you can't convince me that sin has no consequences. I came frighteningly close to finding out just how devastating sin can be. We really do reap what we sow (Galatians 6:7). Sin may satisfy for the short term, but in the long run it offers nothing but pain and heartache (Hebrews 11:25). The consequences of sin are never in our favor.

7. When your icon is finished, thank God that his mercy has granted you the grace to paint the holy images.

When the Work Is Done, Give Thanks to God

During my days as a church music director, our arts teams prayed before every service, beseeching God to bless and anoint our efforts. Then when we were finished with our part of the service, we'd all bolt for the parking lot, myself included, hoping to beat the traffic home. Now, as I look back on it, I wish we had taken a couple minutes before leaving to thank the Lord for answering our prayers.

Don't ever assume that our God doesn't notice or appreciate those who give thanks. Jesus healed ten lepers, but only one, a Samaritan, returned to thank him. Jesus commended the grateful ex-leper and blessed him, but took exception to the other nine. "Jesus asked, 'Were not all ten cleansed? Where are the other nine? Was no one found to return and give praise to God except this foreigner?'" (Luke 17:17–18).

I've heard some pastors label those nine as ungrateful, but I'm not sure that's accurate. After all, they had just been healed of the most hideous disease of their day. I doubt they were ungrateful. I bet they all went out and celebrated. But they still failed to say "thanks" to the one who healed them. This convicts me. I must ask God for a dozen things every day. Do I thank him each time my prayers are answered? I'm afraid that, some days, the percentage of my "thank-yous" is no better than those nine lepers.

Cultivating gratitude can also help prevent haughtiness and conceit. It is inappropriate for you and me to take all the credit for something that God empowered us to accomplish. As artists, we partner with God. Apart from him we can do nothing (John 15:5). While speaking out against pride and self-sufficiency, Paul asks, "What do you have that you did not receive? And if you did receive it, why do you boast as though you did not?" (1 Corinthians 4:7). Being an artist involves a lot of hard work, but let's give credit where credit is due: to the God who endowed us with artistic ability in the first place.

8. Have your icon blessed by putting it on the altar. Be the first to pray before it, before giving it to others.

When iconographers finish a work, they have a devotional—using their painting. After all, that's the purpose of an icon, to facilitate prayer and worship. What better way to see if it "works" than to try it out yourself.

Don't Just Rehearse Worship . . . Worship

If you create a piece for worship, find out if it moves *you* to worship. If you're a performer, make sure the substance of the piece captivates you before you present it to others.

For many years, Joe Horness led worship at Willow Creek Community Church, and his office was a few doors down from mine. Every week I heard Joe playing through the worship order for that week's service. But I knew he wasn't just practicing, he was worshiping. By the time Joe led our congregation, he had already been living that particular worship set. Make sure the time you spend leading worship isn't the only time you worship.

9. Never forget: the joy of spreading icons in the world, the joy of the work of icon painting, the joy of giving the saint the possibility to shine through his icon, the joy of being in union with the saint whose face you are painting.

This last rule (written hundreds of years ago) exhibits uncanny wisdom toward those of us with artistic temperaments. We have a tendency to take our work and ourselves too seriously. Perfectionism and negativity often steal our joy. At times we can be moody, negative, and overly sensitive. On top of that, being an artist involves hard work, with plenty of ups and downs, and the "downs" can be excruciatingly painful and discouraging. The adjectives most associated with artists are "tortured," "frustrated," or "starving," certainly not "joyous." For artists in the church, the ongoing pressures of weekly services often leave little time to enjoy the fruits of our labors. Even those who are by nature positive and happy don't always take the time to savor their work. They barely finish one service before starting preparation for the next one.

Savor the Joy of Being an Artist in Ministry

I learned something about joy and contentment the other day. As I was walking through my neighborhood, I saw an old rusty car pull up alongside a dumpster outside a nearby apartment complex. Two little boys jumped out of the car, followed by a young woman whom I assume was their mother. The boys raced over to the dumpster and pulled out a mattress they had apparently spotted from the car. As they struggled to hold up the mattress, the mother carefully examined it. Each boy waited with bated breath. When the mother nodded final approval, the boys jumped up and down with glee. Then all three happily loaded their new mattress in the car and drove off.

The picture of those boys jumping for joy over an old beat-up mattress stayed with me a long time. You see, it didn't take much to make them happy. They were perfectly content sleeping on an old discarded mattress. In that moment, those boys celebrated what they had instead of dwelling on all they didn't have.

How about you? Do you ever focus so much on what you don't have that you can't appreciate all you do have? In spite of all the challenges, this last rule reminds us that there is great joy and reward in combining art and ministry. Creating or performing is fun in and of itself, and bringing truth and beauty to the world is a noble deed. But when your talent is also used in ministry, you are impacting others in ways that are eternal.

I know a businessman who loves playing drums at his church. On many occasions I've heard him say, "I can't believe I get to play drums for the Lord. Is it really legal to have this much fun serving God?" Even if you're not completely fulfilled or satisfied as an artist, don't let that stop you from appreciating the artistic experiences and opportunities you do have.

Follow-up Questions for Group Discussion

1. What do you think is the most valuable lesson we can learn from iconographers regarding art and worship?

2. Why is it important for artists to forgive those who reject our talent or criticize our work?

3. Do you agree that the artist's penchant for detail is worthwhile or valid? Why or why not?

4. How can an artist avoid becoming overly obsessed with detail?

5. What is the difference between unhealthy perfectionism and the healthy pursuit of excellence?

6. How can artists help each other sustain the rigors of ministry?

7. Are there any spiritual disciplines or practices you've adopted to help prepare your heart and soul for the busy seasons of Christmas and Easter? If so, please describe.

8. How does selfish pride damage a worship team's unity, morale, and effectiveness?

9. Of all the consequences of sin discussed in this chapter, which in your opinion is the most serious?

10. What are some of the rewards and fulfillments that come from combining art and church ministry?

Personal Action Steps

1. Using the "Rules for Iconographers" as an example, compile a list of spiritual guidelines that summarize your own approach to art making or worship leading.

2. Write your own "Artist's Prayer." Feel free to base your prayer on Psalm 90:17 or another passage of Scripture.

3. Is there anything more you can do to prepare better for the rigors of ministry, especially the Christmas and Easter seasons? Enter some of these suggestions into your calendar so as not to forget them when the time comes.

4. Choose one of the hymns or choruses from an upcoming worship service at your church and meditate upon the lyrics.

5. Following the example of the iconographers, create an artistic expression to be used as a tool for meditation and worship.

Epilogue

Worship—Our Most Common Ground

I remember the first time I heard corporate worship in a language other than my native tongue. Every song was in Spanish and though I couldn't understand exactly, I still got goose bumps. It was exhilarating to observe the Holy Spirit manifested beyond my cozy little corner of the kingdom.

Since then, my travels have offered many more opportunities to experience worship in various languages. Again, I may not understand every word, but I still get goose bumps. More and more, I'm astounded at how quickly and effectively worship brings people of diverse backgrounds together in Christ.

I recently visited Taize, the ecumenical monastic community in the south of France that has pioneered a distinctive contemplative approach to worship and prayer. Though Taize is especially popular among young people in Europe, people of all ages and from all over the world flock by the thousands to this little village in the French countryside throughout the year. During my four-day stay, I met Christians from Europe, Africa, North America, and the Far East—Catholics as well as Protestants—and we quickly became friends because of the bond we share in Christ. Three times a day, we all gathered for prayer and worship. Scripture was read and prayers were offered in one language after another. Songs were sung, sometimes chanted, in multiple languages as well. In spite of the cultural barriers, we worshiped as one in the Spirit.

One afternoon, while out for a walk, I heard a group of young people singing praise choruses in German while, not far away, some townspeople who had gathered for church recited the Lord's Prayer together in French. I was struck by the fact that worship is our most common ground. Amid various races, nationalities, languages, and customs—and despite even our theological differences—worship is the tie that binds all believers in Christ.

My fellow artists, may we continue to grow as private worshipers, to experience not only God's presence but also his attributes, and be transformed by the character of God. May we continue to grow in our understanding of who God is and learn from worship leaders who have gone before us. In a world torn by hatred and strife, may we continue to worship as one—with Christians all over the world—bound together by the unfailing love of Christ.

"O Lord, our Lord, how majestic is your name in all the earth!" (Psalm 8:1).

Notes

Chapter 1: Growing as a Private Worshiper

1. C. S. Lewis, *Reflections on the Psalms* (New York: Harcourt Brace, 1958), 95.

2. Lewis, *Reflections*, 96–97.

3. Jerry Bridges, *I Exalt You, O God: Encountering His Greatness in Your Private Worship* (Colorado Springs: Waterbrook, 2001), 10.

4. Jerry Bridges, *I Will Follow You, O God: Embracing Him as Lord in Your Private Worship* (Colorado Springs: WaterBrook, 2001), 33.

5. Bob Rognlien, *Experiential Worship: Encountering God with Heart, Soul, Mind, and Strength* (Colorado Springs: Navpress, 2005), 45.

6. William Barclay, *The New Daily Study Bible: The Letter to the Romans* (Louisville: Westminster John Knox Press, 2002), 184–85.

7. Louie Giglio, *The Air I Breathe: Worship as a Way of Life* (Sisters, Oregon: Multnomah, 2003), 87–88.

8. Jerry Bridges, *The Pursuit of Holiness* (Colorado Springs: NavPress, 1978), 84–85.

Chapter 2: Encountering the Character of God

1. Thomas Brooks, *The Works of Thomas Brooks*, ed. Alexander B. Grosart, vol. 5, reprint (Carlisle, Penn.: Banner of Truth, 1980), 308.

2. William Shakespeare, *Hamlet*, Act 3, Scene 3, lines 97–98.

3. Gary Thomas, *Sacred Pathways: Discover Your Soul's Path to God* (Grand Rapids, Mich.: Zondervan, 2000), 65.

4. Andy Park, *To Know You More: Cultivating the Heart of a Worship Leader* (Downers Grove, Ill.: InterVarsity, 2002), 31–32.

5. Stephen Charnock, *The Existence and Attributes of God* (Grand Rapids, Mich.: Baker, Reprinted 1996), 242.

6. Ray Waddle, *A Turbulent Peace: The Psalms for Our Time,* (Nashville: Upper Room, 2003), 51.

7. Elizabeth Barrett Browning, *Aurora Leigh*, Book Seven, lines 821–25.

Chapter 3: Responding to the Character of God

1. "Spirit of God, Descend Upon My Heart," music by Frederick C. Atkinson, text by George Croly. Public domain.

2. Atkinson and Croly, "Spirit of God."

3. Rick Warren, *The Purpose-Driven Life: What on Earth Am I Here For?* (Grand Rapids, Mich.: Zondervan, 2002), 102.

4. Dietrich Bonhoeffer, *Life Together* (New York: HarperCollins, 1954), 29.

5. C. S. Lewis, *Reflections on the Psalms* (New York: Harcourt Brace, 1986), 95.

6. David Murrow, *Why Men Hate Going to Church* (Nashville: Thomas Nelson, 2005), 116.

7. "Doxology" or "Old Hundredth," music attributed to Louis Bourgeois in the *Genevan Psalter* of 1551, words by Thomas Ken. Public domain.

8. David Murrow, *Why Men Hate Going to Church*, 141.

9. Gary Thomas, *Sacred Pathways: Discover Your Soul's Path to God* (Grand Rapids, Mich.: Zondervan, 2000), 167.

10. Richard Foster, *Celebration of Discipline: The Path to Spiritual Growth*, 20th anniversary ed. (New York: HarperCollins, 1998), 169–70.

Chapter 4: How God's Character Shapes Our Character

1. Richard Foster, *Celebration of Discipline: The Path to Spiritual Growth*, 20th anniversary ed. (New York: HarperCollins, 1998), 173.

2. Howard L. Rice, *Reformed Spirituality: An Introduction for Believers* (Louisville: Westminster, 1991), 198.

3. N. T. Wright, *For All God's Worth: True Worship and the Calling of the Church* (Grand Rapids, Mich.: Eerdmans, 1997), 10.

4. Richard Foster, *Celebration of Discipline: The Path to Spiritual Growth, 20th Anniversary Edition* (New York: HarperCollins, 1998), 159–60.

5. C. S. Lewis, *Reflections on the Psalms* (New York: Harcourt Brace & Company, 1986), 94.

6. C. S. Lewis, *Mere Christianity* (New York: Simon & Schuster, 1980), 176.

7. Brennan Manning, *Abba's Child: The Cry of the Heart for Intimate Belonging* (Colorado Springs: NavPress, 1994), 62–63.

8. Lewis, *Mere Christianity*, 87.

Part 2 Introduction: Worshiping in Truth

1. Andy Park, *To Know You More: Cultivating the Heart of a Worship Leader* (Downers Grove, Ill.: InterVarsity, 2002), 15.

Chapter 5: Who Is God?

1. N. T. Wright, *For All God's Worth: True Worship and the Calling of the Church* (Grand Rapids, Mich.: Eerdmans, 1997), 31.

2. Larry Crabb, "A Trinitarian Understanding of Sin," *Conversations* (Fall 2005), 8.

3. Henri J. M. Nouwen, *Behold the Beauty of the Lord: Praying with Icons* (Notre Dame, Ind.: Ave Maria, 1987), 21–22.

4. J. I. Packer, *Knowing God* (Downers Grove, Ill.: InterVarsity, 1973), 110.

5. Dallas Willard, *The Divine Conspiracy: Rediscovering Our Hidden Life in God* (San Francisco: HarperSanFrancisco, 1998), 94–95.

6. Jerry Bridges, *The Pursuit of Holiness* (Colorado Springs: NavPress,1978), 32.

7. Dallas Willard, *Renovation of the Heart: Putting on the Character of Christ* (Colorado Springs: NavPress, 2002), 151.

8. C. S. Lewis, *The Lion, the Witch, and the Wardrobe* (New York: HarperCollins, 1978), 86.

9. Philip Yancy, *What's So Amazing About Grace?* (Grand Rapids, Mich.: Zondervan, 1997), 70.

10. Julian of Norwich, *Revelations of Divine Love* (New York: Penguin, 1966), 70.

11. Packer, *Knowing God*, 37.

12. George Herbert, "Evensong."

13. Stephen Charnock, *The Existence and Attributes of God*, reprint ed. (Grand Rapids, Mich.: Baker, 1996), 508.

14. Packer, *Knowing God*, 80.

15. Packer, *Knowing God*, 86.

16. Rob Bell, *Velvet Elvis* (Grand Rapids, Mich.: Zondervan, 2005), 31.

Chapter 6: Who Am I?

1. Based on personal testimony at Easter Sunday service. Used by permission.

2. Dallas Willard, *Renovation of the Heart: Putting on the Character of Christ* (Colorado Springs: NavPress, 2002), 71.

3. Dallas Willard, *The Divine Conspiracy: Rediscovering Our Hidden Life in God* (San Francisco: HarperSanFrancisco, 1998), 344.

4. C. H. Spurgeon, *The Treasury of David*, vol. 1 (McLean, Va.: MacDonald), 13.

5. Richard Foster, *Streams of Living Water: Celebrating the Great Traditions of the Christian Faith* (New York: HarperCollins, 1998), 82.

6. Gerald May, *Addiction and Grace* (New York: Harper & Row, 1988), 152–54.

7. Donald Miller, *Blue Like Jazz: Nonreligious Thoughts on Christian Spirituality* (Nashville: Thomas Nelson, 2003), 232.

8. Henri J. M. Nouwen, *Life of the Beloved: Spiritual Living in a Secular World* (New York: Crossroad, 1992), 30–31.

9. Willard, *Renovation of the Heart*, 60.

10. C. S. Lewis, *Mere Christianity* (New York: Macmillan, 1960), 94.

11. Rob Bell, *Velvet Elvis* (Grand Rapids, Mich.: Zondervan, 2005), 114.

12. Bell, *Velvet Elvis*, 141.

Chapter 7: What Is God Inviting Me to Do?

1. Pedro Arrupe, *Pedro Arrupe: Essential Writings/Selected with an Introduction by Kevin F. Burke* (Maryknoll, N.Y.: Orbis, 2004), 8.

2. Rob Bell, *Velvet Elvis* (Grand Rapids, Mich.: Zondervan, 2005), 165.

3. "Worship Leader Boot Camp," *Worship Leader Magazine* (July/August 2005), 19.

4. Rob Bell, *Bullhorn*, Nooma DVD (Grand Rapids, Mich.: Zondervan, 2005).

5. Gary L. Thomas, *Authentic Faith: The Power of a Fire-Tested Life* (Grand Rapids, Mich.: Zondervan, 2002), 141.

6. C. S. Lewis, *The Weight of Glory and Other Addresses* (New York: Simon & Schuster, 1980), 135.

Chapter 8: The Levites

1. Dallas Willard, *The Divine Conspiracy: Rediscovering Our Hidden Life in God* (San Francisco: HarperSanFrancisco, 1998), 65.

2. Philip Yancey, *The Bible Jesus Read* (Grand Rapids, Mich.: Zondervan, 1999), 112–13.

3. Risto Nurmela, *The Levites: Their Emergence as a Second-Class Priesthood* (Atlanta: Scholars, 1998), 9.

4. Peggy Noonan, *What I Saw at the Revolution: A Political Life in the Reagan Era* (New York: Random House, 1990), 37.

Chapter 9: Asaph

1. Robert W. Bailey, *New Ways in Christian Worship* (Nashville: Broadman, 1981), 35–36.

2. C. H. Spurgeon, *The Treasury of David*, vol. 2 (McLean, Va.: MacDonald), 312.

3. Dan B. Allender and Tremper Longman III, *The Cry of the Soul: How Our Emotions Reveal Our Deepest Questions About God* (Colorado Springs: NavPress, 1994), 24.

4. Brennan Manning, *A Glimpse of Jesus: Stranger to Self-Hatred* (San Francisco: HarperCollins, 2003), 106.

5. Nancy Beach, *An Hour on Sunday: Creating Moments of Transformation and Wonder* (Grand Rapids, Mich.: Zondervan, 2004), 201.

6. Renee Grant-Williams, *Voice Power: Using Your Voice to Captivate,Persuade, and Command Attention* (New York: Amacom, 2002), 45–46.

7. *Walk the Line* (Hollywood: Twentieth Century Fox, 2004).

Chapter 10: The Iconographers

1. Michel Quenot, *The Icon: Window on the Kingdom* (Crestwood, N.Y.: St. Vladimir's Seminary Press, 1991), 79.

2. Jim Forest, *Praying with Icons* (Maryknoll, N.Y.: Orbis, 1997), 24.

3. Edward M. Bounds, *Purpose in Prayer* (Grand Rapids, Mich.: Baker, 1991), 37–38.

4. C. S. Lewis, *Mere Christianity* (New York: Simon & Schuster, 1980), 111.

5. John Ortberg, *God Is Closer Than You Think* (Grand Rapids, Mich.: Zondervan, 2005), 42.

6. A. W. Tozer, *The Attributes of God*, vol. 1 (Camp Hill, Pa.: Christian, 1997), 123.